Payroll Administra~

Technical Units 74 t~ ~~

AAT Level 3 Certificate in Payroll Administration (QCF) (Finance Act 2009)

Course Companion

In this August 2009 edition

- Everything you need to get you through the **2003 Standards** at Level 3, as amended in November 2006

- Clear format, with plenty of space for your own notes

- Material up to date at 1 August 2009 including Finance Act 2009 and taking into account all AAT guidance issued

FOR JUNE AND DECEMBER 2010 EXAMS AND SKILLS TESTS

BPP
LEARNING MEDIA

First edition October 2003
Seventh edition August 2009

ISBN 9780 7517 6779 7
(Previous edition 9780 7517 4653 2)

British Library Cataloguing-in-Publication Data
A catalogue record for this book
is available from the British Library

Published by

BPP Learning Media
Aldine House, Aldine Place
London W12 8AA

www.bpp.com/learning media

Printed in Great Britain

We are grateful to the QCA for permission to
reproduce extracts from the Standards of Competence
for Accounting, and to the AAT for permission to
reproduce extracts from the mapping and Guidance
Notes.

Your learning materials, published by BPP Learning
Media Ltd, are printed on paper sourced from
sustainable, managed forests.

BPP
LEARNING MEDIA

Contents

Page

BPP
LEARNING MEDIA

Introduction

How to use this Course Companion

Aims of this Course Companion

> To provide the knowledge and practice to help you succeed in the exam and skills testing for Payroll Administration Technical Units 74 to 76.

To pass the exam and skills tests you need a thorough understanding in all areas covered by the standards of competence.

> To tie in with the other components of the BPP Learning Media Effective Study Package to ensure you have the best possible chance of success.

Course Companion

This covers all you need to know for the exam and skills tests for Payroll Administration Technical Units 74 to 76. Numerous activities throughout the text help you practise what you have just learnt.

Revision Companion

When you have understood and practised the material in the Course Companion, you will have the knowledge and experience to tackle the Revision Companion for Units 74 to 76. This aims to get you through the exam and skills tests, whether in the form of the AAT simulation or in the workplace.

Recommended approach to this Course Companion

(a) To achieve competence in Payroll Administration, you need to be able to do **everything** specified by the standards. Study the Course Companion carefully and do not skip any of it.

(b) Learning is an **active** process. Do **all** the activities as you work through the Course Companion so you can be sure you really understand what you have read. There is a checklist at the end of each chapter, detailing the performance criteria, range statement and knowledge and understanding covered by each activity.

(c) After you have covered the material in the Course Companion, work through the **Revision Companion**.

(d) Before you take the exam or skills tests, check that you still remember the material using the following quick revision plan for each chapter.

   (i) Read through the chapter contents list. Are there any gaps in your knowledge? If so, study the section again.

   (ii) Read and learn the key learning points, which are a summary of the chapter.

   (iii) Do the quick quiz again. If you know what you're doing, it shouldn't take long.

This approach is only a suggestion. Your college may well adapt it to suit your needs.

Quick quizzes

These include true/false and other formats not used by the AAT. However, these types of questions are usually very familiar to students and are used to help students adjust to otherwise unfamiliar material.

Remember this is a **practical** course.

(a) Try to relate the material to your experience in the workplace or any other work experience you may have had.

(b) Try to make as many links as you can to your study of the other Units at Level 3.

(c) Keep this text, (hopefully) you will find it invaluable in your everyday work too!

Payroll administration structure

The competence-based Education and Training Scheme of the Association of Accounting Technicians is based on an analysis of the work of accounting staff in a wide range of industries and types of organisation. The Standards of Competence for Payroll Administration which students are expected to meet are based on this analysis.

The Standards identify the key purpose of the payroll administration occupation, which is to operate, maintain and improve systems to record, plan, monitor and report on the payroll activities of an organisation, and a number of key roles of the occupation. Each key role is subdivided into units of competence, which are further divided into elements of competences. By successfully completing assessments in specified units of competence, students can gain qualifications at Levels 2 and 3.

Whether you are competent in a Unit is demonstrated by means of:

- *Either* an exam (set and marked by AAT assessors)
- *Or* a skills test (where competence is judged by an Approved Assessment Centre to whom responsibility for this is devolved)
- Or *both* an exam *and* a skills test

Below we set out the overall structure of the Level 3 stage, indicating how competence in each Unit is assessed. There is more detail about the exam and skills test on page (xxii).

About the qualification

This qualification is for people already working within, or wishing to pursue a career in, payroll administration. It develops a mixture of specialist payroll skills, as well as essential IT, communication and management skills. **This Course Companion covers only the specialist payroll skills.** Other BPP Study Texts are available for the IT, communication and management skills, as these are common to other AAT qualifications in Accounting, Business Administration or Management.

The target audience

The qualification will be relevant for those who already work in the payroll function of a large organisation or a small business, who work in payroll bureaux, who are self-employed, or who aspire to become payroll administrators.

Level 3

All units are mandatory

Unit of competence	Elements of competence

Unit 74 Managing the payroll function

Element 74.1	Applying controls to the payroll function
Element 74.2	Resolve queries and produce management information
Element 74.3	Implement redundancy pay procedures

Skills testing *only*

Unit 75 Completing year-end procedures

Element 75.1	Produce payroll year-end returns
Element 75.2	Identify reportable benefits and expenses in the context of income tax and National Insurance
Element 75.3	Produce reports of benefits

Exam *and* skills testing

Unit 76 Maintaining working relationships with external bodies

Element 76.1	Facilitate the transfer of funds to external bodies
Element 76.2	Provide information to authorised agencies

Skills testing *only*

Unit 21* Working with computers

Element 21.1	Use computer systems and software
Element 21.2	Maintain the security of data

Skills testing *only*

Unit 22* Contribute to the maintenance of a healthy, safe and productive working environment

Element 22.1	Monitor and maintain a safe, healthy and secure working environment
Element 22.2	Monitor and maintain an effective and efficient working environment

Skills testing *only*

Unit 23 Achieving personal effectiveness

Element 23.1	Plan and organise your own work
Element 23.2	Maintain good working relationships
Element 23.3	Improve your own performance

Skills testing *only*

*This unit can be completed at either Level 2 or Level 3.

BPP
LEARNING MEDIA

Level 3 Standards of competence

The structure of the Standards for Level 3

Each Unit commences with a statement of the **knowledge and understanding** which underpin competence in the Unit's elements.

The Unit of Competence is then divided into **elements of competence** describing activities which the individual should be able to perform.

Each element includes:

(a) A set of **performance criteria**. This defines what constitutes competent performance.

(b) A **range statement**. This defines the situations, contexts, methods etc in which competence should be displayed.

(c) **Evidence requirements**. These state that competence must be demonstrated consistently, over an appropriate time scale with evidence of performance being provided from the appropriate sources.

(d) **Sources of evidence**. These are suggestions of ways in which you can find evidence to demonstrate that competence. These fall under the headings: 'observed performance; work produced by the candidate; authenticated testimonies from relevant witnesses; personal account of competence; other sources of evidence.' They are reproduced in full in our Revision Companion for Level 3.

The elements of competence for Level 3 are set out below. Knowledge and understanding required for the unit as a whole are listed first, followed by the performance criteria and range statements for each element. Performance criteria are cross-referenced below to chapters in this Level 3 Course Companion.

Unit 74 Managing the Payroll Function

What is the unit about?

This unit is about your responsibility to control the accuracy and compliance of the payroll, to provide information to employees and managers and to implement redundancy pay procedures.

The first element requires you to ensure that rates for permanent and temporary payments and deductions, including statutory payments and deductions, are correctly set in the computerised payroll system. You also need to calculate exceptional payments and ensure that directors' National Insurance contributions are deducted correctly.

The second element is about providing information to management and resolving employees' queries about their pay. You need to show that you can extract data from the computerised payroll system and present information in a medium and format appropriate to the data being presented and the intended recipient.

The third element is concerned with the implementation of redundancy pay procedures. You need to show that you calculate redundancy pay, taking into account statutory and organisational requirements.

Throughout the unit you need to show that you maintain confidentiality of employees' personal details and that you meet organisational and statutory deadlines.

Elements contained within this unit are:

Element 74.1 Applying controls to the payroll function
Element 74.2 Resolve queries and produce management information
Element 74.3 Implement redundancy pay procedures

Knowledge and understanding

The statutory framework

1. Employment Rights Act legislation in respect of redundancy rights (Element 74.3)

2. Industrial Tribunals legislation in respect of redundancy rights (Element 74.3)

3. Data Protection legislation (Elements 74.1, 74.2 & 74.3)

4. HM Revenue and Customs regulations in respect of:

    – Income tax and National Insurance liability on pay, expenses and benefits (Element 74.1)

    – National Insurance regulations concerning directors (Element 74.1)

    – Income tax and National Insurance regulations relating to 'out of synch' payments (Element 74.1)

    – Income tax and National Insurance regulations concerning termination and lump sum payments (Element 74.1)

    – Legislation controlling attachments of earnings and their interaction with each other (Element 74.1)

The organisation

5. Information flows within the organisation (Element 74.2)

6. Organisational, external agency and employee requirements for information (Elements 74.2 & 74.3)

7. Procedures for the security and confidentiality of information (Elements 74.1, 74.2 & 74.3)

8. Sources of information for the resolution of discrepancies (Elements 74.1, 74.2 & 74.3)

Element 74.1 Applying controls to the payroll function

Performance criteria		Chapters in this Text
A	Ensure the treatment of all **allowances** and enhancements is correctly identified with respect to tax, National Insurance and pensions deductions	1
B	Update rates for permanent and temporary payments and deductions against agreed scales for each type of employee affected	1
C	Calculate **exceptional payments** in accordance with organisational requirements, to the deadlines agreed	1
D	Reconcile the National Insurance liability for directors against the National Insurance actually paid	1
E	Monitor compliance with **attachments to earnings** legislation	1
F	Ensure **termination payments** are processed accurately and in accordance with legislative requirements	1
G	Reconcile total charges to organisational budgets against aggregate payroll totals and correctly code them for allocation	1

Range statement

1	**Routine payments:** payments; expenses and benefits; permanent; temporary	1
2	**Exceptional payments:** payments not made on the due day such as late payments to new starters; special one-off bonus not paid with normal pay; payments made to employees after they have left employment	1
3	**Attachments to earnings:** Council tax orders; Scottish arrestments of earnings; child support orders; attachment of earnings orders	1
4	**Termination payments:** pay in lieu of notice; ex gratia payments; statutory redundancy payments; damages; restrictive covenants	1

Element 74.2 Resolve queries and produce management information

Performance criteria		Chapters in this Text
A	Seek clarification or additional information from employees or managers where the nature of their queries is not clear	2
B	Check that individuals raising queries are authorised to receive the information they are requesting	2
C	Agree all requests for information for content, **medium** in which **data** is to be presented, together with the **format** of the information and deadlines for the despatch of information	2
D	Produce accurate information that meets the requirements agreed with the intended recipients	2
E	Respond to telephone or face-to-face enquiries accurately and in accordance with the organisation's customer care requirements	2
F	Refer enquiries to the appropriate person when you do not have the authority or expertise to resolve them	2

Range statement

1	**Reporting medium:** report printed from computerised payroll system; word-processed document; e-mail and electronic file transfer	2
2	**Data:** personal; organizational; financial; statutory; non-statutory	2
3	**Format:** formal report; letter; memorandum	2

Element 74.3 Implement redundancy pay procedures

Performance criteria	Chapters in this Text
A	Ensure all **documentation** relating to the redundancy is checked for compliance with statutory and organisational requirements	3
B	Refer documentation that does not comply with statutory and organisational requirements to the appropriate person for resolution	3
C	Calculate the length of reckonable service, age and value of a week's pay in accordance with statutory rules	3
D	Calculate the amount of any statutory redundancy payment accurately	3
E	Apply the terms of any local, non-statutory scheme to enhance the statutory payment correctly	3
F	Inform the relevant pensions administrator where the redundancy is linked to pensionable retirement, calculate any abatement correctly and apply it to the final payment	3
G	Input to the payroll system all sums due in respect of the redundancy in ways that ensure that payments will be made at the correct time and will receive the appropriate tax treatment	3
H	Ensure all communications relating to redundancy are conducted at an appropriate level of confidentiality	3

Range statement

1	**Documentation:** redundancy notice; statement of redundancy payment; service record; contract of employment; birth certificate; details of organisational redundancy payment scheme	3

Unit 75 Completing Year End Procedures

What is the unit about?

This unit is about producing payroll year-end returns and reports. You need to demonstrate that you use a computerised system to produce these. You also need to show that you can check the taxable value of benefits and expenses manually, for example in response to queries or to check that the system has been set up correctly.

The first element requires you to produce year-end returns and despatch them to employees and external agencies. This includes reconciling cumulative payroll totals to year-end balances to ensure that the information provided on returns will be accurate.

In the second element you need to identify benefits and expenses that are subject to tax and National Insurance contributions as well as the statutory returns applicable to each employee in respect of their benefits and expenses. This includes ensuring that dispensations are up-to-date.

The final element requires you to calculate the taxable value of benefits and expenses and to report these to the HM Revenue and Customs using the statutory forms.

Throughout the unit you need to show that you maintain confidentiality of employees' personal details and that you meet organisational and statutory deadlines.

Elements contained within this unit are:

Element 75.1 Produce payroll year-end returns
Element 75.2 Identify reportable benefits and expenses in the context of tax and National Insurance
Element 75.3 Produce reports of benefits

BPP
LEARNING MEDIA

Knowledge and understanding

The statutory framework

1   Data Protection legislation (Elements 75.1, 75.2 & 75.3)

2   HM Revenue and Customs regulations in respect of:

- Income tax and National Insurance liability on pay, expenses and benefits (Elements 75.1, 75.2 & 75.3)

- Income tax and National Insurance regulations relating to end of year reporting (Elements 75.1, 75.2 & 75.3)

- The methods of submitting end of year returns (Elements 75.1 & 75.2)

- Dispensations, extra statutory concessions, statutory exemptions and HM Revenue and Customs Regulations settlement agreements and their impact on end of year reporting for Income Tax and National Insurance purposes (Elements 75.2 & 75.3)

The organisation

3   Policies for dealing with expenses and benefits (Elements 75.2 & 75.3)

4   Method of payment of expenses (Elements 75.2 & 75.3)

5   Policies, practices and procedures for filing (Elements 75.1 & 75.3)

6   Signatories and authorisations (Elements 75.1 & 75.3)

7   Information flows within the organisation (Elements 75.1 & 75.3)

8   Procedures for the security and confidentiality of information (Elements 75.1, 75.2 & 75.3)

9   Sources of information for the resolution of discrepancies (Element 75.1, 75.2 and 75.3)

10   Principles of payroll accounting and the reconciliation of balances (Element 75.1)

Element 75.1 Produce payroll year-end returns

	Performance criteria	Chapters in this Text
A	Reconcile cumulative pay records to year-end balances	4
B	Reconcile totals of income tax and National Insurance contributions deducted with payments made to the Collector of Taxes, taking into account recoverable sums	4
C	Reconcile the total value of basic and supplementary pension contributions and Additional Voluntary Contributions from each employee with cumulative net taxable pay prior to completion of year-end returns to the Revenue	4
D	Complete all statutory and non-statutory year end **returns** accurately	4
E	Despatch all statutory and non-statutory year end **returns** by the agreed **media** and due dates	4
F	Distribute employee year-end information for employees by the applicable statutory date	4
G	Prepare internal year-end summaries for accounting purposes in an accurate and timely manner	4

Range statement

1	**Returns:** P35; P38A; P60/14; management reports	4
2	**Media:** paper; magnetic; e-mail; internet; disc	4

Element 75.2 Identify reportable benefits and expenses in the context of tax and National Insurance

	Performance criteria	Chapters in this Text
A	Identify the existence of a tax and National Insurance liability for **benefits** and **expenses**	5
B	Identify statutory **exemptions** from liability to income tax and National Insurance	5
C	Ensure that dispensations are up-to-date and are applicable to current organisational procedures	5
D	Identify the relevant **statutory return** to be submitted for each employee	5
E	Identify the correct method of calculating the income tax and National Insurance liability of benefits and expenses	5

Range statement

1	**Benefits:** assets transferred; payment of employee's own debts; vouchers; credit cards; cars; fuel for cars; loans; vans; in-house benefits; shares; living accommodation	5
2	**Expenses:** travel and subsistence; qualifying and non-qualifying relocation; mobile telephones; employee's own telephone; hotel expenses; staff and client entertaining	5

Element 75.3 Produce reports of benefits

Performance criteria		Chapters in this Text
A	Correctly **calculate** the value of taxable **benefits**	6
B	Report the value of taxable benefits and **expenses** accurately, taking into account **non-reportable items**	6
C	Calculate the Class 1A National Insurance liability accurately in accordance with statutory timescales	6
D	Calculate the tax and Class 1B National Insurance liability on benefits where the organisation has agreed to meet the liability	6
E	Complete all **statutory** and **non statutory** year end returns accurately	6
F	Despatch all **statutory** and **non-statutory** year end returns by the due dates	6
G	Ensure all year-end information for employees is made available by the applicable statutory date	6
H	Produce internal year-end summaries for management accounting purposes in an accurate and timely manner	6
Range statement		
1	**Benefits:** assets transferred; payment of employee's own debts; vouchers; credit cards; cars; fuel for cars; loans; vans; in-house benefits; shares; living accommodation	6
2	**Expenses:** travel and subsistence; qualifying and non-qualifying relocation; mobile telephones; employee's own telephone; hotel expenses; staff and client entertaining	6
3	**Statutory returns:** form P11D; form P11D(b); form P9D	6
4	**Non-statutory returns:** internal end of year reports	6

Unit 76 Maintaining Working Relationships with External Bodies

This unit is about your responsibility for liaising with external bodies such as HM Revenue and Customs (HMRC).

The first element requires you to make payments to external bodies. This involves reconciling payroll records with the organisation's financial reports to ensure that the amounts paid agree with the amounts due, as well as arranging the payments.

The second element is about providing information to authorised agencies. You are required to show that you can communicate via a variety of media and that you do so in a courteous, clear and timely fashion.

Throughout the unit you need to show that you maintain confidentiality of employees' personal details and that you meet organisational and statutory deadlines.

What is the unit about?

Elements contained within this unit are:

Element 76.1 Facilitate the transfer of funds to external bodies
Element 76.2 Provide information to authorised agencies

Knowledge and understanding

The statutory framework

1 Data Protection legislation (Elements 76.1 & 76.2)

2 PAYE regulations in respect of deadlines for Tax and NI payments (Element 76.1)

3 Reporting requirements in respect of attachments of earnings (Elements 76.1 & 76.2)

Payroll legislation changes on a regular basis. To ensure the qualification is always testing the current legislation any future legislation changes impacting on this Unit are to be considered as reflecting on the underpinning knowledge and understanding required to meet the standards from the date on which the legislation comes into effect.

The organisation

4 Policies, practices and procedures for filing (Element 76.2)

5 Signatories and authorisations (Elements 76.1 & 76.2)

6 Timescales and schedules for updating, presenting and despatching data (Elements 76.1 & 76.2)

7 Information flows within the organisation (Element 76.2)

8 Procedures for the security and confidentiality of information (Elements 76.1 & 76.2)

9 Systems for the transmission of disbursements to external agencies (Elements 76.1 & 76.2)

10 External agency requirements for information (Elements 76.1 & 76.2)

11 Sources of information for the resolution of discrepancies (Elements 76.1 & 76.2)

Element 76.1 Facilitate the transfer of funds to external bodies

Performance criteria		Chapters in this Text
A	Reconcile payroll records with the organisation's financial reports	7
B	Make **payments** to **statutory bodies** in accordance with statutory deadline dates and ensure they are accompanied by the applicable statutory documentation	7
C	Make payments to non-statutory bodies in accordance with business agreements and ensure they are accompanied by the applicable documentation	7
D	Ensure all payments are made in accordance with organisational regulations and procedures	7
Range statement		
1	**Payments:** cheque; electronic lodgement	7
2	**Statutory bodies:** Collector of Taxes; Local Authorities; Child Support Agency; Courts	7

Element 76.2 Provide information to authorised agencies

Performance criteria		Chapters in this Text
A	Deal with enquiries from statutory agencies and non-statutory bodies in accordance with the organisation's customer care requirements	8
B	Comply with all aspects of the provision of information covered by current Data Protection legislation	8
C	Respond to enquiries in the required **medium**	8
D	Obtain employee authorisation where required prior to the release of information	8
E	Supply information within the specified timescale	8
F	File copies of responses in a logical and accessible manner and in accordance with the requirements of the organisation	8
G	Follow up requests for information from other departments or individuals in an appropriate manner	8
H	Verify the source of all enquiries prior to the release of information	8
Range statement		
1	**Medium of communication:** proformas; letters; telephone calls; face to face; e-mail; internet	8

Assessment strategy

Units 74 and 76 are assessed by skills testing. Unit 75 is assessed by exam *and* skills testing.

Skills Testing *(More detail can be found in the Revision Companion)*

Skills testing is a means of collecting evidence of your ability to carry out practical activities and to operate effectively in the conditions of the workplace to the standards required. Evidence may be collected at your place of work or at an Approved Assessment Centre by means of simulations of workplace activity, or by a combination of these methods.

If the Approved Assessment Centre is a workplace you may be observed carrying out accounting activities as part of your normal work routine. You should collect documentary evidence of the work you have done, or contributed, in an accounting portfolio. Evidence collected in a portfolio can be assessed in addition to observed performance or where it is not possible to assess by observation.

Where the Approved Assessment Centre is a college or training organisation, skills testing will be by means of a combination of the following.

(a)   Documentary evidence of activities carried out at the workplace, collected by you in an accounting portfolio

(b)   Realistic simulations of workplace activities; these simulations may take the form of case studies and in-tray exercises and involve the use of primary documents and reference sources

(c)   Projects and assignments designed to assess the Standards of Competence

If you are unable to provide workplace evidence, you will be able to complete the assessment requirements by the alternative methods listed above.

Exam *(More detail can be found in the Revision Companion)*

The exam is set and marked by the AAT and consists of a short case study and a number of short answer questions. The exam is undertaken under controlled conditions at specific times.

Exams are designed to collect supplementary evidence that you have the necessary knowledge and understanding which underpins competence and that you can apply your skills to a range of contexts. Exams test the application of knowledge and understanding, not the recall of facts and figures.

Building your portfolio

What is a portfolio?

A portfolio is a collection of work that demonstrates what the owner can do. In AAT language the portfolio demonstrates **competence**.

A painter will have a collection of his paintings to exhibit in a gallery, an advertising executive will have a range of advertisements and ideas that she has produced to show to a prospective client. Both the collection of paintings and the advertisements form the portfolio of that artist or advertising executive.

Your portfolio will be unique to you just as the portfolio of the artist will be unique because no one will paint the same range of pictures in the same way. It is a very personal collection of your work and should be treated as a **confidential** record.

What evidence should a portfolio include?

No two portfolios will be the same but by following some simple guidelines you can decide which of the following suggestions will be appropriate in your case.

(a)   **Your current CV**

This should be at the front. It will give your personal details as well as brief descriptions of posts you have held with the most recent one shown first.

(b)   **References and testimonials**

References from previous employers may be included especially those of which you are particularly proud.

(c)   **Your current job description**

You should emphasise financial **responsibilities and duties**.

(d)   **Your student record sheets**

These should be supplied by AAT when you begin your studies, and your training provider should also have some if necessary.

(e)   **Evidence from your current workplace**

This could take many forms including **letters, memos, reports** you have written, **copies of accounts** or **reconciliations** you have prepared, **discrepancies** you have investigated etc. Remember to obtain permission to include the evidence from your line manager because some records may be sensitive. Discuss the performance criteria that are listed in your Student Record Sheets with your training provider and employer, and think of other evidence that could be appropriate to you.

(f)   **Evidence from your social activities**

For example you may be the treasurer of a club in which case examples of your cash and banking records could be appropriate.

(g)   **Evidence from your studies**

Few students are able to satisfy all the requirements of competence by workplace evidence alone. They therefore rely on simulations to provide the remaining evidence to complete a unit. If you are not working or not working in a relevant post, then you may need to rely more heavily on simulations as a source of evidence.

(h)   **Additional work**

Your training provider may give you work that specifically targets one or a group of performance criteria in order to complete a unit. It could take the form of questions, presentations or demonstrations. Each training provider will approach this in a different way.

(i)   **Evidence from a previous workplace**

This evidence may be difficult to obtain and should be used with caution because it must satisfy the 'rules' of evidence, that is it must be current. Only rely on this as evidence if you have changed jobs recently.

(j)   **Prior achievements**

For example you may have already completed the health and safety unit during a previous course of study, and therefore there is no need to repeat this work. Advise your training provider who will check to ensure that it is the same unit and record it as complete if appropriate.

How should it be presented?

As you assemble the evidence remember to **make a note** of it on your Student Record Sheet in the space provided and **cross reference** it. In this way it is easy to check to see if your evidence is **appropriate**. Remember one piece of evidence may satisfy a number of performance criteria so remember to check this thoroughly and discuss it with your training provider if in doubt.

To keep all your evidence together a ring binder or lever arch file is a good means of storage.

When should evidence be assembled?

You should begin to assemble evidence **as soon as you have registered as a student. Don't leave it all** until the last few weeks of your studies, because you may miss vital deadlines and your resulting certificate sent by the AAT may not include all the units you have completed. Give yourself and your training provider time to examine your portfolio and report your results to AAT at regular intervals. In this way the task of assembling the portfolio will be spread out over a longer period of time and will be presented in a more professional manner.

What are the key criteria that the portfolio must fulfil?

As you assemble your evidence bear in mind that it must be:

- **Valid**. It must relate to the Standards.
- **Authentic**. It must be your own work.
- **Current**. It must refer to your current or most recent job.
- **Sufficient**. It must meet all the performance criteria by the time you have completed your portfolio.

What are the most important elements in a portfolio that covers Level 3?

You should remember that the unit is about **payroll administration**. Therefore you need to produce evidence not only demonstrating that you can carry out certain tasks, but also you must show that you can exercise control.

For Unit 74 *Managing the payroll functions* you not only need to show that you can prepare a report, you also need to demonstrate that you have used the relevant information and have met deadlines. Covering letters or memos can provide the necessary evidence of timescales and information required.

The main evidence that you need for Unit 75 *Completing year-end procedures* are copies of P60s, P35s and forms P11D that you have produced. Remember that names should be withheld to protect employee confidentiality.

To fulfil the requirements of Unit 76 *Maintaining working relationships with external bodies* you need to demonstrate that you have used various sources of evidence to assess whether the external body can receive information. You also need to provide evidence of active involvement in communication with external bodies through letter, telephone call, meeting etc.

Finally

Remember that the portfolio is **your property** and **your responsibility**. Not only could it be presented to the external verifier before your award can be confirmed; it could be used when you are seeking **promotion** or applying for a more senior and better paid post elsewhere. How your portfolio is presented can say as much about you as the evidence inside.

For further information on portfolio building, see the BPP Learning Media Text *Building Your Portfolio*. This can be ordered via the Internet: www.bpp.com/aat

BPP
LEARNING MEDIA

P A R T   A

Managing the payroll function

chapter 1

Management
controls in payroll

Contents

Performance criteria

74.1.A Ensure the treatment of all **allowances** and enhancements is correctly identified with respect to tax, National Insurance and pensions deductions

74.1.B Update rates for permanent and temporary payments and deductions against agreed scales for each type of employee affected

74.1.C Calculate **exceptional payments** in accordance with organisational requirements, to the deadlines agreed

74.1.D Reconcile the National Insurance liability for directors against the National Insurance actually paid

74.1.E Monitor compliance with **attachments to earnings** legislation

74.1.F Ensure **termination payments** are processed accurately and in accordance with legislative requirements

74.1.G Reconcile total charges to organisational budgets against aggregate payroll totals and correctly code them for allocation

Range statement

1   **Routine payments:** payments; expenses and benefits; permanent; temporary

2   **Exceptional payments:** payments not made on the due day such as late payments to new starters; special one-off bonus not paid with normal pay; payments made to employees after they have left

3   **Attachments to earnings:** Council Tax orders; Scottish arrestments of earnings; child support orders; attachment of earnings orders

4   **Termination payments:** pay in lieu of notice; ex gratia payments; statutory redundancy payments; damages; restrictive covenants

Knowledge and understanding

3   Data Protection legislation (Elements 74.1, 74.2 & 74.3)

4   HMRC regulations in respect of:

- Income tax and National Insurance liability on pay, expenses and benefits (Element 74.1)
- National Insurance regulations concerning directors (Element 74.1)
- Income tax and National Insurance regulations relating to 'out of synch' payments (Element 74.1)
- Income tax and National Insurance regulations concerning termination and lump sum payments (Element 74.1)
- Legislation controlling attachments of earnings and their interaction with each other (Element 74.1)

7   Procedures for the security and confidentiality of information (Elements 74.1, 74.2 & 74.3)

8   Sources of information for the resolution of discrepancies (Elements 74.1, 74.2 & 74.3)

Signpost

Unit 74 is aimed at the higher level clerk, with more responsibility, but not necessarily a payroll manager.

1 The problem

At Level 2, you dealt with the day to day running of payroll. Level 3 will consider the more complex problems involved.

This element deals with some of the problems mentioned at Level 2, but deferred until Level 3.

- How do you deal with NICs for directors?
- What are attachment of earnings orders?
- How do attachment of earnings orders work?
- How do I deal with exceptional payments?
- What about termination payments?

2 The solution

Most payroll departments use computers for payroll processing. So far, we have assumed that the parameters used are correct. Section 3 deals with setting up and checking the parameters.

Section 4 looks at exceptional payments, those outside the normal payroll routine. For example, late payments to starters and special one-off bonuses paid separately from normal payroll payments.

Section 5 looks at the special rules for calculating directors' NICs and Section 6 deals with the working of attachment of earnings orders.

Termination payments are subject to special rules, dealt with in Section 7. However, redundancy payments, a special form of termination payment, will be the subject of Chapter 3.

Finally, Section 8 deals with control of payroll costs by comparison to budget; something that was mentioned in passing at Level 2.

3 Payroll parameters

3.1 What are payroll parameters?

Most payrolls are processed by computer, even in the smallest businesses. As we saw at Level 2, permanent information is kept on the employee's master file and temporary information (eg overtime, Statutory Sick Pay) is entered before each pay run.

In order to process the payroll, the computer also needs standard information and this is the information meant by the words 'payroll parameters'. Examples of payroll parameters include the following.

- Rates of pay for hourly paid workers according to grade
- Overtime rates
- Pension scheme standard percentage rates
- Rates of Statutory Payments (eg SSP)
- Tax rates
- NIC rates, according to category
- Rates of other deductions (eg trade union subs)

The system will also need to know and identify which payments are subject to tax, NICs and pension deductions.

3.2 Setting up and amending the parameters

The system should already be programmed with the latest tax and NIC rates. However, when starting a new tax year, the program supplier will send an update which needs to be run before calculating any wages for the new tax year. This update should also include the latest rates for statutory payments (eg SSP, SMP, SPP, SAP).

For monthly paid salaried workers, the employee's master file will include annual salary and the programme will use this information to calculate the monthly pay. However, any changes, whether permanent (salary increase) or temporary (overtime, temporary promotion), must be entered in the records before carrying out the payroll run.

With hourly paid workers, the usual procedure is to include the grade in the employee's master file. The computer is then programmed with the pay rates for each grade. When pay rates change, this list of hourly rates for each grade must be updated.

Similarly, approved overtime rates may be set by grade. Alternatively overtime rates may be part of the employee's master file. Some systems may operate both methods, eg hourly overtime rates set by grade but overtime for monthly paid employees included in their individual master files. The programme will need updating for any changes.

3.3 Checking the parameters

Before each payroll run, the payroll parameters must be checked.

- Correct tax and NIC rates
- Correct rates of hourly pay according to grade
- Correct overtime rates
- Correct statutory payment rates
- Correct standard deduction rates

If the wrong rates are being used, these need to be updated before the pay run.

3.4 Identifying payments

Every payment needs to be correctly identified for deduction purposes.

- Tax
- NIC
- Pension

We have already looked at this, at Level 2.

3.4.1 Taxable payments

All wages and salary payments are taxable, whether permanent or temporary.

- Wages, salary, bonuses and commission
- Backpay
- Shift pay, overtime, unsocial hours, stand-by payments
- Piecework
- Temporary promotion
- Statutory payments (SSP, SMP, SPP, SAP)

If you are not sure what these terms mean, go back to your Level 2 text and revise them.

However, some deductions are made **before** the tax is calculated. You should be able to remember these from your Level 2 studies.

- Company pension scheme deductions (basic and AVCs)
- Give as you earn (GAYE)

Some employers also make non-cash 'payments' to their employees called benefits. These benefits are recorded and entered on form P11D. Any taxable benefits will then be taxed by an adjustment to the employee's tax code (remember K codes from Level 2). Benefits are dealt with in Chapters 5 and 6 of this text.

3.4.2 NICable payments

All the taxable payments listed above are also NICable ('nickable'). From your Level 2 studies, you should remember that pension payments, and GAYE contributions are **not deductible** for NIC purposes.

Example: Pay for NIC purposes

Mary Shelley has gross pay of £1,000 for May 20X2. She contributes £50 per month to the employer's pension scheme and £5 per month to GAYE.

(a)   What is her taxable pay?

(b)   What is her NICable pay?

Solution

(a)   **Taxable pay**

	£
Gross	1,000
Pension scheme	(50)
GAYE	(5)
Taxable pay	945

(b)   **NICable pay**

As the pension and GAYE contributions are not allowable for NIC purposes, the NICable pay is £1,000.

Many expenses and benefits are subject to Class IA NICs at the year end. This will be dealt with in Chapters 5 and 6 of this text.

However, some expenses are included in pay for Class 1 NICs instead. A selection is shown below. A full list is given in Appendix I of booklet CWG 5, which can be downloaded from the HMRC website at www.hmrc.gov.uk/employers/emp-form.htm. You do not need an employer's reference number to use this facility.

Type of expense or benefit	Induce in gross pay for NICs
Vouchers (with some exceptions)	Yes
Telephone – employer is subscriber	No
Telephone – employee is subscriber: • Phone used exclusively for business • Phone exclusively for private use • Mixed business/private use	No Yes Rental – yes on full amount Calls – yes on full amount less any purely business calls (evidence needed such as call log).
Mileage payments – any profit element	Yes

Type of expense or benefit	Induce in gross pay for NICs
Travel and subsistence expenses:	
• Specific business expenses	No
• Any profit element (unless covered by a dispensation)	Yes

The expenses listed in the table above are those that you need to know according to the AAT guidance. Dispensations are dealt with in Chapters 5 and 6 of this text.

You may find the following table helpful.

Payment	Payroll		P11D	
	Tax	Class 1 NICs	Tax	Class 1A NICs
Cash or readily converted to cash	✓	✓	✗	✗
Vouchers, use of credit cards, payments on employee's behalf	✗	✓	✓	✗
Benefits where the contract is with the employer	✗	✗	✓	✓
Reimbursed business expenses	✗	✗	✗ (Enter on P11D if no dispensation, but no tax to pay)	✗

3.4.3 Pensionable payments

At Level 2, we looked at pensionable pay in detail. The following should be revision.

Pension contributions are based on **pensionable earnings**. These may be different from gross pay.

(a) Pensionable earnings may be those at a **particular date** (eg 1 January each year). So pensionable earnings would not increase until 1 January of the following year, even if there had been a pay rise in June.

(b) Pensionable earnings may **exclude** bonuses and commission. If included, these may be averaged over a number of years.

(c) The maximum amount on which tax relief can be claimed by the employee is the **greater** of net earnings and £3,600.

(d) For tax relief purposes, there is an **annual allowance** (£245,000 for 2009/10). Therefore tax relief can only be obtained on total employee and employer contributions up to £245,000. Any excess will be taxed at 40%.

Activity 1.1

Martin Bayside is a member of his firm's pension scheme. Basic contributions are 10% of salary, based on the salary at 1 January each year. Bonuses are ignored for the purposes of calculating pensionable salary. At 1 January 20X3, Martin's salary was £36,000 pa. In September 20X3, his salary increases to £37,500 pa. In October 20X3, he receives a bonus of £500. He also makes the following contributions each month.

- AVCs £25 pm
- Sharesave £20 pm
- GAYE £75 pm

Tasks

For the month of October 20X3 calculate the following:

(a) Pensionable earnings
(b) Taxable earnings
(c) NICable earnings

Tutorial note. AVCs are additional voluntary contributions to the firm's pension scheme.

3.5 Security and confidentiality

3.5.1 Data protection legislation

If you are using a computer to process payroll, then this is exempt from notification under the Data Protection Act 1998. However if you are using payroll files for any other purpose, then the rules of the Data Protection Act 1998 may apply.

Remember that the features of this legislation are:

(a) Everyone now has the right to go to court to seek redress for **any breach** of data protection law, rather than just for certain aspects of it.

(b) Filing systems that are structured so as to facilitate access to information about a particular person now fall within the legislation. This includes systems that are **paper-based** or on **microfilm** or **microfiche**. Personnel records meet this classification.

(c) Processing of personal data is **forbidden** except in the following circumstances.

(i)   With the **consent** of the subject (person).
(ii)   As a result of a **contractual arrangement.**
(iii) Because of a **legal obligation** (eg payroll).
(iv)   To **protect the vital interests** of the subject.
(v)   Where processing is in the **public interest.**
(vi)   Where processing is required to exercise **official authority.**

(d)   The processing of **'sensitive data'** is forbidden, unless express consent has been obtained or there are conflicting obligations under employment law. Sensitive data includes data relating to **racial origin**, **political opinions, religious beliefs, physical or mental health, sexual proclivities** and **trade union membership**.

(e)   Data subjects have the right to a **copy of data** held about them and also the right to know **why** the data are being processed.

Important!

For the purposes of your portfolio, you may need to include payroll documents that you have produced. This is allowed, but you need to preserve confidentiality. Therefore, the AAT recommend that personal details are either excluded from the print out or Tippex-ed out. Witness testimony will then confirm that the documents were correctly prepared.

3.5.2 Confidentiality

Payroll information is very sensitive and must be kept securely.

Unauthorised people must not have access to employee records, or information from those records, without permission. Remember, from Level 2, that no information can be given to third parties without the employee's express (written) permission; unless they have statutory authority to demand information (eg HMRC, Child Support Agency).

Employee records may be kept manually, on computer or by a mixture of both.

However the records are kept, access must be restricted to authorised personnel only. Manual files should be kept in a locked cabinet and the key kept in your possession (not in the lock!). Computer files should be protected by restricted access to that part of the programme, by password or by both.

Never leave employee files open (either manual or computer), when you are away from your desk.

Activity 1.2

Jacob Mendez is the local union representative and wants information about employees' pay to ensure that agreed pay scales are being used.

Tasks

(a)   Jacob wants to see a schedule of hourly rates of pay by grade of employee. He does not want details of individual employee's pay.

(b)   Jacob wants details of Judith Chance's pay, as he has heard that she is not receiving the correct pay for her grade.

What is your response in each case?

Activity 1.3

Judith Chance visits you with a query about her pay. She is Grade D and such employees should receive £5.50 per hour. According to her last payslip, she is only being paid £5.00 per hour. What do you do?

4 Exceptional payments

By exceptional payments, we mean those payments made outside the usual payroll run. The range statement specifies three types of exceptional payment.

    (a)   Starter joins too late to be paid in one pay period and so is paid for the odd days in the next pay period.

    (b)   Special one-off payments (eg bonus) not paid with normal pay.

    (c)   Payments made to employees after they have left employment.

In each case, you need to know the tax and NIC rules.

4.1 Late paid starters

An employee may start a few days before the end of a pay period. He joins too late to be included on that payroll run. Therefore the following pay period, he receives a full period's wages plus the extra few days. How are the extra days treated for tax and NIC purposes?

4.1.1 Tax treatment

If the employee has a cumulative tax code, there is no problem. Simply use the tables for the date of payment. Calculate the tax due and deduct the tax paid to date as shown on form P45 (if any).

For week 1/month 1 codes you need to calculate the week number for the date of payment and then deduct the week number for the week before the date of joining. The result gives the week number to be used for calculating tax.

Example: Non-cumulative tax codes

An employee joins in week 42, too late to be paid in that month's pay run. The next pay period is week 47. Which tax tables are used if his code is 146L W1/M1?

Solution

Week of payment	47
Week before week of commencement	41
Week number to be used	6

Therefore pay is calculated using week 6 tables. Subsequently, month 1 tables will be used.

4.1.2 NIC treatment

For NIC purposes, you must treat the payment as if it had been made on the normal pay days, and calculate the NICs on each part separately.

You should use whichever of the exact percentage method or NI tables that is normally used when processing the payroll.

Example

Max (a monthly paid employee) joins Parsifal Ltd during June 20X3. He is paid £2,000 at the end of July 20X3, being salary of £500 for June and £1,500 for July. How are NICs calculated?

Solution

The NICs are calculated separately on the two amounts of £500 (June) and £1,500 (July), using the monthly earnings limits and thresholds.

Activity 1.4

Maria joins Parsifal Ltd on 25 September 2009 on a monthly salary of £2,650. She is paid her first salary of £3,260 on 31 October 2009. She is NIC category letter A.

Task

Calculate the NIC due.

Your payroll system uses the exact percentage method for calculating NICs.

Tutorial note. The table A rates are as follows. Calculate employees' NIC and employer's NIC separately. Employees' NICs on earnings between the ET and UEL: 11% and on earnings above the UEL: 1%. Employer's NIC on all earnings above the ET: 12.8%. For 2009/10, monthly ET is £476 and UEL is £3,656.

4.2 Special payments not made with usual payroll

Where extra payments are made on a separate day to the normal payroll run, care must be taken not to give tax and NIC allowances as if it were a normal payday.

4.2.1 Tax treatment

Remember only one amount of free pay can be given in any pay period. In the case of K codes, only one amount of additional pay can be added in any pay period.

Strictly tax should be operated at the time any additional payment is made, using the tables for that week or month.

However, this could lead to an employee receiving a tax refund and then effectively repaying it on the normal pay day. Therefore, where the extra payment is paid **before** normal pay day, **and** the code is **cumulative**, use the following procedure.

    (a)   For suffix codes

        (i)   Enter the full amount on the deduction card in the week of payment

        (ii)   Calculate tax in the usual way for the tax week that the **normal payment** would take place

        (iii)   If there is tax to pay, deduct it

        (iv)   If there is a tax refund, ignore it. Cross out the figure in col 7 of P11 and **add** the repayment to the total tax due in col 6. Use this figure as the starting point for the next tax calculation.

        (v)   On normal pay day, calculate tax as normal.

    (b)   For K codes

        (i)   Enter the extra payment on the deduction card for the week of payment

        (II)   Add 'additional' pay for the **normal pay day** and calculate tax, using the regulatory limit

        (iii)   On normal pay day, do **not** add any more 'additional pay', calculate tax on pay using tables SR, B to D as necessary.

4.2.2 NIC treatment

Calculate NICs on the extra payment at the time of payment. Then, on normal pay day, recalculate NICs on the total payments and deduct the balance of NICs due.

Example: NICs on extra payment

Max receives a bonus of £500 on 12 February 2010. He is paid his usual salary of £2,000 on 28 February 2010. His NIC category is A.

Tasks

(a)   Calculate the NICs due on 12 February 2010.

(b)   Calculate the NICs due on 28 February 2010.

Extracts from monthly table A are given in the appendix.

Solution

(a) Max is usually paid monthly and so monthly table A is used. Payment takes place in week 45 and is entered on the deduction card for that date. Employees' NICs of £2.86 are deducted from the £500.

(b) Payment takes place in week 47 and is calculated on £500 + £2,000, ie £2,500. The entry for week 45 is crossed through, but must still be legible. Employees' NICs deducted from the payment on 28 February are £220.00 (£222.86 – £2.86).

Week	1a	1b	1c	1d	1e	1f
44						
45	~~412~~	~~64~~	~~24~~	~~0~~	~~0.19~~	~~2.86~~
46						
47	412	64	2,024	0	482.19	222.86

Activity 1.5

Complete the tax side of form P11 for Max if his tax code is (a) 461L and (b) K461.

Extracts from Table A

Code 461:		
	Week 44	3,908.52
	Week 45	3,997.35
	Week 46	4,086.18
	Week 47	4,175.01
	Month 11	4,234.12

Tax code		Amended			
461L		WK/mnth			

				K codes				K codes			K codes
W e e k	M o n t h	Pay in the week	Total pay to date	Total free pay to date	Total additional pay to date	Total taxable pay to date	Total tax due to date	Tax due at end of current period	Regulatory limit	Tax deducted in the week	Tax not deducted owing to the regulatory limit
		2	3	4a	4b	5	6	6a	6b	7	8
43	10	2,000.00	20,000.00	3,849.20		16,150.80	3,230.00			323.00	
44											
45											
46											
47	11										

		Tax code		Amended							
		K461		WK/mnth							
					K codes				K codes			K codes
W e e k	M o n t h	Pay in the week	Total pay to date	Total free pay to date	Total additional pay to date	Total taxable pay to date	Total tax due to date	Tax due at end of current period	Regulatory limit	Tax deducted in the week	Tax not deducted owing to the regulatory limit
		2	3	4a	4b	5	6	6a	6b	7	8
43	10	2,000.00	20,000.00		3,849.20	23,849.20	4,769.80	476.98	1,000.00	476.98	
44											
45											
46											
47	11										

4.3 Payments made to the employee after they have left employment

We dealt with this at Level 2. If an employee receives a further payment after he or she has left, and form P45 has been issued, then tax is deducted at the basic rate (20%). For NICs use the following rules:

- Final salary payment – use same NI table letter and earning period as when the employee left but use rates at date of payment.
- Irregular payments – use same NI table letter but **weekly** rates
- Payment made more than six weeks after date of leaving, use Table A.

5 Directors' NICs

5.1 Introduction

Special rules apply for employees who are directors or who are deemed by HM Revenue and Customs (HMRC) to be acting as directors. The NIC system for directors is, effectively, **cumulative**. This is to prevent directors artificially reducing NIC liabilities by paying themselves large sums at infrequent intervals and so avoiding the majority of employees' NICs by only paying 1% on amounts above the UEL.

Example: Abuse

Marcus is a director of his company. He pays himself a salary of £400 per month. In December 2009, he pays himself £100,000. What is his NIC liability under the normal rules?

Solution

Marcus pays no NICs for 11 months of the year as £400 per month is below the ET. In December he would pay (£3,656 – £476) × 11% + (£100,000 – £3,656) × 1% = £1,313.24

So Marcus will have paid NIC of £1,313.24 on total earnings of £104,400. If the salary had been evened out over the year (ie £8,700 per month), he would have paid 12 × [(£8,700 – £3,656) × 1% + (£3,656 – £476) × 11%] ie. £4,802.88. Therefore Marcus has saved NIC of £3,489.64.

Most employees have a weekly or monthly **earnings period** for NIC purposes but a director's earnings period is:

- **Annual** (where the director was in office on 6 April even if the director leaves during the year), *or*
- **Pro-rata annual** (if they become directors during the tax year) running from the tax week of their appointment to the end of the tax year.

Whether the earnings period is annual or pro-rated, NICs are calculated on the total earnings to date. For example, in Month 4:

	£
NICs on total earnings in months 1-4	X
Less: NICs already paid in months 1-3	(X)
NICs now due in month 4	X

This has the following effects.

- No NICs are paid by the director until the annual ET is reached (£5,715).
- Once a director has earned the annual ET, then NICs are payable at the rates in the contribution tables.
- No NICs are paid by the company until the annual Earnings Threshold is reached (£5,715)

5.2 Using the exact percentage method

Assessment focus point

The Chief Assessor has indicated that only the exact percentage method will be used to calculate NIC in skills tests and exams.

The exact percentage method makes the logic of this procedure clearer. We will deal first with an annual earnings period and then look at a pro-rated annual earnings period.

5.2.1 Annual earnings period

You approach the calculation of a director's NICs as follows.

Step 1   As usual, establish the earnings subject to NI this pay day and the Table letter you will use.

Step 2   Add these to the earnings subject to NI already paid this tax year so that you know total earnings for the tax year to date.

Step 3   Now compare this total with:

- The LEL for the whole tax year.
- The ET for the whole tax year.
- The UAP for the whole tax year.
- The UEL for the whole tax year.

Step 4   If earnings to date do not exceed the LEL, then no NICs are due yet from the director.

Step 5   If earnings to date exceed the LEL, but do not exceed the employee's ET, open a P11 but do not deduct any NICs yet.

Step 6   If earnings to date are above the ET then calculate NICs at the usual rates on total earnings between the ET and up to the UEL and at 1% above the UEL (employees' NICs).

Step 7   If earnings to date are above the ET then calculate NICs at the usual rates on earnings above the ET (employer's NICs).

Step 8   Now deduct from these figures the NICs paid in this tax year up to last pay day. The remainder is the NIC due on this pay day.

Remember that the UAP will come into play if the contracted out rates are used (see Level 2 text).

Example: Annual earnings period, exact percentage method

Molly Paterson is a longstanding director of your company. She is paid £1,000 per month. Your company has no pension scheme. Molly's earnings are subject to NIC at Table A rates. In June 2009 she received a bonus of £3,000 in addition to her normal salary payment. In July 2009 she received another bonus of £20,000.

What NICs are payable on Molly's salary in 2009/10?

Solution

In **April 2009** Molly receives £1,000. This is below the annual ET so no NICs are due in April – or in May, as the cumulative total is only £2,000.

In **June 2009**, total earnings for the year to date are:

	£
Salary (3 months)	3,000
Bonus	3,000
	6,000

Employees' NICs: (£6,000 − £5,715) × 11% = 31.35

Employer's NICS: (£6,000 − £5,715) × 12.8% = 36.48

Total NICs due to date, all payable this month as none have been paid in earlier periods = 67.83

July 2009

	£
Earnings, April – June	6,000
Salary, July	1,000
Bonus, July	20,000
Total earnings to date	27,000

	£
Employees' NICs: (£27,000 − £5,715) × 11%	2,341.35
Less: NICs deducted April – June	(31.35)
Due this pay day	2,310.00

	£
Employer's NICs: (£27,000 − £5,715) × 12.8%	2,724.48
Less NICs deducted April – June	(36.48)
Due this pay day	2,688.00

Total NICs due this pay day	4,998.00

August 2009

	£
Earnings, April – July	27,000
August salary	1,000
	28,000

	£
Employees' NICs: (28,000 − 5,715) × 11%	2,451.35
Less: NICs deducted April-July	(2,341.35)
Due this pay day	110.00

	£
Employer's NICs due to date on (£28,000 − £5,715) at 12.8%	2,852.48
Less NICs deducted: April–July	(2,724.48)
Due this pay day	128.00

Total NICs due this pay day	238.00

September 2009 – March 2010

As earnings to date are £29,000, £30,000, £31,000, £32,000, £33,000, £34,000 and £35,000 respectively which are all below the UEL, the amount due will be the same as in August ie.

	£
Employees' NIC	110.00
Employer's NIC	128.00
Total NICs due this pay day	238.00

Totals for 2009/10

Employees' NIC (£2,451.35 + (7 × £110.00)) = £3,221.35

Employer's NIC (£2,852.48 + (7 × £128.00)) = £3,748.48

Activity 1.6

Molly's sister Polly is also a director of your company. She is paid £10,000 per month. She receives a bonus of £4,000 in June 2009. Calculate the NICs due on her earnings in April, May and June 2009 at Table A rates.

5.2.2 Director joining in the year: Pro-rated Annual Earnings Period

When a director is **appointed** during the tax year, you must work out how many tax weeks are **left** in the tax year so that you can use the right figures for the LEL, ET, UAP and UEL.

Take the weekly rates of LEL and UAP from the tables and multiply by the number of weeks. However, the ET and UEL are calculated by taking the annual figure (of £5,715 and £43,875 respectively), dividing it by 52, multiply by the number of weeks and **round up** to the nearest whole pound.

Example: pro-rated annual earnings period.

(a) Dolly becomes a director on 6 March 2010. This is the last day of tax Week 48. So there are 5 tax weeks left in the tax year (**you ignore week 53 for these purposes and include the week of appointment**).

(b) Dolly receives a salary payment of £4,950 at the end of March 2010. How much NIC is due on this assuming she is paying table A rates?

Solution

(a) First you must calculate the various limits pro rata for Dolly's earnings period.

LEL: £95 × 5 = £475

ET: £5,715/52 × 5 = £550

UAP: £770 × 5 = £3,850

UEL: £ 43,875 /52 × 5 = £4,219

So Dolly's earnings for the tax year to date exceed the UEL prorated for her earnings period. As she is not contracted-out, you can effectively ignore the UAP.

(b)   Employees' NICs due: $(£4,219 - £550) \times 11\% + (4,950 - 4,219) \times 1\% = £410.90$

Employer's NICs: $(£4,950 - £550) \times 12.8\% = £563.20$

Total NICs due this period $= £974.10$

Activity 1.7

Here is a list of the directors of your company on 6 April 2010.

Name	Date of appointment
John Birch	21.1.91
Sally Hill	3.4.09
Bill Rogerson	10.5.09
Lucille James	12.11.09
Arun Misra	6.4.10

Arun Misra replaces Sean Heaney who was appointed on 1 January 1998 and resigned on 10 December 2009. What is the earnings period for each director for the tax year 2009/10?

Activity 1.8

Your company has two directors.

- Peggy Ainsworth has been a director for many years and currently earns £45,000 per annum. She is 45 years old and has a personal pension plan as the company has no occupational pension scheme.

- On 1 August 2009 Vijay Parmar was appointed to the board. He is 30 years old and will earn £32,000 per annum. He also has a personal pension plan.

Calculate the NICs **due to date** on each director's salary at the end of August.

5.3 Administrative arrangements for assessment of director's NICs

There is an optional arrangement for calculating directors' NICs when all these conditions are met.

- The director normally receives his or her earnings at **regular intervals** (eg monthly) so that he or she has a regular earnings period like other employees.

- The director's earnings normally exceed the lower earnings limit for the pay period concerned (eg where paid monthly, the director must normally be paid more than £412).

- The director agrees to have his or her NICs assessed as if the earnings period was the regular pay period, not the annual or pro-rata annual period normally used.

All this means is that all through the tax year until the last pay period the director's NICs are calculated in the same way as everyone else's with no reference to NICs paid in other periods in the current tax year.

However, **in the last pay period of the tax year** (or in the last pay period before a director resigns) the payroll officer must **reassess the NICs due** in respect of the director's earnings in the tax year, using an annual or pro-rata annual earnings period as appropriate.

You work out the NICs due for the whole earnings period, deduct the NICs already paid and pay the balance to HMRC with the other NICs and PAYE due for the period.

If the director receives a bonus during the year, or changes to a different contribution rate, you may reassess the NIC due at that point to avoid delaying a large payment or refund until the end of the tax year. Once having made a reassessment, however, you must then apply an annual or pro-rata annual earnings period in the usual way for the remainder of the tax year.

Example: Administrative arrangements for assessment of directors' NICs

Pearl Ltd has three directors. Eric receives a monthly salary of £2,500. Elizabeth receives a quarterly fee of £300. William receives occasional irregular payments. Can any of the three directors be paid using the administrative arrangements?

Solution

Elizabeth's earnings are at regular intervals but below the LEL. William's earnings are not paid at regular intervals. Their earnings must be assessed for NICs using an annual earnings period. Eric, however, earns above the LEL and is paid monthly. If he agrees, his earnings for Months 1 to 11 can be assessed to NICs in the normal way. In Month 12 the payroll officer will reassess his earnings using an annual earnings period.

Example: Bonus paid in year

Let's consider the situation if Eric is paid £1,000 pm and receives a bonus of £18,000 in month 6.

Month 1

	£
Employees' NICs: (£1,000 − £476) × 11%	57.64
Employer's NICs: (£1,000 − £476) × 12.8%	67.07
Total NICs due for the month	124.71

Months 2 − 5 and 7 − 11 will all be assessed like this.

Month 6

	£
Employees' NICs: (£3,656 − £476) × 11% + (£19,000 − £3,656) × 1%	503.24
Employer's NICs (£19,000 − £476) × 12.8%	2,371.07
Total NICs due for the month	2,874.31

Month 12

Total earnings for the year: £12,000 salary + £18,000 bonus = £30,000

	£
Employees' NICs due: (£30,000 − £5,715) × 11%	2,671.35
Paid in Months 1 to 11: (£57.64 × 10) + £503.24	(1,079.64)
Payable now	1,591.71

	£
Employer's NICs due: (£30,000 − £5,715) × 12.8%	3,108.48
Paid in Months 1 to 11: (£67.07 × 10) + £2,371.07	(3,041.77)
Payable now	66.71

Eric's NIC for Month 12 exceeds his salary! It would have been better to reassess his NIC at the end of Month 6. There would then have been a large NIC liability which could have been deducted from his bonus.

It would be good practice, if the reassessment is not done until Month 12, to explain to Eric that there will be a large NIC liability then.

HMRC requires employers to pay over the whole amount due, even if the director's earnings are insufficient to cover it.

6 Attachments of earnings

Although the standards refer to attachments **to** earnings (in pc 74.1.E), we are looking at attachment **of** earnings orders (AEOs). These were mentioned at Level 2, but now you will see how these orders work in practice.

Remember from Level 2, that attachment of earnings orders are **statutory deductions** and so must be made.

6.1 Child Support Agency

The Child Support Agency (CSA) administers the system of child maintenance. It will assess the amount an absent parent should pay towards the child's maintenance.

The CSA will issue a Deduction from Earnings Order (DEO) direct to an employer. The DEO will show the amount to be deducted and sent to the CSA. Failure to comply with a DEO is an offence under section 32(8) of the Child Support Act and could lead to prosecution.

Example of a DEO

A DEO indicates that the normal deduction rate is £30 per week and the protected earnings rate is £100. The employee's net earnings are £120 for the first week and £160 for the second week. How much is deducted under the DEO?

_____

Solution

The protected earnings rate is £100. This means that any deductions under the DEO cannot take the employee's pay below £100 per week.

First week

	£
Net pay	120
Protected earnings	(100)
Leaves	20

Therefore you would only deduct £20 in the first week and carry forward the balance of £10 not deducted.

Second week

	£
Net pay	160
Protected earnings	(100)
Leaves	60

As the amount available exceeds the normal deduction (£30) and shortfall brought forward (£10), you would deduct a total of £40 in the second week, with nothing carried forward.

Note that only shortfalls in deductions are carried forward. Any shortfalls in protected earnings are lost. However, for DEOs issued prior to 2003, shortfalls in protected earnings are carried forward.

Example of amounts carried forward

Andy DiMaggio has a DEO showing a protected earnings rate of £500 per month and a deduction rate of £150 per month. The DEO starts on 1 September 2009. Pay for the first four months after the order comes into effect is as follows.

	£
September 2009	900
October 2009	450
November 2009	650
December 2009	1,000

What is deducted each month?

Solution

Month	Attachable pay	Protected earnings	Available pay	Arrears of deduction b/f	Deduction in month	Arrears of deduction c/f
Sept	900	500	400	–	150	–
Oct	450	500	(50)	–	–	150
Nov	650	500	150	150	150	150
Dec	1,000	500	500	150	300	–

An employer is allowed to take up to £1 from wages each pay period towards administrative costs of making the deductions. This deduction is additional to the DEO and is kept by the employer. Note that this charge is taken after the DEO and can reduce the income below the protected rate.

So, in the first example, the employer could still take £1 administrative costs in the first week, even though this would reduce net pay to £99.

However the administrative cost cannot be taken for any pay period where no deductions are made. In the example above, the administration cost could be taken in September, November and December, but not in October.

Activity 1.9

You are the payroll assistant for Harris Ltd. You have received a DEO for Mr Tweed. The DEO shows a normal deduction rate of £50 per week and a protected earnings rate of £100 per week. Harris Ltd will take the £1 per week administrative fee from Mr Tweed's pay. What is Mr Tweed's net pay for weeks 1-4, if his pay after tax and NICs is as follows?

(a)   Week 1   £150
(b)   Week 2   £175
(c)   Week 3   £100
(d)   Week 4   £250

6.2 Court orders

6.2.1 Introduction

A court can make an Attachment of Earnings Order (AEO) in respect of an unpaid debt, eg maintenance debts.

Court issued AEOs can be priority or non-priority orders

Priority

- Maintenance debts
- Court fines

Non-priority

- Judgement debts

A priority order will be deducted before a non-priority order. If there is insufficient pay to cover both types of orders, then it is usually the priority order that is deducted. However, if the protected earnings rate for the priority order exceeds the pay, then the non-priority orders may be deducted.

If there are two or more orders in a category, then they are taken in date order. Note that a DEO is treated as a priority order for these purposes. So if an employee has a DEO from January 2004, a priority AEO from September 2000 and a non-priority AEO from January 2000, the order will be:

1   Priority AEO – September 2000
2   DEO – January 2004
3   Non-priority AEO – January 2000

Example of priority and non-priority orders

Frances Di Maggio has two court orders. The first is for deductions of £20, with a protected earnings rate of £150. The second is for deductions of £20, but with a protected earnings rate of £100. The first is priority, the second non-priority. Frances' earnings for the current week are £125.

Solution

No deduction can be made under the first order, as Frances' earnings are below the protected earnings rate. As this is a priority order, both the protected earnings and deduction shortfalls are carried forward. However, the deductions under the second order can be made, as this will leave £25 available and the deduction is £20.

	Attachable pay	Protected earnings	Available pay	Deduction	Arrears of protected earnings c/f	Arrears of deduction c/f
First order (priority)	125	150	(25)	–	25	20
Second order (non-priority)	125	100	25	20	–	–

The employer is obliged to make the deductions under the AEO and to pay them to the court (or as directed in the order). As seen above, the AEO is similar to the DEO in that it will show a normal deduction rate and the protected earnings rate.

With a priority AEO both the protected earnings and deductions are cumulative. So shortfalls of **both** protected earnings **and** deduction are carried forward. However, non-priority orders are **not** cumulative. So each pay period is considered in isolation without bringing forward under-deductions or arrears of protected rate.

6.2.2 Types of orders

In **England and Wales**, Attachment of Earnings Orders (AEOs) can be made under the following Acts.

- Attachment of Earnings Act 1971 – orders can be priority or non-priority (AEO)
- Community Charge Regulations 1989, 1992 and 1993 – mainly irrelevant now (CC)
- Council Tax (Administration and Enforcement) Regulations 1992 – priority orders (CT)
- Child Support (Collection and Enforcement) Regulations 1992 and 1993 – priority orders (DEO)
- Schedule 5 AEO (from April 2004) – priority orders (S5)

In **Scotland**, the orders are called Arrestment of Earnings Orders. They are made under the following Acts.

- Debtors (Scotland) Act 1987

    - Current Maintenance Arrestments (CMA)
    - Earnings Arrestments (EA) for debts and fines
    - Conjoined Arrestment Order (CAO)

- Child Support (Collections and Enforcement) Regulations 1992 and 1993 – DEO on same basis as England and Wales.

In Scotland, an employer can only operate one order at a time. If a second order comes in, it can only be operated if it is a CAO.

In **Northern Ireland**, the legislation parallels that in England and Wales.

6.2.3 Attachable earnings

Earnings that can be 'attached' (ie have orders deducted from them) are as follows in England and Wales.

- Wages
- Salary
- SSP (but **not** SMP, SPP or SAP)

Orders are deducted after tax and NIC.

- AEOs – specified rate and protected earnings, priority orders carry forward arrears of deductions and protected earnings
- CC/CT/S5 – percentage table (see Section 6.3)
- DEOs – like priority AEOs prior to 2003, for orders issued from 2003: arrears of protected earnings are not carried forward

The employer can levy a £1 administration charge per pay period.

6.2.4 Arrestable earnings

In Scotland, arrestable earnings are the same as attachable earnings in England and Wales.

Orders are deducted after tax and NIC.

- CMAs – fixed amounts with some protected earnings
- EAs – fixed amounts drawn from tables
- CAOs – combination of both the above orders
- DEOs – specified rate with protected earnings, arrears of both deductions and protected earnings can carry forward

The employer can charge £1 per pay period for administrative costs.

6.3 Council Tax orders

A council can recover arrears of Council Tax by applying to a Court for one of the following.

- Distraint of goods by a bailiff
- Distress warrant
- Attachment of earnings order (AEO)

For payroll purposes, you are interested in the AEO.

Council Tax AEOs are issued by the charging authority in a set format. They operate in a completely different way to Court Orders, as there is no deduction or protected earnings rates. Instead Council Tax AEOs use a set of percentage deduction tables, similar to Student Loan Deductions.

Schedule 5 AEOs work in exactly the same way.

7 Termination payments

7.1 What are termination payments?

Termination payments are made when an employee's contract is ended, usually without the period of notice specified in the contract.

The employee may also be made **redundant**, in which case there is a minimum statutory payment, statutory redundancy pay.

Redundancy will be dealt with in detail in Chapter 3 of this Text. However, the point to note now is that redundancy means that the employee's job no longer exists. Whereas termination means simply that the employee has been asked to leave, his or her job may still be there and he or she may be replaced.

Termination payments can include many elements. The following list includes the most common ones.

- Pay in lieu of notice
- *Ex-gratia* payments
- Redundancy – statutory and occupational (see Chapter 3)
- Damages for breach of contract
- Restrictive covenants
- Compromise agreements
- Golden handshakes
- Garden leave

7.2 Tax and NIC treatment

Some termination payments are exempt, others partly exempt and most are entirely taxable and NICable. It is essential that **each element** of the termination package is **considered separately** to determine the tax and NIC status.

7.2.1 Contractual payments

Contractual payments are fully taxable and NICable. Contractual payments may include amounts not mentioned in the contract but that are usual in the trade or that the employer is in the habit of making.

- Payments for work done (eg terminal bonus to ensure employees stay to the end of the notice period)
- Payments for doing extra work during a period of notice
- Pay in lieu of notice (where stated in the contract or where the payment is made automatically)
- Payments for extending a period of notice
- Holiday pay
- Compensation for loss of office (if stated in the contract)

These are all taxable and NICable in full and should be entered on the deduction card on the date of leaving.

7.2.2 Non-contractual and other payments

Non-contractual payments, also called *ex-gratia* payments, should come as a complete surprise to the employee. They are made at the employer's discretion and are **not** to reward work, loyalty or staying on after a period of notice to finish a job. Be aware that the employer should not have promised these payments to the employee, either verbally or in writing, otherwise they become contractual. (Remember that contractual payments are taxable in full.)

Other payments on termination including the following.

- Compensation for loss of office (where not mentioned in the contract)
- Redundancy pay

Ex-gratia payments and these other payments are **partly exempt**. They would not normally be subject to the PAYE rules because they are not payments in return for services. Therefore special legislation was introduced to bring them into the PAYE rules.

The first £30,000 is exempt and any excess is taxable, but **not NICable**.

As you will see in Chapter 3, statutory redundancy pay is not taxable but does form part of this £30,000 exemption.

If termination payments are received over a period of time, then the £30,000 limit is allocated to earlier payments first. **Benefits** that continue after termination are taxable when received. However they can form part of the £30,000 exemption. The exemption is set against cash first, then benefits.

Example: Benefits

Bill Bowles was made redundant on 5 April 20X1. He was paid a total of £25,000 in redundancy pay and was allowed to keep his company car until 5 April 20X2. The taxable benefit for the car is £8,500 pa.

What is the taxable amount in (a) 20X0/20X1 and (b) 20X1/X2?

Solution

(a) **20X0/X1**

	£
Redundancy payment	25,000
Exempt	(25,000)
Taxable	NIL

(b) **20X1/X2**

	£
Benefit	8,500
Exempt (£30,000 – £25,000 used in 20X0/X1)	5,000
Taxable	3,500

Activity 1.10

Jennifer Jones has been made redundant. In addition to her redundancy package, she is given an additional payment of £35,000. She is not contractually entitled to this payment and it comes as a complete surprise to her. Is it an *ex-gratia* payment?

Activity 1.11

The letter enclosing the cheque for £35,000 in Activity 1.10 above, thanks Jennifer for all her hard work and states that this extra payment is due to her loyalty over the past 10 years. Does this make any difference to your answer to activity 1.10?

7.2.3 Exempt payments

Very few payments are fully exempt from tax and NICs. They are:

- Lump sum payments from approved pension schemes
- Lump sum payments for disability
- Lump sum payments for service abroad

7.2.4 Recording payments

Any termination payments that are taxable should be included on the P45 and the Tax Office notified of the details.

If any payments are made after the issue of the P45, tax must be deducted at the basic rate (code BR). The employee and Tax Office must be notified of the payment and deduction.

7.3 Pay in lieu of notice (PILON)

The employee's contract may state that he or she is entitled to one month's notice. Quite often on a termination, the employee is given little or no notice.

Obviously this could lead to a court case for breach of contract and therefore the employer will usually offer pay in lieu of notice (called PILON for short). So if the employee is entitled to six weeks' notice and only receives one week's notice, he will usually be paid PILON amounting to five weeks' wages.

Note that some contracts of employment still say one month's notice. This is correct for up to 4 years' service. After this, an additional week is added for each year's service up to a maximum of 12 weeks (3 months).

If PILON is mentioned in the contract of employment, it will be subject to tax and NICs as usual and is included on the deduction card on the date of leaving. If the employer is in the habit of paying PILON, even though it is not mentioned in the contract, then this is also fully taxable and NICable.

However, if PILON is paid as damages, then it is treated as partly exempt. No NIC is due and the PILON forms part of the termination package, so only amounts over £30,000 are taxable. The same applies to non-contractual PILON.

7.4 Damages

Damages for breach of contract are not subject to NICs. However, damages are taxable if the total payment on termination exceeds £30,000.

7.5 Restrictive covenants

An employee may accept a limitation on his or her future conduct or activities in return for a payment.

For example, the employee may agree not to set up his or her own business, in direct competition to the former employer, for one year after leaving or within five miles of the former employer's offices.

Any payments made under a restrictive covenant are fully taxable and NICable.

7.6 Compromise agreements

This is the situation where the solicitors for the employer and employee agree a payment in lieu of the employee suing for damages. If the agreement is contractual, then it is full taxable and NICable. However if it is not contractual, then it is partly exempt (as part of the £30,000 limit) but not NICable.

7.7 Golden handshake

Some businesses will make an extra payment when terminating an employee's job. These are usually called 'golden handshakes'

If specified in the contract, or the employer usually pays them, they are fully taxable and NICable. Otherwise they form part of the total payment subject to the £30,000 exemption.

7.8 Garden leave

Sometimes it is in the employer's best interests to have an employee leave the place of employment immediately, but not to take up a new employment until the period of notice specified in the contract is finished. This is usually known as 'garden leave'. The idea is that the employer continues to pay the employee, but the employee stays at home and works in his or her garden. Salary is paid as usual (as if the employee was actually working his or her notice period) and is fully taxable and NICable.

8 Budgets

A business will attempt to control costs by setting a budget. Budgets are usually set by department and will include payroll costs.

The budget will estimate the payroll costs for each month based on the number of employees and their salaries, wages, etc. Pay rises may be included in the budget.

Therefore the payroll manager should be able to compare the actual payroll costs to budget and provide a reconciliation of any discrepancies.

Example: Comparison to budget

Parsifal Ltd's total payroll costs for May 20X5 are £120,000. Budget for the same month is £110,000. The payroll manager is asked to reconcile the actual costs to budget.

Solution

On investigation, the payroll manager discovers that the factory staff worked overtime over one weekend in May 20X5 in order to fulfil an urgent order. This overtime was not included in the budget.

The additional (unbudgeted) overtime amounted to £8,420 gross. It is assumed that employer's NIC amounts to 12.8% of this figure.

In addition, employer's pension contributions will total 5% of this figure.

Reconciliation of May 20X5 wages to budget

	£	£
Budget		110,000
Extra costs:		
Overtime to fulfil urgent order	8,420	
Employer's NIC @ 12.8%	1,078	
Employer's pension costs @ 5%	421	
		9,919
		119,919
Unreconciled difference		81
Actual wages		120,000

Activity 1.12

In June 20X5, there is a further discrepancy between Parsifal Ltd's actual payroll costs of £135,000 and budget of £120,000.

Comparison between budget and actual reveals that unbudgeted bonuses of £12,733 gross were paid during June 20X5. Employer's NIC and pension contributions are not included in this figure. Complete the following reconciliation.

Parsifal Ltd
Reconciliation of actual payroll costs to budget for June 20X5

	£	£
Budget		
Unbudgeted costs:		
Bonuses		
Employer's NIC @ 12.8%		
Employer's pension costs @ 5%		
	_____	
Unreconciled difference		_____
Actual wages		_____

Key learning points

☑ **Payroll parameters** are used by computerised systems in order to process payroll.

- Rates of pay for hourly paid workers by grade
- Overtime rates
- Pension scheme standard percentage rates
- Rates of other standard deductions

☑ Payroll parameters need to be **set up and checked** before each payroll run.

☑ Payroll payments need to be **identified for deduction purposes**.

- Taxable
- NICable
- Pensionable

☑ Some **expenses** need to be included in pay for NIC purposes.

☑ All payroll records must be kept **secure and confidential**.

☑ You need to know the tax and NIC treatment of **exceptional payments**.

☑ There are special rules for **directors' NICs**.

☑ You must know how to deal with **DEOs** and **AEOs**.

- Protected earnings
- Deduction rates
- Whether shortfalls are cumulative or not

☑ **Termination payments** may be wholly taxable and NICable, wholly exempt or partly exempt.

☑ **Partly exempt payments** have to be totalled. The first £30,000 of this total is exempt from tax. However, all partly exempt payments are exempt from NICs.

☑ Payroll costs may be **controlled** by comparison to **budget**.

☑ You may be required to perform a **reconciliation** between budget and actual costs.

BPP LEARNING MEDIA

Quick quiz

1   Directors' NICs are calculated differently from those of other employees. What is the principal difference?

2   A director in office on 6 April is leaving your company before the end of the tax year, so you calculate his NIC as for any other employee. True or false?

3   Does the employer receive any compensation for the work involved in a DEO?

4   An employee's total of partly exempt payments on leaving is £50,000. How much is taxable and how much NICable?

Answers to quick quiz

1   Directors have an annual earnings period. This is pro-rated for directors appointed during the year. The effect of this is that directors' remuneration is subject to NICs calculated on a cumulative basis.

2   False. Even if a director leaves during the tax year, his or her remuneration must be dealt with on an annual earnings basis for NIC purposes.

3   Up to £1 per pay period that a deduction is made can be taken from net pay to cover the employer's administrative costs.

4

	£
Total payments	50,000
Exempt	(30,000)
Taxable	20,000

The whole £50,000 is exempt from NICs.

Activity checklist

This checklist shows which performance criteria, range statement or knowledge and understanding point is covered by each activity in this chapter. Tick off each activity as you complete it.

Activity

1.1 ☐ This activity covers performance criteria 74.1.A.

1.2 ☐ This activity covers knowledge and understanding point 7.

1.3 ☐ This activity covers knowledge and understanding points 7 and 8 and performance criteria 74.1.B.

1.4 ☐ This activity covers performance criteria 74.1.C.

1.5 ☐ This activity covers performance criteria 74.1.C and range statement 2.

1.6 ☐ This activity covers performance criteria 74.1.D.

1.7 ☐ This activity covers knowledge and understanding point 4 regarding NI regulations for directors.

1.8 ☐ This activity covers performance criteria 74.1.D.

1.9 ☐ This activity covers performance criteria 74.1.E.

1.10 ☐ This activity covers performance criteria 74.1.F and knowledge and understanding point 4 on termination payments.

1.11 ☐ This activity covers performance criteria 74.1.F and knowledge and understanding point 4 on termination payments.

1.12 ☐ This activity covers performance criteria 74.1.G.

chapter 2

Queries and management information

Contents

Performance criteria

74.2.A Seek clarification or additional information from employees or managers where the nature of their queries is not clear

74.2.B Check that individuals raising queries are authorised to receive the information they are requesting.

74.2.C Agree all requests for information for content, **medium** in which **data** is to be presented, together with the **format** of the information and deadlines for the despatch of information

74.2.D Produce accurate information that meets the requirements agreed with the intended recipients

74.2.E Respond to telephone or face-to-face enquiries accurately and in accordance with the organisation's customer care requirements

74.2.F Refer enquiries to the appropriate person when you do not have the authority or expertise to resolve them

Range statement

1   **Reporting medium:** report printed from computerised payroll system; word-processed document; e-mail and electronic file transfer

2   **Data:** personal; organizational; financial; statutory; non-statutory

3   **Format:** formal report; letter; memorandum

Knowledge and understanding

3 Data Protection legislation (Elements 74.1, 74.2 & 74.3)
5 Information flows within the organisation (Element 74.2)
6 Organisational, external agency and employee requirements for information (Elements 74.2 & 74.3)
7 Procedures for the security and confidentiality of information (Elements 74.1, 74.2 & 74.3)
8 Sources of information for the resolution of discrepancies (Elements 74.1, 74.2 & 74.3)

Signpost

This element is about providing information to management and resolving employees' queries about their pay.

1 The problem

The payroll department is responsible for producing payroll reports for management. In addition, individual employees will have queries about their personal pay.

How are these queries to be resolved? What about confidentiality and security of information?

2 The solution

In this chapter, we will be looking at the types of information that may be required within an organisation. Remember that because payroll contains sensitive (confidential) data, information can only be given to **authorised** people.

Employees' enquiries are likely to require different handling than management enquiries.

Employees are often genuinely concerned about the information held on computer files. So we will look at the provisions of the Data Protection Acts.

3 What information is required?

As a payroll assistant, you will probably receive many requests for information. When a request is made from within your organisation you will need to decide the following points.

- Is the person requesting the information authorised to receive it?
- Exactly what information is needed?
- When is the information needed?

3.1 Authorisation

You may receive a request for information from your supervisor. If the information is for your supervisor's own use, then there is no problem with authorisation. Your supervisor is obviously authorised to receive payroll information!

Suppose your supervisor has passed on a request for information from someone outside the payroll department. It is likely that the third partly is authorised to receive the information, otherwise your supervisor would not have passed on the request. However it does no harm to check authorisation to the authorised signatory list, as your supervisor may be busy and did not realise exactly what information was requested.

An **authorised signatory list** is a list of people in the organisation authorised to provide payroll data (eg authorising overtime) and to receive it. By each name, there should be a specimen signature.

You may also receive a request for information direct from another department, eg accounts. The accounts department will normally receive a monthly (or weekly) summary of total gross pay and deductions for each pay period. This is usually a total for all employees, rather than individual figures. However, the accounts department do need details of individual director's pay and benefits at the company year end (as these figures have to be disclosed in the company's published accounts).

Therefore you will soon get to know which individuals and departments are authorised to receive payroll information on a regular basis. What happens when you receive a request from someone outside this regular circle, or if a regular contact requests unusual information?

If someone who is not authorised requests payroll information, you must always refer the request to your supervisor for authorisation. Similarly, if someone that you know is authorised requests unusual information, once again you should refer the request to your supervisor pointing out that the information requested is unusual.

In summary, never give out payroll information unless authorised to do so. If in doubt, refer the request to your supervisor.

Activity 2.1

Your supervisor passes you a request for the salary details of Alan Smith. The request is signed by A Brown. The personnel manager is Arthur Brown, but this does not look like his signature. In addition, the information is to be sent to A Brown's home address. What do you do?

Activity 2.2

The sales manager, Alice Cooper, is preparing a salary review for her sales reps. She sends you a request for details of commission paid during the last twelve months. Do you let her have the information?

3.2 Content

Once you are satisfied that the request is authorised, you will need to verify exactly what information is needed. Remember that one of the payroll department's criteria is **accuracy.** It is no use producing details of deductions for month 2, if the request is for deductions in **week** 2.

Most times a request for information will make it clear exactly what information is required. However, bear in mind that people outside the payroll department may use terms differently.

For example, a request for details of deductions from the accounts department would normally mean both statutory and voluntary deductions. However a similar request from the pensions department or trustees would probably mean that they needed details of pension deductions only.

Therefore it is important to keep in mind who is requesting the information and what they are likely to mean by this request. If in doubt, always go back to the person requesting the information to clarify exactly what they need.

In the example above, it would be a waste of your time to provide details of all deductions (both statutory and voluntary), when the pensions department only wanted the pension deductions. Similarly the pensions department will be annoyed to receive a lot of information that they do not need.

3.3 Deadline

It is essential to find out whether there is a deadline for the information. If the pensions department need details of pension deductions for a meeting at 10.00 on Thursday, it is no use giving the information at 10.00 on the following Friday.

You also need to know about any deadlines in order to plan your work. If two reports have been requested at the same time, you need to know which is needed first.

Remember another of the payroll department's criteria is **timeliness**. It is no use producing a highly detailed, accurate report, if it is sent out too late for the recipient to be able to use it. This is a complete waste of your time. It is far better to get accurate information that is less detailed (but fulfils what is needed) to the person on time.

4 What format should the reply take?

The format of your reply needs to be **appropriate** to the request. You will normally reply in one of the following ways.

- Paper (eg letter, memorandum, report printed by the computer)
- Disc (eg word-processed document or spreadsheet)
- Electronically (eg e-mail, fax)

You should check the format required at the same time as you verify the content of the report. However, if the deadline is close, you may need to check if an alternative format can be used (eg faxing a report instead of sending a paper copy by internal mail).

4.1 Paper reports

A paper report can be in the form of a letter, a memo or a printout of a computer schedule. Paper reports can be used whether the payroll system is manual or computerised.

A letter is useful for formal answers. An employee may want a letter confirming his or her income for presentation to a bank or a landlord. Alternatively an employee on maternity leave may have queried her Statutory Maternity Pay and a letter will set out her entitlement better than a phone call (which can be forgotten or misunderstood).

A memo is used for informal answers. The Chief Executive may want details of the employees who have received gross pay in excess of £40,000 during the year. There is no need to write a formal letter, but a memo can be put in an envelope marked 'private and confidential' to ensure that the information is not seen by anyone except the Chief Executive.

Memos are also useful for sending information to all employees. If, for example, your organisation is just about to change from paying wages by cheque to direct credit, a memo can be used to inform all employees and to request bank or building society details.

If the report is complex, then it may be easier to produce a spreadsheet of the information required. Spreadsheets can be produced manually or by computer depending on the system used by your organisation. Also, if your organisation uses computer software to process the payroll, it may be easier to just use one of the standard reports produced by the software. In either case, the report can then be given to the person requesting the information.

Remember the confidential nature of payroll information and do not leave the reports lying around. If the person requesting the information is not at their desk, either put the report in an envelope marked 'private and confidential', or leave a message that the report is ready and take the report back with you. You can then lock the report away until it is collected.

4.2 Disc reports

In the case of computer produced reports (whether a spreadsheet produced by you or a report produced by a payroll processing software package), it will save paper if the report is downloaded onto disc.

Downloading the report onto a disc is more secure, as the report can be password protected.

Discs are also useful if the person requesting the information needs to process the figures himself. He can download the disc onto his computer and then manipulate the information into whatever format he wishes.

Activity 2.3

You are preparing a commission report as requested by Alice Cooper in activity 2.2. It was agreed that you would send Ms Cooper a print out by 2.00 pm on Thursday. However, the printer has stopped working and the repairman is not due until 11.30 am on Thursday. What do you do?

4.3 Electronic reports

Reports can also be sent electronically by e-mail and fax.

A fax can be useful if the person needing the report is out of the office (eg working at home or at another office). Due to the confidential nature of payroll information, you should telephone before sending the fax to ensure that the recipient is there and can wait by the machine to take the fax as soon as it is sent.

E-mail is a useful way of sending information to one or more people within the organisation. It is an electronic form of memo and can be used in the same circumstances. Also schedules or spreadsheets can be sent as an e-mail attachment, saving the need to send paper copies or discs by internal post, for example. If everyone in the organisation has e-mail, it is an effective way of sending out general information.

E-mails can also be encrypted to ensure privacy and that only the recipient can open them. Therefore e-mails can be a useful way of sending sensitive payroll information.

Reports sent to HMRC may need to make use of electronic file transfer. We will look at this in detail in Chapter 4.

Activity 2.4

Ms Cooper is at a customer's office when you phone her in activity 2.3. She gives you the option of getting her secretary to print out the report and then faxing it to her, or of sending the report file via e-mail to her laptop. Which option do you use?

5 How should the report be distributed?

If the report is to go to one person, then it can be distributed in any of the ways detailed in Section 4 on the format of the report.

However, sometimes a report needs to go to a number of people (for example, to all the members of the Board prior to a Board Meeting). Once again, confidentiality must be maintained, but also timeliness needs to be considered.

Therefore it is important that the method of distribution be agreed in advance with the recipients.

Example: Board meeting

The Board are meeting in two day's time to agree the directors' salaries for the next year. You have been requested to provide a report of the directors' salaries and benefits for the past year. There are five board members and you contact each to find out how the report should be sent to them. Their replies follow.

T. Blair	Send to home address
G. Brown	In office
A. Campbell	In office
N. Chamberlain	Travelling, so fax or e-mail to hotel
P. Mandelssohn	On holiday

Solution

Some of the replies were not very helpful! T Blair wants the report sent to his home address, but the meeting is in two days' time so can you trust the post? You know he has a laptop computer, so you ask his secretary to find out if you can e-mail the report to his laptop instead. She tells you that his laptop is in the office and recommends that you send paper copies, via courier, to his home address, as that is how she is sending other Board Meeting papers to him.

G Brown and A Campbell are both in the office. Therefore you could take paper copies to them. However, if the report is bulky, it may be better to e-mail it.

N Chamberlain is in Europe on business, staying in hotels. He has suggested that you fax or e-mail the report to his hotel. He does not have a laptop and will be flying into the UK just before the meeting, so does not want the report left in his office or sent to his home. Ask his secretary to find out when he will be at his hotel and arrange to fax the report when he can be there to receive it. Do not e-mail to the hotel, as you do not know how many people will have access to the information before it is passed to Mr Chamberlain.

P Mandelssohn is on holiday. You speak to his secretary and find out that he is due home the day before the meeting. He is not expected in the office until the meeting. He has told his secretary that he wants some other reports couriered to him the day he gets home. So you arrange for your report to be couriered at the same time.

The above example shows some of the problems that can arise in distributing reports. Most of the problems arose because of the short notice given to you and the fact that the method of distribution was not given with the request. However this is the kind of problem you are likely to meet in practice. Note how useful senior managers' secretaries can be in providing information on how to contact their boss.

These reports are for internal use, we will be looking at information requests from external bodies in Part C of this Text.

6 Employee enquiries

As a payroll assistant, a fair amount of your time will be spent dealing with employee enquiries. These may come from past, present or potential employees.

Each will have their own problems. However, make sure that you understand the exact nature of the enquiry **before** replying. Remember that replies must be accurate, timely and relevant.

If your organisation has a **customer care policy**, then its requirements must also be followed for employee enquiries, including past and future employees.

6.1 Past employees

Past employees will include the following categories.

- Retired employees now receiving a pension
- Retired employees who did not qualify for a pension
- Past employees who have changed jobs
- Past employees who are currently unemployed
- Past employees who have been made redundant
- Past employees who were sacked for misconduct

In the final two categories, there may be employees who are taking your employer to an Industrial Tribunal for unfair dismissal or unfair selection for redundancy. However, in all categories, you must ensure that any reasonable request for information is answered.

Activity 2.5

Anna Christianson was dismissed for improper conduct and is taking your employer to the Industrial Tribunal for unfair dismissal. She has written to you requesting details of her overtime payments for the past year to produce as evidence at the Tribunal. Do you reply to this query?

Past employees may contact you with enquiries about their P45. Remember, from your Level 2 studies, that you should never alter or reissue a form P45.

If the former employee has lost their P45, then you can provide a letter setting out the information shown on the P45. If the former employee insists that there is an error on the form P45, you will have to explain that you can not alter a P45 once it has been sent to HMRC.

Activity 2.6

George Jones telephones you to say that he has found an error on his form P45 and he wants a revised form to take to his new employer. Do you issue a revised form P45?

Former employees may need to contact you for details of their pay if they have lost their P60 (details of gross pay and PAYE and NI deductions for a tax year). HMRC rules now allow you to issue a duplicate P60 (see Chapter 4 of this Text).

Former employees may also need details of their past pay for pension purposes, although the request may come from the pension fund.

In all cases, requests for **reasonable** information from past employees should be answered. However, **unreasonable** requests (eg for details of pay from ten years ago) should be politely refused. Your organisation is allowed to make a charge for providing information (maximum £10) as recompense for the time and effort involved.

Activity 2.7

Rosemary Clark left employment with your firm two years ago. She writes to you saying that she lost all of her P60s during a move and wants details of her pay and deductions for the six years she was employed by your firm. Is this a reasonable request?

6.2 Current employees

Current employees are more likely to have the following types of queries.

- How was my net pay calculated?
- What are all these deductions for?
- Why hasn't my pay rise been put through this month?
- Why haven't I been paid this month?

All enquiries for information from current employees need to be dealt with promptly and courteously, even if they do seem silly. If the employee has asked the question, then it is obviously important to the employee to have a proper explanation of the point. Remember you are the payroll professional, lay people often have little idea of the tax rules.

However, employees are only entitled to information about their own pay. If they want information about other employees, then this cannot be given without authorisation.

Activity 2.8

Jack Smith, the union representative, comes to see you about Sid Sanderson, one of his members. He is concerned that Sid is being paid less than the agreed union rate for his work and wants details of Sid's current pay rate. Do you give him this information?

Activity 2.9

Sid Sanderson turns up at your office furious that you have not given his pay details to Jack Smith. What do you do?

6.3 Future employees

Future employees may contact you to find out what information they need to bring with them when they start with your organisation. Usually, they should have been given this information by whoever hired them, or by personnel. However, this may not have happened or the future employee may have lost or forgotten the instructions.

The information required will depend on the data needed to complete the employee records. This will usually include the following.

- Form P45 (if the new employee comes from a previous job)
- Name
- Title
- Address
- Telephone number
- Tax code
- Date of birth
- Gender
- NI number
- NI table letter
- Bank/building society account details (for direct credit)

Other information should be sent to you by personnel (eg job title, date of commencement, salary details, overtime rates, etc).

Once the employee has joined the firm, you can find out other things like voluntary deductions (eg pension fund, payroll giving, etc).

6.4 Summary

Regardless of whether the employee is past, current or future, you should always deal with enquiries as follows.

- Make sure you understand the query before replying.
- Make sure that the person requesting the information is authorised to receive it.
- Make sure that it is a payroll query (and not personnel, for example).
- If you cannot deal with the enquiry yourself, refer it to your supervisor or the appropriate department.
- Make sure that replies are accurate, timely and relevant.
- Ensure that you maintain confidentiality and security of information.
- Keep records of face-to-face and telephone enquiries in case of future queries.

7 Methods of making enquiries

You will have to be very careful, when receiving employee enquiries, that you are dealing with the person concerned. Methods of making contact include the following ways.

- Person-to-person
- Telephone
- Letter or memo
- Fax
- E-mail

7.1 Person-to-person

Person-to-person enquiries occur when the employee comes to see you in person. This may seem a safe way of giving information if you work in a small organisation and know all the employees personally.

However, what about a large organisation with a thousand employees? It is very unlikely that you will know even 100 employees personally. So you will need to check that the person is exactly who he or she says.

One way is to ask them to provide personal information, such as their employee number, their home address, their date of birth or their bank account details.

You should only answer the query when you are sure that you are speaking to the employee concerned. If in doubt, say that you will send the information to their home address. Always keep a record of any person-to-person enquiries for future reference.

7.2 Telephone

Once again the question of identity arises. Even if they are using the correct extension number, you can not be sure that an unauthorised person is not using the employee's phone.

You should carry out similar checks as above. Never answer the query over the telephone, if you are in any doubt about the caller's identity. Use an alternative method, such as sending a memo by internal mail, or a letter to the employee's home address.

Once again keep a record of all telephone conversations for future reference.

Activity 2.10

You receive a phone call from someone saying that they are Reeza Longah and asking for details of their payrise due this month. Your phone system shows that the call is from Reeza's extension. However, how can you be sure that you are actually talking to Reeza?

7.3 Letter or memo

A query by letter or memo should be checked to employee records for details such as the following.

- Home address
- Telephone number (if given)
- Signature (many organisations ask new employees to sign a starter form)

Only when you are satisfied that you have a genuine employee enquiry, should you send a reply.

7.4 Fax

Similar details should be used as for letters. Additional checks can include the fax number used, if it is the employee's home fax or an office fax number.

If replying by fax, always ensure that the recipient will be by the machine to ensure confidentiality.

7.5 E-mail

Enquiries by e-mail may seem safe, if the employee is following normal computer safety rules. However, you cannot be sure that the employee has not left their desk with the computer still on, and someone else is using their e-mail for unauthorised purposes.

Therefore even e-mail messages do need to be checked. If in doubt, reply by some other means, eg letter to home address or ask for written confirmation of the query.

8 Third party enquiries

You may be approached by third parties with requests for information about an employee.

- HM Revenue and Customs (HMRC)
- Pension trustees
- Banks and building societies
- Mortgage suppliers
- Child Support Agency (CSA)

Where the third party has **statutory** authority to make the enquiry (eg HMRC, CSA), then you must give that information even if the employee has forbidden you to provide it.

Activity 2.11

One of your employees has come to see you, as he is being investigated by the Child Support Agency. He tells you that he is not the father they are seeking and not to give them any information. What do you do?

Where the third party does not have statutory authority, then you can only provide information when the employee gives you authorisation.

9 Data Protection Acts 1984 and 1998

9.1 Security

As a payroll officer, one of your tasks is to ensure that not only are employees paid the right amounts, but that the payroll records and files are kept **secure** and **up to date**.

Payroll information is some of the most **sensitive information** that is produced. In many companies, employees at certain grades do not know what their colleagues are paid. Also, many higher paid employees prefer to keep their salaries a secret.

Whatever you feel about how desirable it is to keep these matters confidential, **it is necessary for you to do so**.

- Do **not discuss employees' personal details,** other than as is necessary for your job.

- Ensure that payroll files, tapes and disks are **locked away**, unless you are using them at the time, or they are **supervised by appropriate personnel** (eg computer room staff) if authorised.

- Ensure that only **authorised personnel** have access to the files.

Similar considerations apply to the employer's **cheque book** and **cash**, if these are used for paying wages. They should be kept in a safe.

In some organisations where employees are paid in cash, the payroll office will be **locked** for the entire period that cash is being counted and the paypackets prepared.

9.2 The Data Protection Act 1984

Any business which uses computers is likely to have to comply with the provisions of the Data Protection Act 1984. This sets **standards for the holding of personal data** and gives certain **rights to the individual**. It aims to **prevent misuse** of computer-held information to the disadvantage of the person concerned.

Businesses may hold data about individuals for a wide range of purposes. Sensitive examples are assessments of **customers' creditworthiness** or of the **reliability of suppliers**. One area that is of relevance to almost every business holding personal information on computers, is the holding of data about **employees**.

To a very limited extent, the processing of such data may be exempt under the Act. **There is an exemption for payroll processing if that is all the data is used for**. However, if a company holds data about employees for any other purpose (eg personnel), it is caught by the Act.

It is clear that companies can use employee data for a wide range of purposes other than payroll processing, including the following.

- Employee assessment
- Career planning
- Manpower planning
- Training purposes

- Recording of holidays
- Job scheduling
- Provision of references

It is therefore most unlikely that an employer is able to take advantage of the exemption in practice.

9.3 Practical implications of the Data Protection Act 1984

Because the exemptions are so narrow, most businesses will not be able to rely on them and therefore the Act will apply. How does this affect payroll officers?

In order to ensure compliance with the Act, all relevant staff must be made fully aware of its implications and made to realise that it will inevitably affect the performance of their work with computers. You should therefore be aware of the **data protection principles**.

There are eight **Data Protection Principles**. All eight apply to **personal data held by data users**, and the eighth applies additionally to personal data in respect of which services are provided by **computer bureaux**.

The eight principles are as follows.

1   The information to be contained in personal data shall be obtained, and personal data shall be processed, fairly and lawfully.

2   Personal data shall be held only for one or more specified and lawful purposes.

3   Personal data held for any purpose or purposes shall not be used or disclosed in any manner incompatible with that purpose or those purposes.

4   Personal data held for any purpose or purposes shall be adequate, relevant and not excessive in relation to that purpose or those purposes.

5   Personal data shall be accurate and, where necessary, kept up to date.

6   Personal data held for any purpose or purposes shall not be kept for longer than is necessary for that purpose or those purposes.

7   An individual shall be entitled:

   (a)   at reasonable intervals and without undue delay or expense:

      (i)   to be informed by any data user whether he holds personal data of which that individual is the subject; and

      (ii)   to access to any such data held by a data user; and

   (b)   where appropriate, to have such data corrected or erased.

8   Appropriate security measures shall be taken against unauthorised access to, or alteration, disclosure or destruction of, personal data and against accidental loss or destruction of personal data.

A specified and lawful purpose (principle 2) seems a broad term. In fact there are a number of purposes related to commercial life, including employee data, statutory audit requirement and so forth.

As a payroll administrator, how do you think these purposes affect you? Some of the principles are a matter of company policy, but others are clearly relevant in all cases.

The **length of time** personal data is kept varies from situation to situation. You are required to keep **PAYE personal data** for at least three years. In other instances, it may not be necessary: for example, do you need to keep the personal file of somebody who left your organisation several years ago?

Security measures do concern you. In a payroll department you will be responsible for maintaining security. Issues of **confidentiality** arise, too. You cannot, for example, disclose your boss's salary to your friends (unless of course he or she tells you to do so). If in doubt, you would be best advised to ask the person concerned.

An individual who is the subject of personal data has a **right of access**, which means that he can request a **copy of the information** constituting personal data held by a data user. He should make his request **in writing** and may be asked to pay a **fee**. The statutory maximum fee is currently set at £10. It is unlikely that you would ask a current employee to pay a fee to find out what information was in your files but it might not be unreasonable to charge an ex-employee who wanted these details, because you might have to go to some trouble to recover the data and print it out. Find out your organisation's policy in this respect.

9.4 Data Protection Act 1998

The Data Protection Act 1998 brings the UK into line with the rest of Europe.

The data protection principles extend to **all personal data**, in any form – so all employee records are covered.

Sensitive data (such as racial origin or religious belief) can only be processed in future with the **express consent** of the person concerned, unless this conflicts with employment obligations.

The processing of other personal data is **forbidden** unless one of the following applies.

- The subject freely gives specific and informed agreement.
- A contractual arrangement provides for it.
- There is a legal obligation (as there is on employers to collect tax and NICs).
- Protection of the vital interests of the subject requires it.
- The public interest requires that it be processed.
- The exercise of official authority requires it.

Activity 2.12

There are several problems to be dealt with today in the Payroll Office. How would you deal with each one, and why?

(a) Mona Lott has come in to complain that she is not paid as much as others doing what she considers to be work of equivalent responsibility. She wants you to give her a list of all the employees of her grade and length of service, stating the basic salary etc of each employee.

(b) Jim Jones, one of the union officials, says he has heard that the managing director has awarded a huge pay increase to himself, while refusing to authorise any pay increase for the staff Jim represents. He asks you as a favour to give him all the details of directors' salaries and perks. (Jim Jones is a family friend.)

(c) Sharon Brown tries to get into the office to borrow some tea bags. The office is locked because you are making up the weekly pay packets for the few dozen staff who still insist on this method of payment. Sharon has not been with the company long and has previously seemed very interested in finding out all about the arrangements for paying employees in cash.

(d) Harry Ellis, who recently left the company, asks to see your computer records about him. He is worried that they may be inaccurate. You think he may be confusing payroll with personnel but he will not listen when you attempt to explain. He insists on receiving a printout at once. You cannot do this as you are in the middle of a long print run.

10 Payroll reports

So far, we have mentioned computer produced reports. However, how do you extract information from the system?

To demonstrate the basic operations of a payroll system we will look at the menus you can find on a payroll package. Generally speaking, when it is time to run a payroll, the following tasks have to be carried out.

- Amend permanent data (if necessary) on employee records.
- Input wages data for processing.
- Calculate the payroll details.

In addition, from time to time it may be necessary to provide additional information.

- Print a special report of some kind.
- Alter something which affects the whole system (eg income tax rate changes).
- Answer enquiries on payroll data.

The main menu for a typical payroll package is as shown below.

```
                            PAYROLL
                          MAIN MENU
DATA FILE MAINTENANCE ------------------------------------------------------- 1

PAYROLL CALCULATION RUN ----------------------------------------------------- 2

REPORTING ------------------------------------------------------------------- 3

ENQUIRIES ------------------------------------------------------------------- 4

FILE SECURITY --------------------------------------------------------------- 5

SYSTEM MAINTENANCE ---------------------------------------------------------- 6

CLOSEDOWN                                                          <RETURN>

PLEASE SELECT A FUNCTION
```

In this Unit, we concentrate on reporting.

10.1 Produce a report

In order to produce a report, the main menu option to select is option 3: 'reporting'. The computer will provide you with this sub-menu.

```
                            PAYROLL
                     REPORT REQUEST MENU
CURRENT PAYROLL REPORTS ----------------------------------------------------- 1

END OF YEAR DATA ------------------------------------------------------------ 2

COMPANY/EMPLOYEE PERM DATA -------------------------------------------------- 3

EXIT                                                              <RETURN>

PLEASE SELECT A FUNCTION
```

Which of these options you select depends on what kind of report you want. All sorts of reports are available to you. Reports usually summarise information for the whole company or for a department.

If you select Option 1: current payroll reports, this will enable you to access the following types of report.

- Employee details
    - Net pay for last pay period and cumulative to date
    - Cumulative deductions (itemised)
    - Gross pay to date
    - Pension contributions
    - SSP, SMP, SPP and SAP

- Departmental analyses
    - Pay to date
    - SSP, SMP, SPP and SAP
    - Deductions
- Student Loan Deductions
- Income tax for last pay period and cumulative to date
- Employee NICs for last pay period and cumulative to date
- Employer's NICs for last pay period and cumulative to date
- SSP, SMP, SPP and SAP recoveries

You can also create your own reports on most systems eg analysis of wages by financial code.

Option 2 will provide end of year reports needed to complete the end of year returns. Option 3 enables you to provide print outs of permanent data, such as gross salaries, number of employees in the pension scheme etc.

Reports can be concerned with different types of data.

- Personal (Fred Blogg's payslip)
- Organisational (a list of hourly pay rates by grade of employee)
- Financial (a posting summary)
- Statutory (tax deductions)
- Non-statutory (pension contributions)

10.2 Make enquiries

As you might expect, enquiries are answered by selecting Main Menu option 4: 'enquiries'. The following sub-menu will appear on the screen.

```
                              PAYROLL
                          ENQUIRIES MENU
  COMPANY PAYROLL DATA --------------------------------------------------- 1
  EMPLOYEE PERMANENT DATA ----------------------------------------------- 2
  EMPLOYEE CUMULATIVE DATA ---------------------------------------------- 3
  EMPLOYEE ACCUMULATORS ------------------------------------------------- 4
  EMPLOYEE TEMPORARY DATA ----------------------------------------------- 5
  CLOCK CARD DATA ------------------------------------------------------- 6
  EMPLOYEE SICK PAY ----------------------------------------------------- 7
  EMPLOYEE END OF YEAR DATA --------------------------------------------- 8
  EXIT                                                        <RETURN>
  PLEASE SELECT A FUNCTION
```

You will then select the appropriate option needed for your enquiry eg option 7 for a sick pay enquiry. 'Enquiries' are usually used to obtain information about individual employees.

☑ Any information must be:

– Accurate
– Timely
– Authorised
– Confidential

☑ When a request for information is received, you need to check the following.

– Authorisation
– Content
– Deadline

☑ The format should be appropriate to the request.

– Paper
– Disc
– Electronic

☑ Distribution of the report should be agreed in advance.

☑ Employee enquiries can come from **past**, **present** or **future** employees.

☑ Always ascertain the **exact** nature of the query **before** replying.

☑ Refer non-payroll enquiries to the appropriate person or department.

☑ Replies must be:

– Accurate
– Timely
– Relevant

☑ Computer files and the information that must be given to employees is governed by the Data Protection Acts 1984 and 1998.

☑ Third party enquiries can come from two sources.

– Statutory
– Non-statutory

☑ All non-statutory third party enquiries have to be authorised by the employee.

☑ No matter how an enquiry is received, check that the person making the enquiry is authorised to receive the information.

Quick quiz

1   Should information be given to anyone who asks for it?

2   What are the two most important considerations about the information in a report?

3   Should payroll information ever be faxed?

4   If a report contains confidential information, can it be left on the recipient's desk?

5   How should reports be distributed?

6   If an employee spots an error on their P45, you should issue a new form. True or false?

7   A new employee should always give you their last P60. True or false?

8   What qualities should a reply to a query have?

9   Third party enquiries must be authorised by the employee. True or false?

10   Is it safe to assume that e-mails are from the person show on the header?

11   If your employer uses a computer payroll package, will the Data Protection Act 1984 apply?

1   No. Payroll information is confidential and so can only be given to authorised people.

2   It must be accurate and it must be timely.

3   Only if the recipient can be standing by the machine when the fax is received.

4   Never! Leave a message that the report is ready and take it back to your office.

5   Agree the method of distribution in advance.

6   False. You should never amend or issue a new form P45. If the error is fundamental, then you should inform your tax office.

7   False. They should give you their P45. However, if they do not have a P45 (because they have been unemployed for some time), then details such as the NI number can be taken from a P60.

8   All replies should be accurate, timely and relevant.

9   False. All **non-statutory** enquiries must be authorised by the employees. However, bodies like HMRC and the CSA have **statutory** authority to demand information without the employee's permission.

10   No. Someone can be using another person's e-mail to send the message. For example, an employee could leave their computer switched on while away from their desk and someone else takes the opportunity to send e-mail in the employee's name.

11   If the employer holds employee data on computer **only** for payroll processing, then the Act does not apply. However, this is unlikely to be the case in practice.

Activity checklist

This checklist shows which performance criteria, range statement or knowledge and understanding point is covered by each activity in this chapter. Tick off each activity as you complete it.

Activity

2.1		This activity covers performance criteria 74.2.B and 74.2.F.
2.2		This activity covers performance criteria 74.2.B and 74.2.F.
2.3		This activity covers performance criteria 74.2.C.
2.4		This activity covers performance criteria 74.2.C and knowledge and understanding point 7.
2.5		This activity covers performance criteria 74.2.B and 74.2.D.
2.6		This activity covers performance criteria 74.2.E.
2.7		This activity covers performance criteria 74.2.D.
2.8		This activity covers performance criteria 74.2.B.
2.9		This activity covers performance criteria 74.2.E.
2.10		This activity covers performance criteria 74.2.B and 74.2.E and knowledge and understanding point 7.
2.11		This activity covers performance criteria 74.2.E and knowledge and understanding point 6.
2.12		This activity covers performance criteria 74.2.B, 74.2.E and 74.2.F

chapter 3

Redundancy payments

Contents

Performance criteria

74.3.A Ensure all documentation relating to the redundancy is checked for compliance with statutory and organisational requirements

74.3.B Refer documentation that does not comply with statutory and organisational requirements to the appropriate person for resolution

74.3.C Calculate the length of reckonable service, age and value of a week's pay in accordance with statutory rules

74.3.D Calculate the amount of any statutory redundancy payment accurately

74.3.E Apply the terms of any local, non-statutory scheme to enhance the statutory payment correctly

74.3.F Inform the relevant pensions administrator where the redundancy is linked to pensionable retirement, calculate any abatement correctly and apply it to the final payment

74.3.G Input to the payroll system all sums due in respect of the redundancy in ways that ensure that payments will be made at the correct time and will receive the appropriate tax treatment

74.3.H Ensure all communications relating to redundancy are conducted at an appropriate level of confidentiality

Range statement

1   **Documentation:** redundancy notice; statement of redundancy payment; service record; contract of employment; birth certificate; details of organisational redundancy payment scheme

Knowledge and understanding

1   Employment Rights Act legislation in respect of redundancy rights (Element 74.3)
2   Industrial Tribunals legislation in respect of redundancy rights (Element 74.3)
3   Data Protection legislation (Elements 74.1, 74.2 & 74.3)
6   Organisational, external agency and employee requirements for information (Elements 74.2 & 74.3)
7   Procedures for the security and confidentiality of information (Elements 74.1, 74.2 & 74.3)
8   Sources of information for the resolution of discrepancies (Elements 74.1, 74.2 & 74.3)

Signpost

This is the sole element dealing with redundancy payments.

1 The problem

Unfortunately redundancy can happen at any time and some employees may well have the misfortune to be made redundant more than once in their working lives. For payroll purposes, there are special rules for redundancy payments.

2 The solution

Section 3 will look at redundancy in general, including the rules on when an employee is entitled to redundancy pay.

Under the Employment Rights Act 1996, an employee is entitled to a minimum payment on being made redundant. This is called statutory redundancy pay and is dealt with in Section 4.

The employer may have a scheme to pay more redundancy than the statutory minimum. In addition, an employee may be entitled to other payments. Those payments are looked at in Section 5.

3 Redundancy

3.1 Legal position

An employee has the legal right to a redundancy payment (as compensation) if he is made redundant. Redundancy occurs for the following reasons.

(a)   The employer has ceased, or intends to cease, to carry on the whole business, or the local office or factory is closed.

(b)   Trade requirements have altered so that less or no employees are needed to carry on the business (eg automation of a production line).

The businesses of associated employers are usually treated as one business for this purpose.

If the employee's contract requires him to work at other places than his present place of employment, and the employer *under the terms of the contract* requires him to move to a different place of work because there is no longer work at his present place of employment, that is *not* a case of redundancy. Where there is no such clause an employee may reject a proposed relocation and claim a redundancy payment.

The proper test to see if an employee is redundant is whether there has been a reduction of the employer's requirements for employees to work at the place where the person is normally employed.

In considering whether the requirements for staff have reduced, it is the overall position which must be considered. If, for example, A's job is abolished and A is moved into B's job and B is dismissed, that is a case of redundancy although B's job continues.

If the employer reorganises his business, or alters his methods so that the same work has to be done by different means which are beyond the capacity of the employee, that is not redundancy. The test is whether the job still exists.

3.2 Offer of further employment

The employer may offer a redundant employee alternative employment. If the employee then **unreasonably** refuses the offer, he loses his entitlement to redundancy pay.

The offer of alternative employment must be in the same capacity, at the same place and on the same terms and conditions as the previous employment. If it differs in any such respect, it must be suitable employment in relation to the employee.

The employee is entitled to a four week trial period in the new employment. If either party terminates the new contract during the trial period, it is treated as a case of dismissal for redundancy at the expiry date of the previous employment.

If the employee accepts the offer and continues in the new employment after the expiry of any trial period, his service is treated as continuing from the old employment.

3.3 Resignation

An employee is not entitled to redundancy if he resigns voluntarily.

He may keep his entitlement to redundancy pay if, after the employer gives him notice of dismissal, the employee gives notice of termination to expire at an earlier date than the employer's notice. On receiving the employee's notice the employer may, by a further written notice, require the employee to withdraw his notice (and continue in service until the dismissal takes effect). The employee who fails to comply is not entitled to redundancy pay, unless an employment tribunal decides that he should be.

An employer may warn the employee that he will shortly make him redundant, but does not at that stage give him notice of redundancy. The employee obtains another job and then resigns; that is a voluntary resignation and so he loses his claim to redundancy pay.

If the employer, by his conduct, breaks the contract of employment, the employee may treat this as constructive dismissal and is entitled to redundancy pay if he leaves with or without giving notice.

3.4 Early retirement

The case law is not clear as to whether early retirement amounts to redundancy. However if an employee has been given a redundancy notice but then accepts early retirement, this is an implied withdrawal of the redundancy notice. So the employee is not entitled to redundancy pay.

3.5 Consultation with employees

Regulations introduced in October 1995 mean that the employer is required to appoint an employee representative, whom the employer must consult and inform. The Regulations replaced the previous minimal requirements to inform and consult trade union representatives – obligations an employer could avoid by refusing to recognise or by derecognising the trade union.

Every employer is required to inform and consult the employee representative where:

- A business transfer is proposed.
- More than twenty employees are to be made redundant over ninety days or fewer.

The consultation will include consideration of ways in which to:

- Avoid or reduce the proposed redundancies.
- Mitigate the consequences thereof.

These obligations are in addition to requirements to give written details of:

- The reasons for the proposals.
- The numbers and descriptions of employees it is proposed be made redundant.
- The proposed method of carrying out the redundancies.
- The proposed method of calculating any redundancy payment.

The requirements specify consultation with a view to reaching agreement. There is no obligation for an employer to consult with both a recognised trade union and an employee representative and he may select which of the two representatives he wishes to consult.

The law concerning redundancy is very complicated. You are not expected to know the detailed rules for your assessment. However you will be expected to know a general outline of redundancy, as this gives you guidance on the type of evidence of entitlement to redundancy payments.

4 Statutory redundancy pay

4.1 Qualifying conditions

In order to obtain a redundancy payment, the following conditions must be met.

- (a)   The employee must have been continuously employed for at least two years.
- (b)   He must have been dismissed (or laid off or put on short time).
- (c)   The reason for dismissal must be redundancy.

Some employees are excluded from entitlement. These include fishermen remunerated by a share of the catch and those employed outside the UK.

A person who enters into a contract for a fixed period of at least two years may, by that contract (or subsequently before its expiry), agree in writing to exclude any claim for redundancy payment if the contract is not renewed on its expiry date.

An employer must give a redundant employee a formal written notice of dismissal. Within six months from the relevant date (the date of expiry of the dismissal notice or equivalent event such as expiry of a fixed-term contract) the **employee** must either:

- Obtain payment
- Make written claim for payment by notice in writing to the employer
- Secure that his claim (if in dispute) is referred to an employment tribunal
- Make a complaint of unfair dismissal to a tribunal

If this is not done within the six months the entitlement to redundancy pay is lost unless, within the next six months, the employee persuades a tribunal that it is just and equitable to permit a claim out of time.

On making a redundancy payment (other than under the award of a tribunal), the employer must give to the employee a written statement showing how the amount has been calculated.

4.1.1 Age discrimination regulations

The Employment Equality (Age) Regulations 2006 came into force on 1 October 2006. These regulations removed the upper age limit for redundancy rights, so that older workers now have the right to claim redundancy unless it is a genuine retirement.

The regulations also removed the lower and upper age limits for SRP.

4.2 Calculation of SRP

Statutory redundancy pay is calculated on the following scale.

- (a) One and a half week's pay for each complete year of continuous employment above the age of 40.
- (b) One week's pay for each such year of employment between the ages of 22 and 40.
- (c) Half a week's pay for each such year of employment below the age of 22.

The compulsory school leaving age means that most people will be 16 years old when they leave school. However, some children may be only 15¾ when they leave school if their 16th birthday is before 1 September. Therefore it is possible for someone to have 2 full years' employment while still 17 years old. Though most people will not qualify until they are 18 years old.

You should be able to ascertain the length of service from the employee's **service record** with your employer. Age needs to be checked to the employee's **birth certificate**.

The Department for Business, Innovations and Skills (BIS) oversees redundancy pay. The BIS issues online guidance on redundancy payments, which includes a ready reckoner for calculating the number of week's pay due. It can be found on the Directgov website www.berr.gov.uk/whatwedo/employment/employment-legislation/employment-guidance/page33157.html

(The Directgov (www.direct.gov.uk) website covers minimum wage and working time regulations as well.)

A week's pay (subject to a specified maximum adjusted annually in line with inflation) is taken as the pay of the final week of employment prior to the redundancy notice being issued. If earnings fluctuate, then the week's pay is taken as the average of the 12 complete weeks prior to the redundancy notice being issued. The **contract of employment** should help here.

The maximum number of years that can be counted is twenty. The period of service is counted backwards from the redundancy date. So if an employee has more than twenty years' service, the last twenty years count.

The current maximum for a week's pay is £350 from February 2009, making the maximum statutory payment £350 × 1½ weeks × 20 years = £10,500. From 1 October 2009, the maximum for a week's pay will rise to £380, making the statutory maximum payment £11,400 (£380 × 1½ × 20).

An employment tribunal may decide any dispute over the amount of a redundancy payment. An employee of an insolvent employer who claims that his employer is liable to pay him a redundancy payment may, if the whole or part of the payment remains unpaid, apply to the Secretary of State for payment from the National Insurance Fund. The Secretary of State then has the right to recover the payment from the employer.

Protective awards, which are orders of a tribunal that an employer shall continue to pay remuneration of employees, may be made against an employer who, in a redundancy situation, fails to consult trade unions or to give notice of impending redundancies to the Department of Business, Innovations and Skills.

Example: Redundancy payment

Jack Jones is 62 years old. The normal age of retirement for your firm is 65. Jack is made redundant on 01 January 20X0, having been employed for 30 years. His normal salary is £10,000 per year. What redundancy payment is he entitled to receive?

Solution

Jack Jones has worked for 30 years, the last 21 years since the age of 41. Therefore he is entitled to 1½ weeks pay for the maximum of 20 years. His weekly pay is £10,000/52 = £192.31. Therefore his statutory redundancy pay is £5,769.30 (£192.31 × 1½ × 20).

Activity 3.1

Calculate the statutory redundancy pay due to the following employees, assuming the redundancy takes place in August 2009.

(a)   Martha Marshall who has worked for the firm for 10 years and is now 52 years old. She earns £390 per week.
(b)   Simon Lebon is now 28 years old and has worked for the firm for 5 years. He earns £130 per week.
(c)   Ranjit Singh who has worked for the firm for 20 years and is now 40 years old. He earns £200 per week.

4.3 Steps to take in calculating SRP

Calculating SRP can be time consuming. It will help if you take the following steps.

Step 1   Calculate length of reckonable service

In SRP calculations, only full years of employment are counted. So if an employee has been with the firm for 11 years 11 months, only 11 years count as 'reckonable service'. You will need to know the date employment started and this should be in your employee records or the contract of employment. If the maximum of 20 years is exceeded, use the last 20 years in looking at the age factor. Remember to count backwards from the redundancy date.

Step 2   Determine age factor

You need to know the employee's date of birth for the following reasons.

- Employment before the year in which the 22nd birthday occurs will attract half a week's pay per year.

- Employment from the first full year of employment after the 22nd birthday to the year in which the 41st birthday occurs will attract one week's pay per year.

- Employment from the first full year of employment after the 41st birthday will attract one and a half week's pay per year.

If the employee records do not show the date of birth, you should ask for the employee's birth certificate.

Step 3   Determine the value of a week's wage

For annual salary, a week's wage is 1/52 of the annual figure. Where weekly pay fluctuates, an average of the last twelve weeks' wage is taken. Remember the statutory maximum is £350 per week until 30 September 2009 and £380 per week thereafter.

Step 4   Calculate SRP

Using the last 20 years of employment, if total employment is over 20 years, multiply the week's wage by the age factor and the number of years.

Example: SRP

Jason King was born on 25 June 1970. He started work on 1 July 1990 and is being made redundant on 31 December 2009. Calculate his SRP, if his salary is £10,000 pa.

Solution

Step 1   Calculate length of reckonable service

Start date: 01.07.90
Redundancy date: 31.12.09

Number of full year's service: 19 years (from 01.01.91 to 31.12.09)

Step 2   **Determine age factor**

Date of birth: 25.06.70
Date reached 22: 25.06.92
Date reached 41: not applicable

When he joined on 01.07.90, he was 20 years old.

The first full year of service after his 22nd birthday commences on 01.01.93.

Therefore he qualifies for 2 years at ½ a week's pay per year and 17 years at 1 week's pay per year.

Step 3   **Determine the value of a week's wage**

Salary: £10,000 pa

One week's pay is £10,000/52 = £192.31

Step 4   **Calculate SRP**

SRP = (2 × ½ × £192.31) + (17 × 1 × £192.31) = £3,461.58

Activity 3.2

Now calculate the statutory redundancy pay (SRP) due to these employees on 1 January 2010.

(a)   Alnoor Patel born 26 June 1960. He has worked for the company since 1 January 1981 and his weekly pay is £500.

(b)   Janet Long born 31 March 1990. She has worked for the company since 1 July 2006 and her weekly pay is £140.

(c)   Mark Canter born 27 September 1948. He has worked for the company since 1 July 1968 and his weekly pay is £390.

4.4 Paperwork

As indicated in 4.1 above, each redundant employee must receive a formal written notice of dismissal. This is called a **redundancy notice**. This is likely to be issued by the personnel department, but a copy should be sent to payroll in order to authorise any redundancy payment due. The **minimum** notice period required by law is one week for each year of service, up to a maximum of twelve weeks.

When the employee receives his or her redundancy payment, then he or she must also receive a **statement of redundancy payment** showing how it has been calculated (see 4.3 above). In the case of Jason King (see example above), the statement of redundancy payment could be something like this.

STATEMENT OF REDUNDANCY PAYMENT

Jason King
Date of birth: 25.06.70
Date of commencement of employment: 01.07.90
Date of redundancy: 31.12.09

For each full year of employment up to 22, you are entitled to one half week's pay. For each full year of employment over 22 but under 41, you are entitled to one week's pay.

Your salary is £10,000 pa, which is equivalent to £192.31 per week (£10,000/52).

(a)	17 years' service after the age of 22 (01.01.93 to 31.12.09)	
	17 × 1 × £192.31	£3,269.27
(b)	2 full years' service between 01.01.91 and 31.12.92	
	2 × ½ × £192.31	£192.31
	Payment enclosed	£3,461.58

(**Note.** Part year's service does not count for statutory redundancy pay)

Assessment focus point

If you are asked to produce a statement of redundancy payment in the assessment, a blank form will be provided showing the detail required. You will just need to calculate SRP and complete the statement.

If you are asked to prepare a redundancy payment for an employee for whom you do not hold a copy redundancy notice, then you should query this with your supervisor. Remember that all payroll payments (including SRP) have to be properly authorised.

4.5 Redundancy and pensions

Assessment focus point

Although pc 74.3.F still includes regulations relating to abatement, this no longer applies to redundancies on or after 1 October 2006.

Under the age discrimination regulations, pensions may not be offset against statutory redundancy payments made to employees dismissed on or after 1 October 2006.

5 Other payments on redundancy

5.1 Payments

When an employee is made redundant, he may be entitled to receive some (or all) of the following.

- Statutory redundancy pay (SRP)
- Organisational redundancy pay (in excess of SRP)
- Compensation for loss of office (eg when a director is made redundant)
- Payments for work done (eg terminal bonuses to ensure employees stay to the end of the notice period)
- Payments for doing extra work during a period of notice
- Payments in lieu of notice (eg the contract of employment states one month's notice but the redundancy notice gives only one week's notice)
- Holiday pay
- Lump sum from pension schemes (if retiring)
- Reimbursement of legal costs (if taking the employer to an Industrial Tribunal)

HMRC publishes a redundancy fact sheet which deals with the tax treatment of all types of payments. If your employer is making employees redundant, you are advised to get this fact sheet, particularly if unusual payments are to be made.

5.2 Tax treatment

Payments made on redundancy may be entirely exempt, partly exempt or entirely chargeable to PAYE (see Chapter 1).

The following payments on the termination of employment are exempt, and are not entered on the deduction card.

- Lump sum payments from registered pension schemes
- Legal costs recovered by the employee from the employer following legal action to recover compensation for loss of employment, where the costs are ordered by the court or (for out-of-court settlements) are paid directly to the employee's solicitor as part of the settlement.

Where payments **are partly exempt: the first £30,000 is exempt; any excess is taxable**. SRP is not taxable, but reduces the £30,000 limit.

Payments and other benefits provided in connection with termination of employment are taxable in the year in which they are received. For example, a director may be allowed to use the company car for a year after redundancy. If he was made redundant on 5 April 20X1, a benefit would arise in 20X1/X2 taxable in that year. (Benefits will be dealt with in detail in Chapters 5 and 6.)

Employers have an obligation to report termination settlements which include benefits in kind to HMRC by 6 July following the tax year end. No report is required if the package consists wholly of cash and does not exceed £30,000. Employers must also notify HMRC by this date of settlements which (over their lifetime) exceed or may exceed £30,000.

The provision of **counselling for unemployment** or to help a redundant employee to find new employment or self-employment is not a taxable benefit, nor is the reimbursement of the cost of such counselling taxable, provided that the employee has been in full time employment for at least two years and similar provision is made for other employees generally or other employees of the same class.

An employee may, either on leaving an employment or at some other time, accept a limitation on his future conduct or activities in return for a payment. Such payments are taxable. However, a payment accepted in full and final settlement of any claims the employee may have against the employer is not automatically taxable under this rule.

A payment to an employee as compensation for the loss of rights under a redundancy scheme is not taxable.

All payments to an employee on termination in cash and in kind should be considered. Non-cash benefits are taxed by reference to their cash equivalent (using the normal rules). Thus if a company car continues to be made available to an ex-employee say for a further year after redundancy he will be taxed on the same benefit value as if he had remained in employment.

If the termination package is a partially exempt one and exceeds £30,000 then the £30,000 exempt limit is allocated to earlier benefits and payments. In any particular year the exemption is allocated to cash payments before non-cash benefits.

Example: Redundancy package

Jonah is made redundant on 31 December 2009. He receives (not under a contractual obligation) the following redundancy package.

- Cash in total of £40,000 payable as £20,000 in January 2010 and £20,000 in January 2011
- Use of company car for period to 5 April 2011 (benefit value per annum £5,000)

Solution

In 2009/10 Jonah receives as redundancy:

	£
Cash (1/10)	20,000
Car (£5,000 × $^3/_{12}$)	1,250
	21,250

Wholly exempt (allocate £21,250 of £30,000 exemption to cash first then benefit).

In 2010/11 Jonah receives:

	£
Cash (1/11)	20,000
Car	5,000
	25,000
Exemption (remaining)	(8,750)
Taxable	16,250

Thus of the cash payment £11,250 (£20,000 less £8,750) is taxable and PAYE at the basic rate is deducted. [As this payment is made after Jonah has left, tax is deducted at the basic rate (see your Level 2 studies). Only the amount in excess of £30,000 exemption is put on the deduction card.] The benefit will be included on the year end return (form P11D). Remember, from Chapter 1, that **no NIC** is payable on these amounts.

5.3 Organisational redundancy schemes

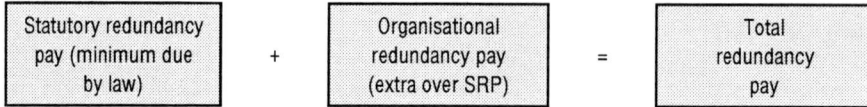

Statutory redundancy pay (minimum due by law)	+	Organisational redundancy pay (extra over SRP)	=	Total redundancy pay

An employer may have an organisational redundancy scheme, or may decide to pay redundancy in excess of SRP. There is no PAYE provided the total redundancy pay (including SRP) does not exceed £30,000. If the total exceeds £30,000, then the **excess** is entered on the deduction card and is taxed under PAYE in the normal way (see your Level 2 studies). However, **no** NICs are due on redundancy payments.

If there is a formal organisational redundancy scheme, then this will usually lay down the redundancy amounts to be paid for each grade of employee. Therefore you will need to check the employee records (contract of employment) to ensure that each employee is being paid the correct redundancy for that grade. If there are discrepancies, these need to be brought to your supervisor's attention.

If there is no formal organisational redundancy scheme, but a decision is made to make payments in excess of SRP, then you should receive instructions from a proper authority (eg the Board or Personnel). You should check the instructions to the authorised signatory list if in doubt.

5.4 Record-keeping

All documents relating to redundancy need to be put on the employee's permanent file and kept for at least three years. In particular, full details are needed of *ex gratia* payments, and other non-taxable payments, so that HMRC PAYE auditors can check that these payments are truly exempt from tax.

Similarly, full details of redundancy payments must be kept, even when these are below £30,000.

Redundancy payments need to be accounted for in the ledger accounts in the usual way. However amounts relating specifically to the redundancy (eg SRP, organisational redundancy pay) should be separately identified from 'normal' wages.

5.5 Confidentiality

Redundancy payments are subject to the usual payroll need for confidentiality. Even if the whole factory is being made redundant, individual redundancy payments still need to be treated as confidential.

Activity 3.3

Jack Jones was made redundant on 01 January 2010 and will receive total redundancy pay of £45,000, £25,000 payable on 1 January 2010 and £20,000 on 1 January 2011. How will this be taxed?

Key learning points

- ☑ If an employee is made redundant, then he must receive a **redundancy notice** in writing and a redundancy payment.

- ☑ An employee must receive at least the amount due under the **statutory redundancy pay** rules.

- ☑ An employee must receive a statement of redundancy pay, showing how the payment has been calculated.

- ☑ An employee may receive other payments on being made redundant including organisational redundancy pay (in excess of the statutory minimum).

- ☑ Any payments on redundancy that are **contractual** are taxable in full on the day of leaving.

- ☑ Redundancy pay (including cash and benefits) is tax-free up to £30,000; payments in excess of £30,000 are taxable and are put on the deduction card when paid.

- ☑ Redundancy documents need to be kept for at least three years for PAYE audit inspection.

Quick quiz

1. Employee A's job disappears. A moves into B's job and B is dismissed. Is B entitled to redundancy pay?

2. Employee B accepts an offer of early retirement during the period of a redundancy notice. Is he still entitled to redundancy pay?

3. Employee C is made redundant. He is 65 and the firm has no stated retirement age. Is C entitled to statutory redundancy pay?

4. Employee D has worked casually for the firm for the last 2 years, generally working during the school holidays. She is 20 years old. Does she qualify for statutory redundancy pay?

5. The maximum weekly wage for statutory redundancy pay purposes is £340. True or false?

6. Are NICs due on redundancy payments?

Answers to quick quiz

1   Yes. Staff requirements have reduced and so B is redundant, even though his job is still there.

2   No. The law treats this as an implied withdrawal of the redundancy notice and so no redundancy pay is due. However B may be entitled to a (greater) tax free lump sum from the pension scheme.

3   Yes, provided the redundancy occurs on or after 1 October 2006, he will be entitled to SRP.

4   No. Employee D has not worked **continuously** for two years.

5   False. It is £350 per week up to 30 September 2009 and £380 per week from 1 October 2009.

6   No. Redundancy payments are exempt from NICs.

Activity checklist

This checklist shows which performance criteria, range statement or knowledge and understanding point is covered by each activity in this chapter. Tick off each activity as you complete it.

Activity

3.1   Covers performance criteria 74.3.C and 74.3.D.

3.2   Covers performance criteria 74.3.C and 74.3.D.

3.3   Covers performance criteria 74.3.E and 74.3.G.

PART B

Completing year-end procedures

chapter 4

Year-end returns

Contents

Performance criteria

75.1.A Reconcile cumulative pay records to year-end balances

75.1.B Reconcile totals of tax and National Insurance contributions deducted with payments made to the Collector of Taxes, taking into account recoverable sums

75.1.C Reconcile the total value of basic and supplementary pension contributions and Additional Voluntary Contributions from each employee with cumulative net taxable pay prior to completion of year-end returns to the Revenue

75.1.D Complete all statutory and non-statutory year end **returns** accurately

75.1.E Despatch all statutory and non-statutory year end **returns** by the agreed **media** and due dates

75.1.F Distribute employee year-end information for employees by the applicable statutory date

75.1.G Prepare internal year-end summaries for accounting purposes in an accurate and timely manner

Range statement

1   **Returns:** P35; P38A; P60/14; management reports

2   **Media:** paper; magnetic; e-mail; internet; disc

Knowledge and understanding

1   Data Protection legislation (Elements 75.1, 75.2 & 75.3)
2   HM Revenue and Customs regulations in respect of:
  –   Income tax and National Insurance liability on pay, expenses and benefits (Elements 75.1, 75.2 & 75.3)
  –   Income tax and National Insurance regulations relating to end of year reporting (Elements 75.1, 75.2 & 75.3)
  –   The methods of submitting end of year returns (Elements 75.1 & 75.2)
  –   Dispensations, extra statutory concessions, statutory exemptions and HM Revenue and Customs Regulations settlement agreements and their impact on end of year reporting for Income Tax and National Insurance purposes (Elements 75.2 & 75.3)
5   Policies, practices and procedures for filing (Elements 75.1 & 75.3)
6   Signatories and authorisations (Elements 75.1 & 75.3)
7   Information flows within the organisation (Elements 75.1 & 75.3)
8   Procedures for the security and confidentiality of information (Elements 75.1, 75.2 & 75.3)
9   Sources of information for the resolution of discrepancies (Element 75.1, 75.2 and 75.3)
10   Principles of payroll accounting and the reconciliation of balances (Element 75.1)

Signpost

Guidance to this element states that, although opening records for the new tax year are not specifically included in the standards, you should be able to do this. In reconciling the cumulative payroll totals to the year-end balances, you are expected to be able to clear totals from the system and so set up the payroll for the first pay-run of the new tax year.

1 The problem

What happens at the tax year end? What returns are needed for management purposes? What are the statutory returns needed by HMRC? How can you be sure that you have paid the correct amounts to HMRC?

2 The solution

In this chapter we will be looking at the year-end returns that have to be made to HMRC. However, first we will take a quick look at dealing with HMRC in Section 3 and month-end returns in Section 4. Month end returns are particularly important as this is, usually, when payments are made and you will need the cumulative total of payments in order to complete the year-end forms.

In Section 5, we will look at annual returns in general and the management reports that you will need prior to completing the returns.

The most important year-end form for an employee is the P60. This forms part of a three form set known as P14. In Section 6, we will complete form P14/P60 and, in section 7, see how these are distributed to employees and HMRC.

The forms P14 are then summarised on the annual return, called a P35. There is a variation called a P38A. The P38A is for listing 'casual' workers and others for whom you did not prepare a deduction card. These forms are dealt with in Sections 8 and 9.

Various miscellaneous items mentioned at Level 2 are dealt with in Section 10.

In Section 11, we will look at opening records for the new tax year.

There are also returns to be made of benefits. Recording benefits are dealt with in Chapter 5 and the year end returns in Chapter 6.

3 Dealing with HMRC

This chapter deals with the **forms** you have to prepare at the end of every tax month and tax year. Some of these you give to employees; some you give to HMRC. HMRC provides **Employer's Help Books** to assist you.

There are four Help Books (E10 to E13), which are sent to all employers and can also be downloaded from HMRC internet site (*www.hmrc.gov.uk/employers/emp-form.htm*).

Important

Filling in these year end returns is a task which might very well be required in your assessment. You need to be meticulously accurate and methodical. Think before you write!

Exams generally appear to be based on HMRC forms. Make sure that you know the most up to date format by checking the HMRC website after February/March 2010, for the 2009/10 year end forms. However the mandatory online filing scheme may lead to a change in exam methods, although the AAT have not yet issued any guidance as to how online filing will affect exams.

3.1 Using HMRC stationery

HMRC provides its own **standard stationery** free of charge so that employers can file the necessary returns without too many difficulties. Some standard forms (eg P45) are provided with the **New Employers Starter Pack.**

Year-end forms were sent out at the end of the tax year, but for 2009/10 onwards must be filed online.

New forms can be obtained quite easily by contacting your PAYE office, or by ordering or downloading from the HMRC website.

3.2 Using your own or a bureau's stationery

Employers are allowed to design their own deduction card (P11). An employer can also use the forms provided by a computer bureau. This stationery must comply with official formats.

- Contain exactly the **same information** as the official form
- Have the **correct reference number**
- Be **easily recognisable**

Approval needs to be sought from a special HMRC management unit if you want to use substitute forms to send to HMRC. **Some forms (such as the P46) cannot be substituted.**

3.3 Photocopying forms

If you run out of forms, **you may photocopy HMRC stationery**. However, the following rules apply.

- The pages must be in **numerical order**.
- The **explanatory notes** accompanying the form must also be photocopied and sent with it.
- The form must have the **correct reference number.**

While it is acceptable to photocopy blank stationery, **it is not acceptable to send in a photocopy of a completed form**.

- If you fill in a form, photocopy it and send in the photocopy, this is not acceptable.
- If you photocopy a blank form, then fill it in and send it, this is acceptable.

3.4 Contacting HMRC

Most of your dealings with HMRC concern **monthly payments, annual returns**, and dealing with **starters** and **leavers**.

When **writing to HMRC,** make sure that you apply the following rules.

- Write to the correct Tax Office.
- Quote your employer's reference number at the top of the letter.
- Quote the employee's NI number, if dealing with a specific employee.

Proper attention to these details ensures that your enquiry will be dealt with as quickly as possible.

If a matter seems to be getting too complicated, then **advise your supervisor** of the problem. In exceptional circumstances, it might be a good idea to arrange a meeting with the Tax Inspector. Your organisation's external auditors will often be involved in sorting out problems of this kind.

3.5 Collectors and inspectors

The **assessment** of an individual's tax liability is dealt with by the **Inspector.** It is separate from the **collection** of the money actually owed. The payment generally goes to the **Collector.**

The **offices** of the Inspector and Collector are usually in completely different parts of the country. There are two collection offices at the moment, based at Shipley (Bradford) and Cumbernauld (Glasgow).

3.6 Computerised processing

If you have a computer-based payroll system, you cannot blame the software supplier or computer bureau for any errors or omissions. Your employer is legally responsible for all returns and so you should check every form before it is submitted.

3.7 Electronic filing

HMRC has developed **Electronic Data Interchange (EDI),** allowing some details to be transmitted between the employer and Tax Office electronically. From April 2002, employers, their agents or payroll bureaux have also been able to file the P35, P14s, P11Ds, P11D(b) and P38A via the **Internet**.

Generally the Internet Service for PAYE (ISP) allows employers to send forms either by sending computer files or by filling forms in on screen before transmission. This is suitable for small employers. EDI allows submission direct from the employer's computer to the HMRC computer and is suitable for large employers, agents and bureaux.

3.7.1 Compulsory electronic filing

All employers will be required to file their end of year PAYE returns (ie P14s and P35) electronically for 2009/10 onwards ie from April 2010.

Electronic filing does **not** include magnetic media (disk/CD ROM or data cartridge). The only means of e-filing are as follows:

- Internet service for PAYE (ISP)
- Electronic Data Interchange (EDI)
- Using an intermediary (payroll bureau or agent) who submits electronically on the employer's behalf.

Larger employers had to e-file by May 2005 and medium-sized ones by May 2006. The timetable is shown below.

Compulsory e-filing depends on the number of employees and this is determined by the number of PAYE employees a business has in the October prior to the filing date.

Number of employees	First compulsory filing	First compulsory return	Deadline
250 or more	2005	2004/05 end of year	19 May 2005
Between 50 and 249	2006	2005/06 end of year	19 May 2006
Less than 50	2010	2009/10 end of year	19 May 2010

Note that size is according to number of employees under each PAYE scheme. Some employers have separate schemes for their directors. So X Ltd may have a PAYE scheme for 2,600 general employees and a separate scheme for 10 directors. The general employee scheme had to submit electronically from 2004/05. However the directors' scheme does not have to file electronically until 2009/10. If the employer submits the directors' scheme electronically from 2004/05, it will receive incentives (see section 3.7.3).

3.7.2 Penalties

For 2008/09 and earlier, there was a penalty of up to £3,000 pa for medium and large employers for failing to e-file when you should have done so. This penalty is **in addition** to any late filing penalty.

3.7.3 Incentives

For employers with less than 50 employees, there are financial incentives to encourage them to adopt e-filing early.

Return	Incentive
2004/05	£250
2005/06	£250
2006/07	£150
2007/08	£100
2008/09	£75

Therefore, a small employer who started e-filing from 2004/05 will earn incentives totalling £825.

3.7.4 Other returns

Note that e-filing is/will be **compulsory only for P14s and P35**. Other forms can still be submitted on paper or by magnetic media (disk, CD Rom, data cartridge), although compulsory e-filing is being phased in from 2009.

From 6 April 2009, medium and large employers now have to submit **forms P45 and P46** electronically; although employers with fewer than 50 employees do not have to submit electronically until 6 April 2011.

Assessment focus point

Remember medium and large employers (ie those with 50 or more employees) must now submit the following forms electronically:

- P14
- P35
- P45
- P46
- P46(Pen)

3.7.5 Non-compliance

Penalties are charged for failing to submit forms P14 and P35 online, based on the number of employees. Employers with over 50 employees may be charged penalties for failing to file forms P45, P46 or P46(Pen) online for the tax quarter ending 5 April 2010 and for the tax year 2010/11.

4 Month end returns

4.1 Paying the Collector

Most employers must pay to the Collector **within 14 days of the end of the tax month** the amounts collected as PAYE, NICs and student loan deductions for that month. Any SSP, SMP, SPP and SAP recoveries are deducted from the amount due.

Tax Month 2, for example, ends on **5 June**. Payment must be made by **19 June**.

The only exception is for **small employers**, who are allowed to pay **every quarter**.

Quarter ending	*Payment due by*
July 5	July 19
October 5	October 19
January 5	January 19
April 5	April 19

You are a **small employer** to HMRC if you estimate that your **average** monthly payment of PAYE tax, student loan deductions and NICs for the year is likely to be **under £1,500.** This means that for some months you might have paid £1,500 or more, but provided the average is less than £1,500 this does not matter.

Activity 4.1

Bob King has a toyshop. He employs a small staff of full and part-time assistants and therefore has to deduct PAYE and NICs from their wages. He estimates that the total of these deductions each month will be as follows:

	£		£
January	1,500	July	1,700
February	900	August	1,700
March	900	September	2,900
April	900	October	2,200
May	900	November	1,500
June	1,900	December	1,000

Can Bob pay his PAYE and NICs every quarter instead of every month?

4.2 Electronic payment

Electronic payment is **compulsory** for employees with 250 or more employees.

- BACS
- CHAPS
- Internet banking
- Telephone banking
- Girobank BillPay

For electronic banking, the **clearance date** is 22nd of each month. Small and medium sized employers can pay by electronic means if they wish and take advantage of this later date.

Where electronic payment is compulsory there are **surcharges** for late payment, which could be as much as 10% of the annual PAYE bill.

4.3 Form P30B

HMRC issues a payslip booklet containing payslips (forms P30B). From 2008/09, the payslip no longer splits the payment between tax and NIC. Instead the payments are allocated at the end of the year, when the P35 is filed.

Therefore all you need to do is add all the deductions together and enter the total payment on the P30B (which is the HMRC equivalent of a bank giro credit form).

There may be occasions when the total figure is **negative** (ie a refund is due). Just write NIL on the P30B and send it without a payment. Deduct the refund from the next month's payment. NIL payments can be notified to HMRC online (www.hmrc.gov.uk/howtopay/paye_nil.htm) **instead of** sending in a blank P30B.

Activity 4.2

The following has been extracted from the Month 2 payroll of Cowry Shells Ltd.

	£
Income tax deducted (gross)	40,000
Income tax refunded	500
Employees' NICs	7,500
Employer's NICs	14,900
Student Loan Deductions	1,500
SSP paid	200
SMP paid	450
SPP paid	500
SAP paid	900

What should be paid to the Collector? Assume that Cowry Shells Ltd is not a small employer for SMP, SPP or SAP recovery purposes.

4.4 Recording the payment

You can pay using any of these methods. Note that large employers **have to pay electronically**.

- **Cheque** (payable to H M Revenue and Customs)
- **Bank giro** at the employer's bank
- **Transfer** from an Alliance & Leicester Giro account
- At a **Post Office**
- **Direct Credit** (BACS)
- Other electronic means (see section 4.2)

Payslips P30B come in **Payslip Booklet P30BC.** You can use the form printed inside the cover as a record of the payment, if you don't want to use form P32 (Employer's Payment Record).

Every time you make a payment this should be recorded on **Form P32** or in the Payslip Booklet P30BC. The example provided on page 84 is filled in with the data from Activity 4.2.

The **date paid** is quite important as well. Remember, the Accounts Office should be paid within 14 days of the end of the tax month (ie by the 19th of the month) or **cleared** by 22nd of the month if paying electronically. There may be penalties to pay if the payment is late.

You need to allow time for the payment to reach HMRC (at least 3 working days from posting a cheque, paying money in at a bank or post office or making a BACS or Giro transfer).

Interest is usually only charged on late payments at the end of the tax year, ie if any payment for the tax year 2009/10 is received after 19 April 2010. It is proposed that interest will be charged on late payments during the tax year. This will be from April 2010, using the risk based approach, so it will be some time before this applies to all employers.

Filling in the P32 is useful, as it helps you with your **year end returns**. We shall consider these next.

HM Revenue & Customs

Employer Payment Record

Employer name

COWRY SHELLS LTD

Accounts Office reference

P

Year ended 5 April   2010
Enter year

You will need information about payments when you complete your form P35 *Employer Annual Return*.

Please fill in this form each time you make a payment. Usually, this will be each week or month - when you make a payment. If you make quarterly payments then you will normally fill in this form every third month. However, you may prefer to fill it in each month (or week), if you do, total your amounts every third month.

For guidance on making payments to HM Revenue & Customs please see Employer Helpbook E13 *Day-to-day payroll*.

Period	Week number	Income Tax (include subcontractor deductions) 1 £	Student Loan deductions 2 £	Net Income Tax (1 + 2) 3 £	Gross National Insurance contributions (NICs) 4 £	Statutory Sick Pay (SSP) recovered 5 £	Statutory Maternity Pay (SMP) recovered 6 £	NIC compensation on SMP 7 £	Statutory Paternity Pay (SPP) recovered 8 £	NIC compensation on SPP 9 £	Statutory Adoption Pay (SAP) recovered 10 £	NIC compensation on SAP 11 £	Total deductions from NICs (total of boxes 5 to 11) 12 £	Net NICs (4 minus 12) 13 £	Amount due (3 + 13) 14 £	Date paid 15
6 April to 5 May	1															
	2															
	3															
	4															
Month 1	Total															
6 May to 5 June	5															
	6															
	7															
	8															
Month 2	Total	39,500 00	1,500 00	41,000 00	22,400 00	-	414 00	-	460 00	-	828 00	-	1,702 00	20,698 00	61,698 00	14/6/09
6 June to 5 July	9															
	10															
	11															
	12															
	13															
Month 3	Total															
6 July to 5 Aug	14															
	15															
	16															
	17															
Month 4	Total															
6 Aug to 5 Sept	18															
	19															
	20															
	21															
Month 5	Total															
6 Sept to 5 Oct	22															
	23															
	24															
	25															
	26															
Month 6	Total															
Totals months	1 - 6															

P32(2008)

HMRC 12/07

BPP LEARNING MEDIA

Period	Week number	Income Tax (include subcontractor deductions) 1 £	Student Loan deductions 2 £	Net Income Tax (1 + 2) 3 £	Gross National Insurance contributions (NICs) 4 £	Statutory Sick Pay (SSP) recovered 5 £	Statutory Maternity Pay (SMP) recovered 6 £	NIC compensation on SMP 7 £	Statutory Paternity Pay (SPP) recovered 8 £	NIC compensation on SPP 9 £	Statutory Adoption Pay (SAP) recovered 10 £	NIC compensation on SAP 11 £	Total deductions from NICs (total of boxes 5 to 11) 12 £	Net NICs (4 minus 12) 13 £	Amount due (3 + 13) 14 £	Date paid 15
Totals months 1 - 6																
6 Oct to 5 Nov	27															
Month 7	28															
	29															
	30															
	Total															
6 Nov to 5 Dec	31															
Month 8	32															
	33															
	34															
	35															
	Total															
6 Dec to 5 Jan	36															
Month 9	37															
	38															
	39															
	Total															
6 Jan to 5 Feb	40															
Month 10	41															
	42															
	43															
	Total															
6 Feb to 5 Mar	44															
Month 11	45															
	46															
	47															
	Total															
6 Mar to 5 April	48															
Month 12	49															
	50															
	51															
	52															
	5															
	Total															
Grand total months 1-12																

5 Complete this line if pay day falls on 5 April (in leap years 4 and 5 April)

Note
The monthly NICs and SSP totals on this form may not be the same as the monthly totals for recovering SSP under the Percentage Threshold Scheme.

Record of funding
If you receive funding from HM Revenue & Customs to pay SSP SMP SPP SAP or to refund tax, you may keep a record in the table below. It will help you to fill in your form P35 *Employer Annual Return* at the end of the year.

Date received from HM Revenue & Customs	Funding to pay SSP/SMP/SPP/SAP £	Funding to refund PAYE Income Tax £
Totals		

5 Annual reports

5.1 Statutory annual returns

Shortly after the end of each tax year, you will need to complete various forms.

- HMRC should receive a **P14** in respect of every employee.

- The employee should receive a **P60**, detailing total pay and total tax and NICs deducted during the year.

- You should also submit one **P35** (a summary covering all employees) for the tax year, together with form **P38A** as appropriate.

We will look at each of these in turn in the rest of the chapter.

HMRC will also want forms dealing with expenses and benefits: forms **P9D** and **P11D**. Employees should also receive copies. These are dealt with in Chapter 6.

Important

When we refer to annual or year-end returns for payroll, these always mean for the **tax year**. Do not prepare year-end returns at the business year-end!

5.2 Reports and reconciliations

Prior to preparing the year-end returns, you need to ensure that **the payroll records are correct**. The easiest way to do this is to prepare **wages control accounts** each month. This will help to ensure that monthly payments to HMRC are correct. See your level 2 studies for this. At the very least a wages control account should be prepared at the year end. You can also prepare **management reports**.

These reports can be extracted manually (if you prepare the payroll manually), or by using computer generated output.

The year-end reports should include these details.

- Cumulative gross pay (excluding SSP, SMP, SPP and SAP)
- Cumulative employee pension deductions (basic and AVCs)
- Cumulative totals of SSP, SMP, SPP and SAP paid
- Cumulative net taxable pay
- Totals of tax and employees' NIC deducted for the tax year (including any rebates)
- Cumulative net pay
- Cumulative totals of employers' NIC (including any rebates)
- Cumulative totals of SSP, SMP, SPP and SAP recovered
- Cumulative totals of SLDs made
- Cumulative employer pension deductions
- Total paid and payable to the collector
- Cumulative totals of GAYE and other voluntary and statutory deductions (eg CSA orders, trade union subscriptions)

With the above reports, you can check the calculation of net taxable pay, net pay and the amounts paid to the collector.

Net taxable pay = Gross pay + SSP + SMP + SPP + SAP – Employee pension deductions – GAYE

Net pay = Net taxable pay – PAYE – Employees' NICs – other deductions

Amount paid and payable to the collector = PAYE + Employees' NICs + Employer's NICs – SSP, SMP, SPP and SAP recovered + SLDs

It is also possible to check the calculation of the SSP, SMP, SPP and SAP recovered. From your Level 2 studies, you should remember that SSP can only be recovered if the SSP paid exceeds 13% of the total Class 1 NICs for that tax month. For SMP, SPP and SAP you can recover 92% at least, and 104.5% if the total Class 1 NICs payable for the year is £45,000 or less.

Example: Year-end reconciliations

The following report has been given to you for the year ended 5 April 2010.

Gross pay (**including** SSP, SMP, SPP and SAP)	£1,276,520
SSP included above	£1,770
SMP included above	£5,300
SPP included above	£1,000
SAP included above	£500
Employee pension deductions	£51,200
Employer pension contributions	£102,400
Cumulative net taxable pay	£1,225,318
PAYE	£224,300
Employees' NICs	£72,100
Employer's NICs	£127,600
Cumulative net pay	£928,920
SSP recovered	£NIL
SMP recovered	£4,876
SPP recovered	£920
SAP recovered	£460
Total paid to the collector (form P32)	£417,744

From the above report, check the following figures.

(a)   Net taxable pay

(b)   Net pay

(c)   Amount paid to collector

(d)   SSP recovered, given that SSP of £720 was paid in month 4 (when total Class 1 NICs were £16,700) and £1,050 was paid in month 5 (when total class 1 NICs were £8,100).

(e)   SMP, SPP and SAP recovered

Solution

(a) Net taxable pay = Gross pay + SSP + SMP + SPP + SAP − Employee pension deductions − GAYE.

In our report above the figure for gross pay **includes** SSP, SMP, SPP and SAP. There are no GAYE deductions.

Net taxable pay = £1,276,520 − £51,200 = £1,225,320.

The figure for cumulative net taxable pay in the report is £1,225,318, a difference of £2 probably caused by rounding, as the report is expressed in pounds only.

(b) Net pay = Net taxable pay − PAYE − Employees' NIC − other deductions
= £1,225,320 − £224,300 − £72,100 − NIL
= £928,920

Note. We have used the figure for net taxable pay calculated in (a), rather than the report figure. You can use either.

(c) Amount paid to the collector = PAYE + Employees' NIC + Employer's NIC − SSP, SMP, SPP and SAP recovered − NIC rebates

= £224,300 + £72,100 + £127,600 − NIL − £4,876 − £920 − £460 − NIL

= £417,744

This agrees to the amount on form P32. If the figure of £417,744 was generated on a report, it should be checked to form P32. This acts as a double-check that the correct amounts are being paid to the collector.

(d) SSP can be recovered if the amount paid exceeds 13% of Class 1 NICs for that month.

Month 4: 13% × £16,700 = £2,171. Therefore no SSP can be recovered
Month 5: 13% × £8,100 = £1,053. So once again, no SSP can be recovered.

(e) As total Class 1 NICs exceeds £45,000, only 92% of SMP, SPP and SAP can be recovered.

SMP: 92% × £5,300 = £4,876
SPP: 92% × £1,000 = £920
SAP: 92% × £500 = £460

5.3 Internal reports

Remember that payroll reports may also be needed for internal management. If management want information in a certain format that also produces the figures you need for the year-end reconciliations, it is worth producing the year-end reports in management format. Otherwise the management report should be produced separately.

You may also need to produce a payroll summary for accounting purposes. This may not be as detailed as your year-end reports, although if you prepare payroll manually then accounts will need all those details.

Always keep deadlines in mind when producing reports. If you do not keep to the statutory deadlines for sending returns to HMRC, your employer will be fined.

5.4 Non-statutory returns

If your employer has a pension scheme, then you will need to make a return to the pension trustees of the following.

- For each employee, the total contributions made by the employee during the year analysed between basic, supplementary and AVCs.

- For each employee, the total employer's contributions made during the year.

This will enable pension trustees to make their annual returns to HMRC. It will also enable you to check your figures of pension contributions.

Activity 4.3

You have prepared a report for the pension trustees, listing pension contributions by employee as follows.

	Basic £	Supplementary £	AVCs £	Employer's £	Total £
N Danvers	8,900	–	2,000	14,400	25,300
C Jackson	5,000	–	–	30,000	35,000
J Baulch	9,000	–	2,000	18,000	29,000
J Edwards	5,000	–	–	10,000	15,000
D Campbell	5,000	–	2,300	10,000	17,300
M Jackson	5,000	5,000	2,000	20,000	32,000

Reconcile this report to the figures given in the example above.

6 Forms P14 and P60

At the end of each tax year (5 April), the payroll department must complete, for each employee including those who have left, the **P14 End of year summary**. These must reach HMRC by **19 May**.

For 2008/09 and earlier, the P14 came in triplicate.

- The **top and second copies** went (together with the summary form P35) to the **PAYE tax office**. The top copy was used for NI purposes and the second copy is for tax purposes.

- The **third copy, called the P60**, had to be given to the **employee by 31 May**. The P60 was identical to the P14 except that it did not have the following boxes.

  - Date of birth
  - NIC box le
  - Date of starting or leaving
  - SSP totals

The **P60** is only given to employees who are working for you on 5 April. If they have **left,** do not prepare one, and if the P60 is the third carbon copy of a set, then destroy it. The reason for this is that it can be used to reclaim tax.

Under online filing, form P14 is completed electronically with exactly the same information as the paper format. Once filed, the P14 is automatically processed by HMRC. A form P60 will still need to be printed out for giving to the employee.

Activity 4.4

Have you ever received a **P60**? Have a look at it and put a copy in your collection of payroll documentation. Also, if you have ever received a P11D put that in your collection too.

6.1 Filling in a P14 and P60

An example of a P14 for tax year 2009/10 is given over the page. HMRC have prepared a sample form to help employers assemble the necessary information prior to completing the P14 online.

Most, although not all, of the information needed can be gleaned from the **deductions working sheet (P11).** The rest can be obtained from your employee records or the **personnel department**. The details entered on a P14 must be **accurate.**

The paper P14 was processed using **Optical Character Recognition (OCR)** equipment. It was very important *not* to use up old HMRC forms as the equipment cannot process these. It was also very important to complete the P14s in ball point pen or something similar so they could be read easily. If you made a mistake, you had to tear up that form and start again on a new form. Alterations could not be made on the form. All entries had to be handwritten or printed – stamps and labels could not be used.

When completing a P14, use the following steps. (Note that these are described using the sample P14 for reference, your computer package may not look quite the same.)

Step 1   The boxes at the top are needed for HMRC administration.

- The employer's name and address.
- The HMRC Office name and reference identifies the PAYE office for the employer.
- The year is the tax year just ended (so for 2009/10 this will be filled in as 2010).

Step 2   Fill in the employee's National Insurance number.

Step 3   Next to the NI number is recorded the employee's date of birth.

Step 4   Fill in the box next to it with M (male) or F (female). If you are unsure, check with the personnel department.

Assessment focus point

Remember that it is now compulsory to include gender and date of birth on form P14. A default date of birth is **not** acceptable.

Step 5 The employee's surname is filled in in capital letters. Underneath show the first two forenames.

Step 6 Many employers, particularly those who operate computerised payroll accounting systems, give an employee a reference number. This can be written as the works/payroll number.

Step 7 The employee's private address should be checked to your employee records. Alternatively the employee can be requested to verify that this is correct, or you can check with the personnel department.

Step 8 In the middle of the P14 are some boxes for NICs.

- The NIC table letter goes in the left hand box.

- The columns labelled 1a to 1f correspond to the columns on the P11 deductions working sheet.

- If contracted out rate contributions are made to a money purchase scheme (COMPS, see your Level 2 study material), the scheme contracted out number must be entered in the right hand box.

If the table letter for NICs has changed during the year, the relevant information for all table letters must be listed separately.

Step 9   Statutory payments (**SSP**, **SMP**, **SPP** and **SAP**) are entered in columns 1g to 1j on the P11 and the figures for SMP, SPP and SAP can simply be taken from there. However for SSP, you should only enter the total amount of SSP paid in those months **when a recovery has been made**.

Step 10   If there were any Student Loan Deductions (see P11 column 1k), these are entered to the right of the statutory payment boxes.

Step 11   The next section of boxes relates to an employee's pay and tax deducted.

- The total for the year should be taken from the bottom of the P11 deductions working sheet.

- Pay and tax in any previous employment can be found on the employee's P45 when he or she joined and these details should have been entered on the P11 at the date of joining. However, if you do not have details of the employee's pay and tax, leave this blank.

- The pay and tax for this employment is the difference between these two.

Note, however, that if the employee has a K Code you should enter in the box for 'This employment' the total of the amounts in column 7 of the P11. Ordinarily this total would be the same as the final figure in column 6 of the P11, but not necessarily with a K code because of the regulatory limit.

Step 12   In the bottom left hand corner of this section, is a small box labelled 'Employee's widows and orphans/life assurance contributions in this employment'. This is a box which will be needed less and less with the passage of time. However, you might need to know what its purpose is.

- Certain types of life assurance premiums used to get tax relief. This relief was abolished for policies issued after 13 March 1984, but still applies to policies issued before that date.

- Some contracts of employment would specify that an employee had to make compulsory contributions to a life assurance policy which gave the employee's widow (or widower) and/or orphans a sum in the event of the employee's death. Premiums paid under that type of policy need to be noted in the box.

Step 13   The employee's final tax code can be found on the deductions working sheet.

Step 14   The payment in Week 53 box in the very bottom right should be marked in the following ways.

- 53 if there was a Week 53 payment.
- 54 if there were 27 fortnightly payments in the year.
- 56 if there were 14 four-weekly payments in the year.

Step 15   If the employee has joined or left during the tax year, note the date in the right-hand boxes. In the case of leavers, the P14 is sent to the Tax Office, so complete one but do not print out a P60. (Destroy it if your computer automatically prints it out.)

Activity 4.5

You are the payroll clerk for BIX Ltd, PAYE reference 123/45678.

Given the information below for Priscilla Bragg, complete P14 using the blank form provided.

The address of BIX Ltd is 5 Bedford Road, Hightown, Bucks AB1 2CD and the tax office name is Hightown. Priscilla's home address is 7 Huntingdon Road, Hightown, Bucks AB1 5XY.

Employee details

Priscilla Mary Bragg
NI Number: AB 12 34 56 C
Date of birth: 1 March 1950
Works number: A29
Date of starting: 1 March 1998

Extracts from P11

Total pay to date (col 3): £12,200.00
Total tax due to date (col 6): £1,352.20
Final tax code: 543L

NIC letter	1a	1b	1c	1d	1e	1f
			End of year summary			
A	4,532	704	5,940	–	1,413.72	653.40
C	412	64	540	–	69.12	–

7 Distributing P14s

For 2008/09 and earlier, once you have filled in the P14/P60 forms, you had to sort them prior to sending them to HMRC.

- Put the forms into alphabetical order of surname, or the order in which you have entered the employees on form P35.

- Separate the form's three parts (if you are using HMRC stationery).

- Make separate bundles of the top (NI) and second (Tax) copies.

- Remove pins or staples.

- Send both the NI and Tax copies to the PAYE tax office with form P35 (see Section 8) in time for it to arrive there by **19 May, to avoid penalties**.

- The third copies (forms P60) must be given to the employees by **31 May**.

Filing forms P14 online removes the need to sort out the P14s. The deadline for filing the P14 electronically remains 19 May and employees still must receive paper forms P60 by 31 May.

If forms P35 and/or P14s are submitted late, the penalty is £100 per 50 employees (or part thereof) per month for up to one year. This applies whether filing by paper (for 2008/09 and earlier) or online (for 2009/10 onwards).

P14 End of Year Summary 2009–10 007

Employer PAYE reference

Tax Year to 5 April 2 0 1 0

INFORMATION ONLY

Employee's details

National Insurance number

Surname

First two forenames

Works/payroll number

Date of birth in figures DD MM YYYY

Gender 'M' male, 'F' female

National Insurance contributions in this employment

(Note: LEL = Lower Earnings Limit, ET = Earnings Threshold, UAP = Upper Accrual Point, UEL = Upper Earnings Limit)

INFORMATION ONLY

Statutory payments included in the pay 'In this employment' figure below

Statutory Sick Pay (SSP)

Statutory Maternity Pay (SMP)

Statutory Paternity Pay (SPP)

Statutory Adoption Pay (SAP)

Pay and Income Tax details

	Pay	Tax deducted
In previous employment(s)		
In this employment		
Total for year		

Employee's Widows & Orphans/Life Assurance contributions in this employment

Final tax code

Expenses payments and benefits paid to directors and employees: Complete form P11D or P9D if appropriate and provide a copy of the information to your employee by 6 July. See booklet CWG2 Employer Further Guide to PAYE and NICs for more details.

Student Loan deductions

Scheme Contracted-out Number

Date of starting DD MM YYYY to 5 April 2010

Date of leaving DD MM YYYY to 5 April 2010

BPP LEARNING MEDIA

7.1 Errors on forms P14/P60

All P14s must be completed **accurately**. HMRC have identified a number of common errors for paper P14s.

- Stationary used has not been approved by HMRC*
- Forms submitted in incorrect or out of date format*
- Employee name omitted*
- National Insurance number omitted and no entries for date of birth and gender*
- No earnings in columns 1a, 1b or 1c*
- Total earnings inserted in just one of columns 1a, 1b or 1c*
- Incorrect earnings figure inserted in columns 1a, 1b or 1c*
- Column 1d used for employer's NICs instead of the total of employees' and employer's NICs*
- Wrong or missing NI category letter (some people inserting the tax code instead)*
- Failure to insert the contracted-out COMPS number
- Correction fluid and/or sticky labels used, preventing it being read by the OCR*
- Student loan deductions should be in whole pounds
- There should always be an entry for tax in this employment
- Death in service counts as a date of leaving
- Do not use continental sevens (7) or n/a as the OCR can not read these

Forms will be rejected if the entries on the forms are unclear, if they have been hole punched over entries or damaged in any other way; if the forms have not been split in two separate bundles; if they are attached together with glue or staples; if the sprockets have not been taken off the forms; or if any of the errors marked with an asterisk(*) above are made. As it is unlikely that any revised forms will be resubmitted before the deadline this will lead to penalties being charged.

Many of these errors can no longer occur with online filing. However the entering of incorrect data is still possible for online forms. Many computer programmes will carry out validation checks, but cannot be expected to pick up all inputting errors. Therefore you still need to double-check information before submitting forms P14.

7.2 Duplicate forms P60

Up to 5 April 2002, HMRC did not allow duplicate P60s to be issued because they could be used in fraudulent tax claims. However for P60s for tax year 2002/03 onwards, duplicates may be issued.

The duplicate P60 must be clearly marked **DUPLICATE**.

HMRC state that there is **no obligation** for employers to provide duplicate P60s, but that it is now **permissible** to do so.

8 Form P35

The P35 is a summary of all your P14s. You must send it with the P14s to HMRC. The P35 lists the summary details of the first ten employees. P35(CS) (ie P35 continuation sheet) is used to record details of additional employees greater than this number. The total of the continuation sheets is added to the P35.

Paper formats of P35 could only be submitted for 2008/09 and earlier. However HMRC do provide a paper format for employers to gather information before submitting electronically. **A blank specimen of a P35 is provided in Activity 4.6.** Your computer package may show a facsimile P35 for completion or may present boxes for completion.

8.1 Completing form P35

You extract the details from the P14s. The figures you fill in relate to **this employment only.**

The **list of employees** should be in the same order on the P35 as the bundle of P14s (**in alphabetical order of surname**). However, you should list **directors first** and identify them with an **asterisk***. Normally the computer package will automatically transfer these details from the files that you have already input.

The P35 also requires you to answer certain **questions** in a checklist in Part 3 of the form 'Yes' or 'No'. Remember that you are committing yourself here, and so if you answer incorrectly, you could be guilty of making a false declaration. You must answer all questions by ticking either the 'No' or the 'Yes' box.

- **Q1** If you answer 'No' (eg you paid someone out of petty cash, or for whatever reason) you should complete **Form P38A**.

- **Q2** If you agree to bear the tax liability of the employees, it is referred to as paying them **free of tax**. In effect you are offering them a net payment. The Tax Office should be consulted so that the amount of true gross pay can be arrived at. As in Q1 above, this should have been sorted out before you arrive at the P35. You may need to refer to this question to your supervisor.

- **Q3** The **expenses and benefits** listed here are generally taxable, and so the employer should be kept informed of payments of this nature.

- **Q4** You are normally required to operate PAYE on **employees from abroad** in the normal way. You will have answered 'no' to the second question only if so instructed by the Tax Office.

- **Q5 All pay to an employee should be included,** even if it was paid to someone else. If in doubt, contact your supervisor or the Tax Office. Note that this question does not include payments such as Child Support Agency orders or Attachment of Earnings Orders.

- **Q6** This question refers to the **IR35 rules**. Basically it applies where someone works for you but bills you via a company or partnership, so that you do not treat them as an employee for PAYE purposes. In this case, the intermediary would tick the 'yes' box. The IR35 rules require the intermediary to pay tax and NIC on deemed payments but this is outside the scope of your level 3 studies.

Part 4 asks for the Employer's Contracting-out Number if the employer has a contracted-out occupational pension scheme (see your Level 2 studies).

You are asked to make a number of **declarations** in part 5.

- You have enclosed **all the forms P14** (or will have sent them in parts).
- You have completed **Form P38A** (which you must do if you answered No to question 1), or it is not due.
- You have completed **P11Ds and P11D(b) where appropriate** (or they are not due).

The P35 form must be signed by hand by an individual. An official stamp or rubber stamp is not good enough. It must also be dated, and the individual must state the capacity in which he or she signed it.

8.2 Rejection of forms

HMRC will reject forms in the following cases.

- The stationary used has not been approved by HMRC (on paper versions for 2008/09 and earlier)
- The P35 is not signed (on paper versions for 2008/09 and earlier)
- The P35 has not been fully completed
- The P14s have been submitted without the P35
- The P35 has been submitted without the P14s
- There is not a P14 enclosed for every employee on the P35

If forms are not correctly resubmitted by the deadline, penalties will be charged (see Section 7).

8.3 Submission of forms

Form P35 must be submitted with forms P14, P38A, P11D(b) and P11D by **19 May** following the end of the tax year ie 19 May 2010 for 2009/10.

Arrangements have been made so that employers can submit forms P35, P38A and P11D(b) via the Internet without the need for a signature (paper versions where still allowed **must** be signed).

Forms P14 and P11D do not include a declaration and so can be submitted in any of the following formats, with the **agreement** of HMRC.

- Paper
- Magnetic tape
- Computer disc
- E-mail
- Electronic data transfer via the Internet

HMRC prefers Internet transmission and this was compulsory for forms P14 and P35 from the year 2004/05 for larger employers (with 250 or more employees), from 2005/06 for employers with 50 to 250 employees and from 2009/10 for employers with less than 50 employees.

Activity 4.6

Degmeter Ltd has four employees. Their completed P14s include the information shown below. Degmeter Ltd has not agreed to bear the employees' tax liability, nor has the company used the services of a person employed by an employer outside the UK. Apart from the P14s provided you are told the following and asked to complete a P35 for 2009/10. Use the blank P35 on the next three pages.

(a) Degmeter Ltd has already paid £8,820.00 in NICs and £9,487.52 in income tax over the year. This is on the P32.
(b) All P11Ds have been prepared and will be sent with the P14s and P35 as will form P11D(b).
(c) Forms P38A are not due.
(d) No one employed by Degmeter Ltd falls under the IR35 rules.
(e) C A Finch is a director of the company.

	C A Finch £	M A Ibis £	G T Heron £	S E Gull £
Total NICs (column 1e)	2,797.80	2,090.20	3,088.68	2,186.88
Pay in previous employment	0	8,712.91	0	0
Tax in previous employment	0	1,670.00	0	0
Pay in this employment	15,053.31	11,312.72	16,500.00	12,000.00
Tax in this employment	2,773.50	2,174.00	3,082.50	1,957.50

HM Revenue & Customs

P35 – Employer Annual Return for

┌ ┐

*
*

└ ┘

Please return to

┌─────────────────────┐
│ For information only │
└─────────────────────┘

Employer PAYE reference   /   Your reference

HMRC office phone number   Accounts Office reference

PAYE Income Tax, National Insurance contributions (NICs) and related payments

If in the tax year you were required to prepare any P11 *Deductions Working Sheets*, you are required by law to:

- complete and sign this Return or send it online. If you send your Return online you must not send this form

- send the 'National Insurance copy' and 'Tax copy' of form P14 *End of Year Summary* (or online equivalent), for each employee for whom you were required to complete a form P11 *Deductions Working Sheet* (or equivalent record) during the year

- send, where applicable, P35(CS) *Continuation Sheets* and form P38A *Employer Supplementary Return*. (Forms P38(S) *Student employees* should not be sent with this Return, but must be kept for at least three years)

- send the Return, including any of the above, in time to reach the above HM Revenue & Customs office by 19 May following the end of the tax year.

You may be charged a penalty if your Return is received late.

Help

For step-by-step guidance on completing this Return:

- see the Employer Helpbook E10 *Finishing the tax year* included on the *Employer CD-ROM*
- go to www.hmrc.gov.uk/employers
- phone our Employer Helpline on 08457 143 143
- contact your HM Revenue & Customs office at the address shown above.

You can get paper copies of all the forms and booklets mentioned on this Return from our Employer Orderline.

- Order online at www.hmrc.gov.uk/employers/emp-form.htm
- Phone 08457 646 646
- Fax 08702 406 406

Other important dates following the end of the tax year

By 19 April – if you do not pay electronically and you post your payment, please pay all outstanding tax and NICs so your payment reaches us no later than 19 April to avoid being charged interest

By 22 April – if you pay by an approved electronic payment method, please pay all outstanding tax and NICs so that cleared funds for your payment reach us no later than 22 April to avoid being charged interest (and a surcharge in the case of employers who have to pay electronically)

By 31 May – give a P60 *End of Year Certificate* to each relevant employee

By 6 July – submit online or on paper, forms:
- P9D *Expenses payments and income from which tax cannot be deducted*
- P11D *Expenses and Benefits*, and
- P11D(b) *Return of Class 1A National Insurance contributions due, Return of expenses and benefits – Employer declaration*
- give a copy of forms P11D or P9D (or equivalent information) to each relevant employee

By 19 July – if you post your payment, please pay any Class 1A NICs so your payment reaches us no later than 19 July

By 22 July – if you pay by an approved electronic payment method, please pay any Class 1A NICs so that cleared funds for your payment reach us no later than 22 July.

Do not include payment with this form. If a payment is due, please use one of our recommended methods to pay direct to our Accounts Office. There is 'How to pay' guidance in your P30BC *Payslip Booklet* notes or in the letter we issue in place of your booklet or go to **www.hmrc.gov.uk/howtopay/paye.htm**   *Now fill in pages 2 and 3* ▶

P35(2008)   Page 1   HMRC 11/07

Part 1   Summary of employees and directors

- If you are sending your form P35 and **all** of your forms P14 on paper you must:
  a. list **each employee or director** for whom you have completed a form P11 *Deductions Working Sheet* (or equivalent record).
     If you have more than ten entries, please prepare P35(CS) *Continuation Sheets*
  b. ensure that all forms P14 are enclosed with this Return.
- If some or all of your forms P14 are not enclosed with this Return because they are being sent by Internet, Electronic Data Interchange (EDI) or magnetic media, there is no need to complete the 'Part 1 Summary of employees and directors' section of this Return. Instead you must begin by completing boxes 3 and 6 of the 'Part 2 Summary of payments for the year' section below.

Guidance notes

Some useful hints are given below. For step by step guidance refer to the 'Help' section on page 1.

If any of the boxes do not apply to you, please leave them blank.

Employee name Put an asterisk (∗) by the name if the person is a director	National Insurance contributions (NICs) Enter the total NICs from **column 1d** on form P11. Write 'R' beside any minus amounts.	Income Tax deducted or refunded in this employment. Write 'R' beside an amount to show a net refund

If you make a mistake and record the wrong entry:
- draw a line through the entry so that it can still be read, and
- record the correct figure alongside

£ 1256 30
10 850
11 2016 30 2106 30

NICs

Total NICs shown above *after deducting amounts marked 'R'* **1** £

Totals from P35(CS) *Continuation Sheets* **2** £

Income Tax

Total tax shown above *after deducting amounts marked 'R'* **4** £

Totals from P35(CS) *Continuation Sheets* **5** £

Part 2   Summary of payments for the year

Total NICs 1 + 2 **3** £

Total tax 4 + 5 **6** £

see Note 2

Advance received from HM Revenue & Customs to refund tax **7** £

Total tax 6 + 7 **8** £

Combined amounts

Total NICs and tax 3 + 8 **9** £

Total Student loan deductions *see Note 3* **10** £

9 + 10 **11** £

Statutory payments recovered
see Note 4

Statutory Sick Pay (SSP) recovered **12** £

Statutory Maternity Pay (SMP) recovered **13** £

NIC compensation on SMP **14** £

Statutory Paternity Pay (SPP) recovered **15** £

NIC compensation on SPP **16** £

Statutory Adoption Pay (SAP) recovered **17** £

NIC compensation on SAP **18** £

Total of boxes 12 to 18 **19** £

Funding received from HM Revenue & Customs to pay SSP/SMP/SPP/SAP **20** £

19 *minus* 20 **21** £

11 *minus* 21 **22** £
see Note 3

For information only

Deductions made from subcontractors *see Note 6* **23** £

Amount payable for the year 22 + 23 **24** £

NICs and tax paid already **25** £

Tax-free incentive payment received during the year *see Note 7* **26** £

NOW PAYABLE   24 *minus* 25 and 26 **27** £

▶ Do not include a payment with this Return. If a payment is due, please make it immediately. See page 1 for notes on how to pay.

Fill in boxes 28 and 29 only if you are a **limited company** that has had CIS deductions made from payments received for work in the construction industry.

CIS deductions suffered *Total of column E on form CIS132* **28** £

Revised amount now payable   27 *minus* 28 **29** £

Note 1

Boxes **1** to **6**   Enter 'R' beside any minus amounts.

Note 2

Boxes **3** and **6**   If you are not required to complete the 'Part 1 Summary of employees and directors' section you should begin by entering the respective NICs and Income Tax totals for **all** employees for whom you have completed a form P11 (or equivalent record).

Note 3

Box **10**   Whole pounds only. Do not enter pence in shaded area.

Note 4

Boxes **12** to **18**   Do not enter the totals paid.
Only enter the amounts you are entitled to recover. You will find this in your P30BC *Payslip Booklet* or your own equivalent payment record.

Note 5

Box **22**   If box **21** is a minus figure then add box **21** to box **11**

Note 6

Box **23**   Enter the total CIS deductions on account of tax from box 4.6 on your CIS300 monthly Returns.

Note 7

Box **26**   If a tax-free payment was credited to your PAYE payment record this year, for having sent any previous year's Return online, enter the amount. If the tax-free payment was repaid directly to you or your adviser by cheque, leave this box blank.

Please now fill in page 4 ▶

Page 2

Page 3

100

BPP LEARNING MEDIA

Part 3 Checklist

You must answer each question

1 Have you sent a form P14 *End of Year Summary* or completed and retained a form P38(S) *Student employees* for every person in your paid employment, either on a casual basis or otherwise, during the tax year shown on the front of this form?

No ☐   Yes ☐

If 'No', please send a form P38A *Employer Supplementary Return*.

2 Did you make any 'free of tax' payments to an employee? In other words, did you bear any of the tax yourself rather than deduct it from the employee?

No ☐   Yes ☐

3 As far as you know, did **anyone else pay expenses**, or in any way provide vouchers or benefits to any of your employees while they were employed by you during the year?

No ☐   Yes ☐

For information only

4 Did anyone **employed by a person or company outside the UK** work for you in the UK for 30 or more days in a row?

No ☐   Yes ☐

If 'Yes', have you sent a form P14 for them?

No ☐   Yes ☐

5 Have you **paid** any of an employee's pay to someone other than the employee, for example, to a school?

No ☐   Yes ☐

If 'Yes', have you included this pay on their form P14?

No ☐   Yes ☐

6 Are you a Service Company?

No ☐   Yes ☐

If 'Yes', have you operated the Intermediaries legislation (sometimes known as IR35) or the Managed Service Companies legislation?

No ☐   Yes ☐

For more detailed information, see CWG2 *Employer Further Guide to PAYE and NICs*.

Part 4 Contracted-out pension schemes   *if applicable*

If you have a Contracted-out pension scheme, enter your Employer Contracted-out number (ECON) from your contracting-out certificate

E 3 ☐ ☐ ☐ ☐ ☐ ☐ ☐

Part 5 Employer certificate and declaration

Tick one box to complete each statement below. *This certificate and declaration covers any documents authorised by us as substitutes for the forms mentioned below. We may penalise or prosecute you if you make false statements.*

I declare and certify that

- forms P14 *End of Year Summary* for each employee or director for whom I was required to complete a form P11 *Deductions Working Sheet* (or equivalent record) during the year,

are all enclosed ☐

or

have been sent separately in one or more parts† ☐

> † If forms P14 have been sent in more than one part, please enter the number of parts sent, **not the total number of forms P14**, and note that only one P35 is required reflecting all P14 parts. For more detailed information, see the *Guide to filing PAYE forms online and paying electronically*.
>
> [   ]

- completed form P38A *Employer Supplementary Return*

is enclosed ☐   is not due ☐

- completed forms P11D and P11D(b) *Returns of expenses payments, benefits and Class 1A contributions*

are due ☐   are not due ☐

All the details on this Return and any forms enclosed or sent separately are fully and truly stated to the best of my knowledge and belief.

Employer signature

[   ]

Please print your name

[   ]

Capacity in which signed

[   ]

Date

[/   /   ]

Please give a daytime phone number. It will help speed things up if we need to talk to you about your Return.

[   ]

By law this Return must reach us by 19 May.

Activity 4.7

Why do you think that HMRC recommend that form P35 is completed by 19 April, when it does not have to be submitted until 19 May?

9 Form P38A

A **P38A** must be filled in when you answer No to question 1 on the **P35**. The P38A is designed to catch **odd situations or casual employees**. For example, you may take on a casual worker for a couple of days, and then arrange for them to work for you again, in a few weeks' time.

For some casual workers, especially for those whose pay is **lower than the thresholds for PAYE or NICs**, you do not need to prepare a P11, so you cannot prepare a **P14**. You are, however, required to keep records and these are what is required for the **P38A**.

All that needs to be entered are the following details.

- Relevant employees' names, addresses and NI numbers (if known).
- The type of employment and its duration.
- The full amount paid in the year.

The form P38A for the year ended 5 April 2009 follows.

The format of P38A for 2009/10 should be available on the HMRC website around February 2010. However it should be very similar. Note that it is divided into two sections: A for employees paid below the NIC threshold and B for other employees.

HM Revenue & Customs

Employer Supplementary Return

To be filled in by the employer

Employer name

HM Revenue & Customs office name

Employer PAYE reference

Accounts Office reference

Workers for whom you have not completed a form P14 or a form P38(S) for the year 6 April 2008 to 5 April 2009

You must complete this form if you answered 'No' to Question 1 of the checklist on your form P35 *Employer Annual Return*.

This form asks for details about payments made to people who worked for you during the year to 5 April 2009, but for whom you did not complete a form **P14** *End of Year Summary* or a form **P38(S)** *Student employees*.

Look at your records for **each worker** and consider whether:

1 you hold a form **P46:** *Employee without a Form P45*, that has been completed at either Statement A or Statement B by the worker

2 the worker was paid less than £90 every week, or £390 if paid monthly.

*Please refer to the *note about pay* on the *right-hand* side of this page.*

If for each of your workers you are able to answer **'Yes'** to both questions above, there is no need to complete the back of this form. Please sign the declaration below and return the form to your HM Revenue & Customs office.

If the answer to either question is **'No'** for any worker, please complete the back of this form for those workers.

Once completed, this form should be sent together with your form **P35** *Employer Annual Return*.

Declaration

I declare that **for each worker** for whom I have not completed a form P14 *End of Year Summary* or a form P38(S) *Student employees*:

- I hold a form P46 that has been completed at either Statement A or Statement B by the worker, **and**
- the worker was paid less than £90 every week, or £390, if paid monthly.

Employer's signature

Date *DD MM YYYY*

***Note about pay.** Pay includes:

- salaries
- wages
- fees
- overtime
- bonuses
- commissions
- pensions
- holiday pay
- payments in lieu of benefits in kind, for example, board wages
- meal vouchers (if worth more than 15p a day)
- lump sum payments when employment ends (if more than £30,000)
- expenses payments or benefits for directors and employees earning at a rate of £8,500 or more a year
- vouchers which can be exchanged for cash, goods and services
- the cost of providing rent-free accommodation
- transport vouchers
- amounts charged to employees' credit cards provided by you
- any other relevant payments to your employees
- any payment which the employee is liable to pay but that you pay for him or her.

This list does not cover all of the items you should treat as pay. For more information see CWG2 *Employer Further Guide to PAYE and NICs*, if you are not sure about an item, ask your local HM Revenue & Customs office.

P38A (2009)

Page 1

HMRC 11/08

If there is not enough space in either section, please continue on a separate sheet. When you have filled in all the details, please sign the declaration below and return the form.

For information on the items that should be treated as pay, please refer to the note about pay overleaf.

Section A

Enter details for:

- any worker who was paid **£90 or more in any week, or £390 or more if paid monthly, or**
- any worker who was taken on for more than a week unless he or she was a harvest worker (who should be entered in Section B – see below).

Full name of person employed, include title of Mr/Mrs/Miss/Ms	Last known address	National Insurance number	Employed as state type of work done	Dates employed if less than a full year		Total pay* for year to 5 April 2009	For official use only
				From	To		

Section B

Enter details for:

- any worker who was paid **more than £100 in total by you in the year** to 5 April 2009, who has **not** already been listed in Section A
- harvest workers. For more information about harvest workers please refer to *CWG2 Employer Further Guide to PAYE and NICs.*

Full name of person employed, include title of Mr/Mrs/Miss/Ms	Last known address	National Insurance number	Employed as state type of work done	Dates employed if less than a full year		Total pay* for year to 5 April 2009	For official use only
				From	To		

Declaration

I declare that to the best of my knowledge and belief:

- I have made no payments that need to be listed above, **or**
- that the details given above, and on the attached sheets, are correct and complete.

Employer's signature

Date *DD MM YYYY*

10 Miscellaneous items

10.1 Refunds due to strikers

At Level 2, you studied tax refunds. You may remember that refunds due to employees on strike were withheld until the strike was over or the employees left your employment.

However what happens if the strike continues over the tax year end?

If the trade dispute continues at the end of the tax year, you need to take the following action.

- Fill in forms P11 as if you had **actually paid** the refunds of tax.

- Complete a form P61 or P62 (obtainable from the local HMRC office).

    - If you complete form P61 (statement of tax withheld), then you only enter a single net figure of tax deducted on form P14. You give the employee both forms P60 and P61.

    - If you enter a separate line on form P60 of the tax refund withheld, then you complete form P62 and give the employee both forms P60 and P62.

- In the new tax year, continue to withhold the tax refund until the trade dispute is settled.

Another case to consider is where the trade dispute is settled within a tax year, but the employee does not return to work after the strike.

In this case, you should pay the withheld tax refund if you know the employee's address. However if you cannot make the payment, you should pay over any tax you cannot refund to the Collector within 42 days of the end of the dispute.

At the tax year end, include the figure as tax not refunded on forms P14 and P35. If the form P35 has already been submitted, then you need to prepare additional forms P14 for each employee involved to show the amount of tax not refunded and send these to the Inspector with a covering list of names, amounts and the total of unrefunded tax.

The tax office will then deal with the tax refunds due.

11 Opening records for the new tax year

Before putting the previous tax year's records into storage, you will need to transfer standing data forward into the new tax year.

Whether the deduction sheets (forms P11) are kept manually or on a computer, certain information needs to be carried forward.

- Employer's name
- Employer's tax office and reference
- Employee's name (surname and first two forenames)
- Employee's NI number
- Employee's date of birth and gender
- Employee's work or payroll number
- NI table letter
- Date of starting

All this information should be taken direct from the previous year's P11.

11.1 Tax codes

In February 2010, HMRC will issue forms P9T for new codes to commence in tax year 2010/11.

Where a form P9T has been issued, the form P11 deduction card for the new year should be noted with the new code. Where more than one P9T is held for the same employee, use the form with the **latest date of issue**.

Where form P9T has not been issued, the code should be taken from the previous year's P11. However, if the code was on a week 1/month 1 basis, the code should be on a cumulative basis for the new tax year. So code 300L week 1/month 1 becomes 300L.

Where a code has not been changed by means of a form P9T, HMRC gives a notice of general uplift in codes, called form P9X. For example, the P9X for 2009 required 44 to be added to any L code brought forward from 2008/09. So code 603L became code 647L in tax year 2009/10.

11.2 Other data

The statutory deductions data for the new tax year will also be needed.

- New tax deduction tables
- New NI tables
- Budget notice (P7X) giving increases in tax codes not already dealt with on form P9X

The P7X tax code changes and new tax tables will all be effective from a certain date (for 2009/10 this was the first pay day in or after Week 1). Until then the brought forward tax codes and existing tax tables should be used. The new NI tables always apply from 6 April of the new tax year.

If you are using a computer to process the payroll, your software supplier will usually give you an update to change the tax and NI rates. However, if you have a special system, you may need to update the tax and NI rates yourself. You should not do this until the date specified by HMRC.

Any other changes introduced by the Budget may need to be processed. For example, payroll giving relief could be extended to NICs. In this case, the correct gross pay figure for NIC purposes would need to be calculated.

Check that all certificates for NIC reduced rate or deferment are still valid. Remember that CA2700 certificates are only valid for a tax year. If a new certificate has not been provided for the new tax year, you will need to make full NIC deductions.

All employee records should be up to date to ensure that the correct details are carried forward into the new year.

- Current salary
- Any continuing periods of SSP, SMP, SPP or SAP, where an employee is sick or on maternity, paternity or adoption leave over the tax year-end
- Any period of SSP within eight weeks of the tax year end (for linking purposes, see your Level 2 material)
- Pensionable salary
- Pension contributions (basic and AVCs)
- Other voluntary deductions
- Any court orders or CSA orders

- Details of Student Loan Deductions
- Any amendments to cost centres and other management information for reports

The payroll system should immediately start new cumulative totals to reflect the new tax year.

• Gross pay	• Other voluntary deductions
• Taxable pay	• Tax
• SSP, SMP, SPP, SAP	• NIC
• Pension contributions	• Non-taxable pay

The cut-off between tax years must be accurate, to ensure that the pay is recorded in the correct tax year.

The previous tax year's cumulative totals must still be available in order to process the end of year returns. They should then be kept (stored) for at least three years. Do not delete old data!

11.3 Leaver's records

Employees who left during the previous tax year should be deleted from the **new tax year's records** to ensure that payments do not continue to be made to them.

This applies to the following types of leavers.

- Resignations
- Dismissals
- Redundancies
- Deaths

However you will need to be careful in the case of those who **retired** during the previous tax year. If your employer runs an occupational pension scheme, then you may need to continue to keep them on the PAYE system. You will be paying them a **pension** instead of wages, but otherwise the PAYE rules are the same. However, NICs are not payable on pensions.

Although leaver's records need to be deleted from the current tax year, you should ensure that copies of the PAYE records are kept for at least three years as required by law. Therefore, if payroll files are kept on computer, do not erase the whole employee file. The records should be archived until they are no longer needed.

11.4 Storing previous year's records

Once the year-end tax returns have been finished, the old cumulative totals need to be cleared down and the records stored. Remember payroll documents need to be kept for **at least three years** by law and preferably longer.

It may be your organisation's policy to keep the last year's records filed in the payroll department for easy reference; while earlier years are archived and may be stored off the premises. Whatever the policy, you will need to ensure that the previous tax year's records are filed and older records archived as necessary.

11.5 Other year ends

It is unlikely that your organisation has a 5 April accounting year-end. Also pension schemes usually run for a calendar year (1 January to 31 December), so you could have to deal with three different types of year ends.

11.5.1 Organisation year end

If your organisation has a 30 June year end, it will need payroll information covering two tax years. For example, the 30 June 2009 year end will need payroll information from 1 July 2008 to 5 April 2009 (tax year 2008/09) and from 6 April 2009 to 30 June 2009 (tax year 2009/10).

The **accounts department** will be recording payroll information for the **organisation's** year end. However, you may be asked to provide the external auditors with details of the directors' pay and benefits for the organisation's year end.

Activity 4.8

You have been asked to provide the auditors with details of the directors' pay and benefits for the company's year end on 30 September 2009. What information do you give?

11.5.2 Pension year end

If there is a pension scheme it may have a calendar year end. You will need to be able to provide lists of individual employee's contributions for the **pension scheme year end**.

In this case, the actual deductions for each employee for each month of the **calendar year** will need to be extracted and totalled to provide the information required. This should cause no problem if you use contribution records (see your Level 2 studies).

In summary the payroll department needs to be able to prepare wages records on a tax year-end basis to comply with the law. However, records must be kept in sufficient detail (and for long enough) to enable data to be extracted for other year ends such as company and pension scheme year ends.

Key learning points

☑   Dealing with HMRC involves:

  –   The **Inspector of Taxes**, who agrees the amounts of tax and NICs due.
  –   The **Collector of Taxes**, to whom payment is made.

☑   By the 19th of the month, employers must pay the Collector what is owing for Income tax and NICs in the month ending 2 weeks before. There is a **Form P30B** payslip for the purpose, the details on which should be recorded on **Form P32**.

☑   After the end of every tax year **Form P14s** must be sent to the authorities and a **Form P60** must be given to each employee. Details for the P14s are collected from the P11s. The P14s are summarised on **Form P35** (which should agree with the P32).

☑   In certain circumstances additional return **P38A** must also be submitted.

☑   Information needed for the new tax year must be carried forward before the old records are closed off.

☑   Amendments may be needed to costing centres for management report purposes.

☑   Leaver's records should be deleted from the new tax year to ensure that no payments are made to them.

☑   Pensioners may need to be kept on the records if there is an occupational pension scheme.

☑   Previous years records should be stored, but records are likely to be needed should be accessible.

☑   Payroll information needs to be available where organisation/accounting or pension scheme year-ends are different from the tax year.

Quick quiz

1   HMRC will accept photocopies of completed forms. True or false?

2   What is a 'small employer' for PAYE purposes? What exception is made for small employers?

3   What happens if you find that the monthly total of PAYE and NIC is a negative figure?

4   What is the P14 used for? When is it filled in?

5   A P60 is issued every month. True or false?

6   When would you have to fill in a form P38A?

7   Tax codes are always carried forward to the next tax year without amendment. True or false?

8   New tax and NI tables should be used from 6 April. True or false?

9   Leaver's records must be deleted. True or false?

10 How long should old records be kept?

11 Payroll departments only provide returns for tax years. True or false?

Answers to quick quiz

1   False. If you run out of forms you can photocopy the HMRC Stationery but you must send them the copy you fill in, not a photocopy of your original.

2   If you estimate that your average monthly payment of PAYE and NICs is under £1,500 (averaged over a tax year), you are a small employer and need only forward your PAYE and NIC once a quarter instead of once a month.

3   You write NIL on the P30B payslip and send it off as normal. You deduct the amount from next month's payment. (If paying electronically, make an online notification of nil payment.)

4   The P14s go with the summary P35 to the tax office by 19 May each year. The P60 is a copy of the P14 which goes to the employee if he or she is still working for you on 5 April. Otherwise it should be destroyed. The P14 and P60 summarise the earnings, PAYE and NICs paid in the year.

5   False. It is issued once a year.

6   Form P38A (Employer's Supplementary Return) must be filled in and submitted with the P35 when the employer has not completed a P14 for one or more employees (usually casuals). You need to list the names, addresses and NI numbers of the employees and to give details of the type and length of the employment and how much each was paid.

7   False. Week 1/month 1 codes need to be altered to the cumulative basis. Also you need to apply any P9T notices and any P9X uplifts.

8   False. New tax codes and tax tables should be used only when HMRC tells you. In the meantime, the old codes and tables should continue to be used. The new NI tables, however, are used from 6 April of the new tax year.

9   True. However, where the leaver has retired, you may need a deduction card if there is an occupational pension scheme. Also old files must be archived, not destroyed.

10   By law at least three years. However, PAYE audits can go back six years, so PAYE records should preferably be kept at least that long.

11   False. Payroll departments provide **PAYE** returns for tax years. However, other returns may be needed where the organisation, pension schemes, etc, have different year-ends.

Activity checklist

This checklist shows which performance criteria, range statement or knowledge and understanding point is covered by each activity in this chapter. Tick off each activity as you complete it.

Activity

4.1		This activity covers performance criteria 75.1.B.
4.2		This activity covers performance criteria 75.1.B.
4.3		This activity covers performance criteria 75.1.C and 75.1.G.
4.4		This activity covers performance criteria 7.5.1.F and range statement point 1.
4.5		This activity covers performance criteria 75.1.D and range statement point 1.
4.6		This activity covers performance criteria 75.1.D and range statement point 1.
4.7		This activity covers performance criteria 75.1.B.
4.8		This activity covers performance criteria 75.1.G.

Benefits: identification

Contents

Performance criteria

75.2.A Identify the existence of a tax and National Insurance liability for **benefits** and **expenses**

75.2.B Identify statutory **exemptions** from liability to income tax and National Insurance

75.2.C Ensure that dispensations are up-to-date and are applicable to current organisational procedures

75.2.D Identify the relevant **statutory return** to be submitted for each employee

75.2.E Identify the correct method of calculating the income tax and National Insurance liability of benefits and expenses

Range statement

1   **Benefits:** assets transferred; payment of employee's own debts; vouchers; credit cards; cars; fuel for cars; loans; vans; in-house benefits; shares; living accommodation

2   **Expenses:** travel and subsistence; qualifying and non-qualifying relocation; mobile telephones; employee's own telephone; hotel expenses; staff and client entertaining

Knowledge and understanding

1   Data Protection legislation (Elements 75.1, 75.2 & 75.3)
2   HM Revenue and Customs regulations in respect of:
    – Income Tax and National Insurance liability on pay, expenses and benefits (Elements 75.1, 75.2 & 75.3)
    – Income Tax and National Insurance regulations relating to end of year reporting (Elements 75.1, 75.2 & 75.3)
    – The methods of submitting end of year returns (Elements 75.1 & 75.2)
    – Dispensations, extra statutory concessions, statutory exemptions and HM Revenue and Customs Regulations settlement agreements and their impact on end of year reporting for Income Tax and National Insurance purposes (Elements 75.2 & 75.3)
3   Policies for dealing with expenses and benefits (Elements 75.2 & 75.3)
4   Method of payment of expenses (Elements 75.2 & 75.3)
8   Procedures for the security and confidentiality of information (Elements 75.1, 75.2 & 75.3)
9   Sources of information for the resolution of discrepancies (Element 75.1, 75.2 and 75.3)

Signpost

This is an element introduced in the 2003 standards. It emphasises the identification of benefits and expenses and their treatment in payroll for tax and NIC purposes.

1 The problem

What is a benefit? Which benefits and expenses are subject to tax and NICs? What annual returns are needed?

Are there any expenses or benefits which can be left off the annual returns?

2 The solution

Section 3 will deal with the identification of benefits and expenses, and how they are returned to HMRC.

In Section 4, we will look at dispensations and exemptions. These items do **not** need to be reported to HMRC.

Finally, in Section 5, we will look at the tax and NIC treatment of benefits and expenses.

3 Identification of benefits and expenses

3.1 Benefits

A benefit is **non-monetary remuneration**. For example, the employee may have the use of a **company car**.

- Employees usually have to **pay tax** on benefits.
- Employees can avoid paying **NICs** on benefits if the benefit is provided properly.
- Employers may have a Class 1A NIC liability on benefits provided.

Suppose that your employer **reimburses** the cost of your business suit (non-uniform). This is not an allowable business expense and **you must pay the tax on the full cost**. It does not matter whether the employer actually buys the suit and gives it to you, with the right to take it back when you leave, or whether you buy it instead and the employer gives you the cash.

For **NICs**, however, if the employer gives you cash to buy the suit yourself, or reimburses you through the payroll, then you pay NICs. If, on the other hand, the employer buys the suit for your use, then you may not have to pay NICs.

3.1.1 Company cars

Your employer may provide company cars for certain employees. If the employee is a director or earns £8,500 a year or more (including the benefit), then a form P46 (car) needs to be completed if the car is available for private use.

The form for 2009/10 is shown overleaf.

The P46 (car) has to be completed when a car is first provided and whenever there are any changes eg a replacement car, or a second car, or the car is withdrawn. Also a form has to be completed if an employee starts to earn more than £8,500 or becomes a director.

Page 1 gives details of the provision, replacement or withdrawal.

The details of the car on page 2 are needed to calculate the taxable benefit.

The details of CO_2 emissions are needed, because the car and car fuel benefits are based on its emissions. This figure should be indicated in the V5 Registration Document for all cars first registered on or after 1 March 2001. For cars registered between 1 January 1998 and 28 February 2001, details can be obtained from the Society of Motor Manufacturers and Traders (www.smmt.co.uk/co2/co2.asp).

A form P46 (car) has to be submitted within 28 days of the end of the quarter in which the change occurred. The relevant quarters are those ending as follows.

- 5 July
- 5 October
- 5 January
- 5 April

Assessment focus point

From 6 April 2009, submission of P46(car) is limited to those situations where a car is provided for the first time or withdrawn or an additional car is provided without the first car being withdrawn. The purpose of the change is to limit compliance costs.

HM Revenue & Customs

Car provided for the private use of an employee or a director

Use from 6 April 2009 onwards

You must complete this form if there is a change that affects car benefits for an employee earning at the rate of £8,500 a year or more, or a director for whom a car is made available for private use. Complete and return this form within 28 days of the end of the quarter to 5 July, 5 October, 5 January or 5 April in which the change takes place.

Employer's details

Name

Phone number

PAYE reference

Employee's or Director's details

Name

National Insurance number

Date of birth *(if known) DD MM YYYY*

Gender

Male ☐   Female ☐

General details

Show here and on Page 2 any changes that have been made.

We provided the employee or director with a car, which is available for private use. ☐

We replaced a car provided to the employee or director with another car which is available for private use. ☐

If the employee has more than one car available for private use please give details of the car that you replaced.

Make and model

Engine size

cc

We provided the employee or director with a second or further car, which is available for private use. ☐

The employee has started to earn at the rate of £8,500 a year or more, or has become a director. ☐

We have withdrawn a car provided to the employee or director and have not replaced it. ☐

If you ticked this box, please complete the boxes below, and then go straight to the declaration overleaf. Do not complete the other sections.

Date withdrawn *DD MM YYYY*

Please give details of the car withdrawn.

Make and model

Engine size

cc

P46 (Car)(2009)   Page 1   HMRC 03/09

BPP LEARNING MEDIA

Details of the car provided:

Make and model

Engine size

cc

Please tick one of these boxes to show the engine size:

up to 1400cc ☐   2001cc or more ☐

1401-2000cc ☐   no engine size ☐

Date first registered *DD MM YYYY*

☐☐ ☐☐ ☐☐☐☐

Emissions

Give details of the approved CO_2 emissions figure at the date of first registration

Grams of CO_2 per kilometre ☐☐☐

If you have not filled in a figure for approved CO_2 emissions, please show the reason:

Car was first registered before 1998, or ☐

1998 or later car, for which there is no approved CO_2 emissions figure *(for example, some personal imports from outside the European Community)* ☐

Type of Fuel or power used

Key letter – use the list of key letters below to find the appropriate key letter and enter it in the box below:

Type:	Key letter
• Petrol	P
• Diesel	D
• Euro IV emissions standard diesel	L
Alternative fuel/power types:	
• Hybrid electric	H
A hybrid electric car combines a petrol engine with an electric motor	
• Electricity only	E
• Bi-fuel	B
For a gas and petrol car that had an approved CO_2 emissions figure for gas at first registration	
• E85	G
For a car manufactured to be able to run on E85, a mixture of petrol and at least 85% bioethanol	
• Conversion or older bi-fuel	C
For a gas and petrol car that only had an approved CO_2 emissions figure for petrol at first registration	

Key letter ☐

If you think that the car uses a type of fuel that is not mentioned above, please contact your HM Revenue & Customs office.

Details of the car provided:

Price and employee contributions

Price of the car (not the price actually paid, but the price for tax purposes – normally the list price at the date of first registration)

£ ☐☐☐☐☐ · ☐☐

Price of accessories not included in the price of the car

£ ☐☐☐☐☐ · ☐☐

Date the car was first made available to the employee
DD MM YYYY

☐☐ ☐☐ ☐☐☐☐

Capital contribution (if any) made by the employee towards the cost of the car and for accessories

£ ☐☐☐☐☐ · ☐☐

Sum that the employee is required to pay (if any) for private use of the car

£ ☐☐☐☐☐ · ☐☐

If so, how often?

Weekly ☐   Quarterly ☐

Monthly ☐   Yearly ☐

Fuel for private use

Is fuel provided for private use?

Tick 'Yes' if the employee is provided with any fuel at all for private use, including any combination of petrol and gas, or petrol for a hybrid electric car.

Do not tick 'Yes' if only electricity is provided.

Yes ☐   No ☐

If 'Yes', must the employee pay for all fuel used for private motoring and do you expect them to continue to do so?

Yes ☐   No ☐

Declaration

I declare that the information I have given is correct according to the best of my knowledge and belief.

Signature

Capacity in which signed

Date *DD MM YYYY*

☐☐ ☐☐ ☐☐☐☐

3.1.2 Other benefits and expenses

The provision of the following benefits or expenses will need to be recorded, as they are included on the year-end returns.

- Assets transferred to the employee
- Payments made on behalf of the employee
- Vouchers
- Credit cards
- Living accommodation
- Mileage allowance and passenger payments
- Cars
- Car fuel
- Vans
- Interest free and low interest loans
- Private medical treatment or insurance
- Relocation expenses
- Services supplied
- Assets placed at the employee's disposal
- Expenses reimbursed by employer (eg travel and subsistence, employee phone costs, entertaining)

We will look at all these in detail (including how to calculate the value of the benefit) in Chapter 6 of this text.

3.2 Statutory returns

3.2.1 P11D

If an employee is a director or earns £8,500 or more per annum (**including** the value of the benefit), then the benefits and expenses are recorded on a form P11D.

The P11D has to be submitted to HMRC by **6 July** following the end of the tax year. So P11Ds for tax year 2009/10 have to be submitted by 6 July 2010. In addition, a copy must be given to the employee by the same date. The forms may be filed online, but this is not yet compulsory.

There are penalties for late submission of form P11D. There is a penalty not exceeding £300 per return, with a further penalty not exceeding £60 per return a day if failure to submit continues.

In addition if an **incorrect return** is made, there is a penalty of up to £3,000 for each incorrect return. The penalty is often related to the amount of the tax lost and interest is charged.

We will look at the completion of forms P11D in the next chapter.

3.2.2 P11D(b)

The P11D(b) is used to calculate Class 1A NICs arising on some benefits.

Various benefits are subject to Class 1A NICs. The P11D indicates exactly which items are chargeable to Class 1A NICs. Therefore, we will look at this in detail in the next chapter.

The form P11D(b) is then used to summarise the total of the benefits subject to Class 1A NICs on all the individual P11Ds.

Class 1A NIC is calculated at 12.8% on those benefits. It is paid only by the **employer**.

The P11D(b) has to be submitted by 6 July following the end of the tax year. There are penalties for late submission of form P11D(b). These are £100 per month (or part month) per 50 employees (or part thereof). The form may be filed online, but this is not yet compulsory.

3.2.3 P9D

Where an employee is not a director and earns less than £8,500 (including benefits) he or she does not need a form P11D.

However certain items still need to be returned and these are entered on a form P9D. We will look at this in detail in Chapter 6 of this text. The following list indicates the items caught.

- Non-business expenses in excess of £25 in total
- Payments made on the employee's behalf
- Gifts (eg Christmas hamper)
- Vouchers and credit cards
- Accommodation

Like the P11D, forms P9D have to be submitted by 6 July following the end of the tax year. They may be filed online, but this is not yet compulsory.

Activity 5.1

Melanie Beale has the use of a company car. The taxable value of the benefit is £2,500 pa. Which annual returns are needed if her salary is

(a)   £5,000 pa?
(b)   £8,000 pa?
(c)   Would your answers differ if Melanie had the use of a company credit card?

4 Dispensations and exemptions

Keeping records of information necessary to prepare forms P11D is time consuming, particularly for employers with large numbers of employees.

Personnel records and contracts of employment need to be consulted for benefit entitlements. The costs to the employer of providing those benefits needs to be separately recorded in the payroll records.

Also records need to be kept of company cars provided (forms P46(car) see Section 3), reimbursed expenses, round sum allowances and assets transferred to the employee.

Then there is the time taken to complete the actual forms themselves in order to meet the 6 July deadline. Therefore dealing with form P11D requirements is a year long, time consuming exercise.

It makes sense, therefore, for employers to take advantage of any legal ways to decrease their administrative burden.

- Dispensations
- Statutory exemptions

4.1 Dispensations

Dispensations are available from your employer's Inspector. A dispensation is a notice from HMRC relieving your employer from reporting certain expense payments and benefits on form P9D or P11D. Also HMRC accept that expenses covered by a dispensation do not count as earnings for NIC purposes.

Any type of expenses (except round sum allowances) and most benefits can be covered by a dispensation.

- Entertaining
- Professional subscriptions
- Non cash vouchers

Although dispensations may be given for travelling and subsistence they are not given for payments for the use of the employee's own car, due to the introduction of authorised mileage rates.

However certain benefits **must** be reported and cannot be covered by a dispensation.

- Car and car fuel benefits
- Vans
- Private medical insurance
- Cheap loans
- Other benefits subject to a Class 1A NIC charge

A dispensation can still save an employer a lot of paperwork and so is worth considering. An expense or benefit covered by a dispensation does not need to be entered on the employee's personal Tax Return either.

Before granting a dispensation, the Inspector must be satisfied that:

- Expenses claims are independently checked and authorised (including directors)
- Where possible, all expense claims are supported by receipts
- No tax is payable on the expenses by your employees (ie they are genuine business expenses)

Dispensations can be granted to cover some employees only. So if the conditions above are met by all employees, but not the directors, the dispensation would cover all employees except directors.

An employer must tell the Inspector of any changes to systems and expenses (eg a change in scale rates) covered by a dispensation. A new dispensation may need to be issued. Therefore employers need to review dispensations at regular interviews to ensure they are still effective. Also, HMRC will review dispensations from time to time to ensure they are still valid.

A dispensation can start from any date, not just the beginning of a tax year. The employer needs to apply using form P11DX, which is obtainable from any Tax Office.

4.2 Statutory exemptions

Even if your employer does not obtain a dispensation, time can still be saved by the use of statutory exemptions.

There is a flat rate deduction for tools and protective clothing in certain industries. Examples include the following.

- Joiners and carpenters £140 pa
- Engineering workers £120 pa
- Nurses £100 pa

The employee claims this allowance where he or she has to bear the cost of upkeep of tools or uniforms or protective clothing. If your employer is in one of the industries covered by the exemption, it is good employee relations to publish the rates so that employees can obtain the correct allowance.

Meal vouchers up to the value of 15p per day are tax free and do not need to be entered on forms P11D. If vouchers of more than this amount are issued, the **excess** is taxable.

Activity 5.2

Comecon Ltd gives its employees luncheon vouchers worth £1.50 per day. How much is taxable?

The following are relaxations of the rule that travel between home and business is not an allowable expense.

(a) A director of two or more companies within the same group is regarded as having one place of normal employment, so travel between the businesses in the course of his duties is allowable.

(b) A director giving his services free to a not for profit company (eg sports club) will not be taxed on the reimbursement of his travelling expenses.

(c) A directorship held as part of a professional practice will not be assessed on reimbursed expenses, provided the company does not claim these expenses against its tax liability.

(d) If a director or P11D employee has health problems that do not disbar him from carrying out his normal duties, but make foreign travel a problem, then his employer can pay the expenses for his wife to accompany him.

Travel expenses in this case include reasonable hotel costs necessarily incurred.

Other important exemptions include the following.

- Free or subsidised canteen facilities available for all staff.
- Taxis provided to take staff home after 9pm (provided that this is not a regular or frequent occurrence) or during public transport disruption.
- Long service awards for 20 years or more service (not exceeding £50 per year of service), provided that a similar award has not been made in the past ten years.
- Annual events for staff, provided the cost does not exceed £150 per head.
- Suggestion schemes, as long as the employee does not work in the department affected by the suggestion, up to £5,000 or 50% of the first year's savings.

- Business gifts bearing the company's name **prominently** up to £50 each year for each recipient (but excluding food, drink, tobacco or vouchers).

- Small gifts from third parties: £250 pa (including entertainment, eg theatre or sporting tickets)

- Mobile phones provided by the employer (see Chapter 6)

- Workplace parking

- Works buses

- Works cycles for travel between one workplace and another

- Workplace nursery

- Childcare vouchers or other childcare provision up to £55 a week (any excess over £55 is taxed)

- Sporting and recreational activities for employees

- Certain accommodation (see Chapter 6)

- Interest-free and low interest loans totalling less than £5,000 (see Chapter 6)

- Incidental overnight expenses (IOE) (see Chapter 6)

- Qualifying removal expenses (see Chapter 6)

- Meals or refreshments provided as part of official 'cycle to work' days

- Welfare counselling available to employees generally

- Training costs

- Equipment provided for disabled employees

- Payments towards additional household costs of employees who work at home, up to £3 per week (£156 pa) without supporting evidence (see Chapter 6)

- Computer equipment provided by employer up to £500, any excess is taxable (see chapter 6)

- Trivial benefits (eg seasonal gift of a turkey or ordinary bottle of wine)

- Pensions advice up to £150 per annum (if the cost exceeds £150, the **whole** amount is taxable).

- Scholarship of up to £15,480 per annum for an **employee** attending full-time university or technical college courses.

Any expense covered by a statutory exemption is omitted from form P9D or P11D.

5 Tax and NIC treatment

5.1 Exemptions

Any amounts covered by a **dispensation** or a **statutory exemption** are omitted from form P9D or P11D. They are also exempt from tax and NICs.

Some benefits may be subject to a PAYE Settlement Agreement (PSA). PSAs are dealt with in detail in Chapter 6. However, basically the employer agrees with HMRC to meet the tax cost of certain benefits provided. The employer will also pay NIC (Class 1B NIC) on these benefits.

Items subject to a PSA or a Taxed Award Scheme (covering third party benefits) are omitted from the annual returns and are exempt from normal PAYE tax and NIC deductions.

5.2 Tax

Generally tax is not deducted at source from benefits or expenses reimbursed. Instead the full taxable amount is included on form P11D. HMRC will then adjust the employee's tax code in order to collect the tax due.

5.3 NIC

Most reimbursed expenses and benefits are not subject to Class 1 NIC in the employee's hands. Instead the **employer** will pay Class 1A NIC on some of these amounts.

5.3.1 Items exempt from Class 1 and Class 1A NICs

- Assets placed at the employee's disposal provided private use is insignificant
- Car parking facilities provided at or near place of work
- Car parking fees paid or reimbursed at or near place of work or for business journeys
- Childcare help (up to the age of 16) provided by employer or where the contract is with the employer.
- Childcare vouchers up to £55 per week
- Protective clothing or uniforms necessary for work
- Computers supplied before 6 April 2006 for private use up to a value of £500 or less
- Credit and charge cards used to purchase goods or services on employer's behalf or for business purposes
- Employee's liability insurance
- Entertaining clients
- Reimbursement of specific and distinct business expenses
- Expenses covered by a dispensation or a statutory exemption
- Medical insurance for employees whose duties are carried out outside the UK
- Mobile phones provided by employer used for business purposes only
- Mobile phones used privately, where contract is with employer (limited to one phone only from 6 April 2006)
- Office accommodation
- Professional subscriptions
- Telephone where employer is subscriber and employee reimburses costs of all private calls
- Telephone where employee is subscriber, but used solely for business purposes.

These items are not included on the deduction card, although some may need to be included on form P11D, see Chapter 6.

5.3.2 Items exempt from Class 1 NIC but liable to Class 1A NICs

These items will be excluded from the deduction card, but will be included on forms P11D. The employer's liability to Class 1A NICs will be calculated on form P11D(b).

They will be dealt with in detail in Chapter 6.

5.3.3 Items liable to Class 1 NICs

These expenses and benefits will need to be included in pay for NIC purposes.

- Reimbursement of car or van fuel for private motoring in a privately owned vehicle
- Car parking fees, unless at or near place of work or for business journeys
- Reimbursement of childcare costs or additional salary to meet those costs
- Childcare vouchers in excess of £55 per week (first £55 is exempt, any excess is NICable)
- Christmas bonus paid in cash
- Clothing that can be worn at any time, when the contract is with the employee
- Employee's Council Tax
- Credit or charge card used to buy items for the personal use of the employee
- Entertaining staff where the contract is with the employee
- Profit element of expenses not covered by a dispensation
- All reimbursed expenses where the contract is in the **employee's** name (ie food, goods, holidays, insurance premiums, medical or dental insurance, personal bills, scholarships, school fees, subscriptions, training payments)
- Income tax paid but not deducted from employee
- Loans written off (at the time loan is waived)
- Meal vouchers (excess over 15p per day)
- Mobile phone under an employee contract
- Readily convertible assets (remuneration provided as gold bullion, shares, share options and other commodities)
- Non-qualifying relocation expenses
- Contributions towards an unapproved retirement benefit scheme
- Round sum allowances
- Telephone where employee is subscriber and phone is used exclusively for private purposes
- Telephone where employee is subscriber and phone is used for both business and private purposes (full amount of rental and full amount of calls unless business calls can be separately identified)
- Vouchers

Key learning points

☑ Taxable benefits are detailed on forms P9D or P11D.

☑ Summary form P11D(b) is used to calculate the employer's liability to Class 1A NIC.

☑ Administration can be reduced by the use of **dispensations** and **statutory exemptions**

Quick quiz

1   Which employees need a P9D?

2   All employees with the use of a company car need a form P11D. True or false?

3   All benefits can be the subject of a dispensation. True or false?

Answers to quick quiz

1   Employees earnings less than £8,500 pa who receive certain benefits

2   False. Only these employees whose salary plus benefits exceed £8,500 pa

3   False. Benefits subject to Class 1A NICs are excluded

Activity checklist

This checklist shows which performance criteria, range statement or knowledge and understanding point is covered by each activity in this chapter. Tick off each activity as you complete it.

Activity

5.1   [   ]   This activity covers performance criteria 75.2.D.

5.2   [   ]   This activity covers performance criteria 75.2.B.

chapter 6

Benefits:
reports

Contents

Performance criteria

75.3.A Correctly **calculate** the value of taxable **benefits**

75.3.B Report the value of income taxable benefits and **expenses** accurately, taking into account **non-reportable items**

75.3.C Calculate the Class 1A National Insurance liability accurately in accordance with statutory timescales

75.3.D Calculate the income tax and Class 1B National Insurance liability on benefits where the organisation has agreed to meet the liability

75.3.E Complete all **statutory** and **non statutory** year end returns accurately

75.3.F Despatch all **statutory** and **non-statutory** year end returns by the due dates

75.3.G Ensure all year-end information for employees is made available by the applicable statutory date

75.3.H Produce internal year-end summaries for management accounting purposes in an accurate and timely manner

Range statement

1 **Benefits:** assets transferred; payment of employee's own debts; vouchers; credit cards; cars; fuel for cars; loans; vans; in-house benefits; shares; living accommodation

Range statement (continued)

2   **Expenses:** travel and subsistence; qualifying and non-qualifying relocation; mobile telephones; employee's own telephone; hotel expenses; staff and client entertaining

3   **Statutory returns:** form P11D; form P11D(b); form P9D

4   **Non-statutory returns:** internal end of year reports

Knowledge and understanding

1   Data Protection legislation (Elements 75.1, 75.2 & 75.3)

2   HM Revenue and Customs regulations in respect of:
   –   Income Tax and National Insurance liability on pay, expenses and benefits (Elements 75.1, 75.2 & 75.3)
   –   Income Tax and National Insurance regulations relating to end of year reporting (Elements 75.1, 75.2 & 75.3)
   –   The methods of submitting end of year returns (Elements 75.1 & 75.2)
   –   Dispensations, extra statutory concessions, and HM Revenue and Customs Regulations settlement agreements and their impact on end of year reporting for Income Tax and National Insurance purposes (Elements 75.2 & 75.3)

3   Policies for dealing with expenses and benefits (Elements 75.2 & 75.3)

4   Method of payment of expenses (Elements 75.2 & 75.3)

5   Policies, practices and procedures for filing (Elements 75.1 & 75.3)

6   Signatories and authorisations (Elements 75.1 & 75.3)

7   Information flows within the organisation (Elements 75.1 & 75.3)

8   Procedures for the security and confidentiality of information (Elements 75.1, 75.2 & 75.3)

9   Sources of information for the resolution of discrepancies (Element 75.1, 75.2 and 75.3)

Signpost

The guidance to this element states that you must have the ability to check the taxable value of benefits **manually** in response to queries or to check that the computer system has been set up properly.

---

1 The problem

In the previous chapter we looked at the identification of benefits and their treatment for tax and NIC purposes. Now we will turn our attention to the end of year reports.

How do we complete forms P11D? How do we calculate Class IA NICs and complete form P11D(b)? What about form P9D?

What is a PAYE settlement agreement and how do we calculate Class 1B NICs?

2 The solution

In this chapter we will be looking at the year-end procedures that have to be carried out in respect of reimbursed expenses and benefits.

Benefits are usually entered on a form P11D, which we will look at in Section 3.

BPP
LEARNING MEDIA

Class 1A NICs are due on some taxable benefits. These are returned on form P11D(b) and we will deal with these in Section 4.

Lower paid workers, whose total pay and benefits are less than £8,500, may need a return on form P9D. See Section 5 for this.

The employer's paperwork can be considerably reduced by the use of PAYE Settlement Agreements (PSAs). These are covered in Section 6.

3 Form P11D

3.1 Employees needing a form P11D

You have to complete a form P11D for all employees who receive taxable 'benefits' and whose total remuneration, **including benefits and expenses** exceeds £8,500. However, a director must have a P11D, even if salary and benefits are below £8,500. In addition, any benefits provided to the family or household of an employee or director must be included on their P11D.

Example: Form P11D

Sally Western has a salary of £5,000 pa. She is not a director. However, she also has the use of a company car. The taxable benefit in respect of the company car is £3,000 pa. Do you have to complete a form P11D? Does it make any different to your answer if Sally's salary is £6,000 pa?

Solution

	£
Salary	5,000
Benefits	3,000
Total	8,000

In this case the total salary and benefits is less than £8,500 and so you would not prepare a form P11D. Nor would you prepare a form P9D (see Section 5).

If Sally's salary is £6,000 pa, then total salary plus benefits is £9,000 pa (£6,000 + £3,000). Therefore, in this case, you would prepare form P11D.

3.2 Taxable benefits

All taxable benefits have to be included on form P11D. The form for 2008/09 is reproduced on the next pages. The form for 2009/10 will not be available until the beginning of 2010, when you will be able to download it from the HMRC website.

HM Revenue & Customs

Please ensure your entries are clear on both sides of the form.

Employer name

Employer PAYE reference

Employee name

Surname

Forename(s)

Works number/department

National Insurance number

P11D EXPENSES AND BENEFITS 2008–09

Note to employer
Complete this return for a director, or an employee who earned at a rate of £8,500 or more a year during the year to 5 April 2009. Send the completed form to your HM Revenue & Customs office by 6 July 2009.

Note to employee
Your employer has filled in this form, keep it in a safe place. You will need it to complete your 2008-09 Tax Return if you get one. The box numberings on this P11D are the same as on the Employment Page of the Tax Return, for example, 13.

If a director tick here ▶

Date of birth *in figures (if known)*

D D M M Y Y Y Y

Gender **M – Male F – Female**

Employers pay Class 1A National Insurance contributions on most benefits. These are shown in boxes which are brown and have a **1A** indicator

A Assets transferred (cars, property, goods or other assets)

	Cost/Market value		Amount made good or from which tax deducted		Cash equivalent	
Description of asset	£	–	£	=	**13** £	**1A**

B Payments made on behalf of employee

Description of payment		**15** £
Tax on notional payments not borne by employee within 90 days of receipt of each notional payment		**15** £

C Vouchers or credit cards

	Gross amount		Amount made good or from which tax deducted		Cash equivalent
Value of vouchers and payments made using credit cards or tokens (for qualifying childcare vouchers the excess over £55 a week)	£	–	£	=	**12** £

D Living accommodation

Cash equivalent

Cash equivalent of accommodation provided for employee, or his/her family or household   **14** £   **1A**

E Mileage allowance and passenger payments

Taxable amount

Amount of car and mileage allowances paid to employee for business travel in employee's own vehicle, and passenger payments, in excess of maximum exempt amounts *(See P11D Guide for 2008–09 exempt rates)*   **12** £

F Cars and car fuel *If more than two cars were made available, either at the same time or in succession, please give details on a separate sheet*

	Car 1	Car 2
Make and Model		
Date first registered	/ /	/ /
Approved CO₂ emissions figure for cars registered on or after 1 January 1998 *Tick box if the car does not have an approved CO₂ figure*	g/km · *See P11D Guide for details of cars that have no approved CO₂ figure*	g/km · *See P11D Guide for details of cars that have no approved CO₂ figure*
Engine size	cc	cc
Type of fuel or power used *Please use the key letter shown in the P11D Guide*		
Dates car was available *Do not complete the 'From' box if the car was available on 5 April 2008 or the 'To' box if it continued to be available on 6 April 2009*	From / / to / /	From / / to / /
List price of car *including car and standard accessories only. If there is no list price, or if it is a classic car, employers see booklet 480*	£	£
Accessories *All non-standard accessories, see P11D Guide*	£	£
Capital contributions (maximum £5,000) the employee made towards the cost of car or accessories	£	£
Amount paid by employee for private use of the car	£	£
Date free fuel was withdrawn *Tick if reinstated in year (see P11D Guide)*	/ /	/ /
Cash equivalent of each car	£	£

Total cash equivalent of all cars made available in 2008–09   **9** £   **1A**

Cash equivalent of fuel for each car	£	£

Total cash equivalent of fuel for all cars made available in 2008–09   **10** £   **1A**

P11D(2009) HMRC 09/08

BPP LEARNING MEDIA

G Vans and van fuel

Total cash equivalent of all vans made available in 2008-09 — **9** £ ____ 1A

Total cash equivalent of fuel for all vans made available in 2008-09 — **10** £ ____ 1A

H Interest-free and low interest loans

If the total amount outstanding on all loans does not exceed £5,000 at any time in the year, there is no need to complete this section.

	Loan 1	Loan 2
Number of joint borrowers *(if applicable)*		
Amount outstanding at 5 April 2008 or at date loan was made if later	£	£
Amount outstanding at 5 April 2009 or at date loan was discharged if earlier	£	£
Maximum amount outstanding at any time in the year	£	£
Total amount of interest paid by the borrower in 2008-09 – *enter "NIL" if none was paid*	£	£
Date loan was made in 2008-09 if applicable	/ /	/ /
Date loan was discharged in 2008-09 if applicable	/ /	/ /
Cash equivalent of loans after deducting any interest paid by the borrower	**15** £ ____ 1A	**15** £ ____ 1A

I Private medical treatment or insurance

	Cost to you	Amount made good or from which tax deducted	Cash equivalent
Private medical treatment or insurance	£	– £	= **11** £ ____ 1A

J Qualifying relocation expenses payments and benefits

Non-qualifying benefits and expenses go in sections M and N below

Excess over £8,000 of all qualifying relocation expenses payments and benefits for each move — **15** £ ____ 1A

K Services supplied

	Cost to you	Amount made good or from which tax deducted	Cash equivalent
Services supplied to the employee	£	– £	= **15** £ ____ 1A

L Assets placed at the employee's disposal

	Annual value plus expenses incurred	Amount made good or from which tax deducted	Cash equivalent
Description of asset ____	£	– £	= **13** £ ____ 1A

M Other items (including subscriptions and professional fees)

	Cost to you	Amount made good or from which tax deducted	Cash equivalent
Description of other items ____	£	– £	= **15** £ ____ 1A
Description of other items ____	£	– £	= **15** £
Income tax paid but not deducted from director's remuneration			tax paid **15** £

N Expenses payments made to, or on behalf of, the employee

	Cost to you	Amount made good or from which tax deducted	Taxable payment
Travelling and subsistence payments *(except mileage allowance payments for employee's own car - see section E)*	£	– £	= **16** £
Entertainment *(trading organisations read P11D Guide and then enter a tick or a cross as appropriate here)* ____	£	– £	= **16** £
General expenses allowance for business travel	£	– £	= **16** £
Payments for use of home telephone	£	– £	= **16** £
Non-qualifying relocation expenses *(those not shown in sections J or M)*	£	– £	= **16** £
Description of other expenses ____	£	– £	= **16** £

The first section asks for the **employer's** details.

- Employer's name
- Employer's PAYE tax reference

Below this, the **employee's** details need to be shown.

- Employee's name (surname and forename(s))
- Tick box if employee is a director
- Works number
- National Insurance number
- Date of birth
- Male (M) or Female (F)

It is now **compulsory** to enter details of the employee's gender and date of birth. A default date of birth is not acceptable.

The details of the benefits are then entered in the various sections below. The numbers by the right hand boxes refer to the section of the employee's Tax Return where these figures are entered.

Remember to omit any item subject to a dispensation or statutory exemption (see Chapter 5).

Where a benefit is liable to Class 1A NICs (see Section 4), the extreme right hand side of the box is indicated '1A'.

Remember any benefit can be assessed in your exam or skills test. Make sure you are familiar with form P11D and its various working sheets which are reproduced in this chapter. Check the HMRC website early in 2010 for the 2009/10 formats.

Important!

All figures entered on form P11D or P9D must **include** VAT.

3.3 Section A: Assets transferred

Any assets transferred to an employee have to be included here, eg car, house, TV set, food hamper at Christmas, business suit. In the first box enter details of the asset.

The cost (or market value for secondhand items) goes in the second box. This is the **cost to the employer**. So if the employer receives a discount, it is the discounted cost that is entered here. Market value of secondhand items is the price the item could have fetched if sold singly on the open market, it is not the written down value in the accounts. So, for example, HMRC will check the market values of cars by reference to trade guides eg Glass's. If there are additional costs (eg delivery costs) in transferring the asset to the employee these are added to the cost or market value.

The employee may make a payment to the employer towards the cost of the asset or the employer may include an amount on form P11 as part of taxable pay. In either case, the gross amount is entered in the third box.

The figure in the third box is deducted from the figure in the second box, to arrive at the benefit, which is entered in the fourth box. This is the amount that will be taxable.

3.4 Section B: Payments made on behalf of employee

This refers to the employee's **personal bills** that are paid by the employer. For example, the payment of an employee's personal credit card bill direct to the credit card company, if the employee does not have to reimburse the employer. A description and the amount involved are entered in this section.

Notional payments include earnings paid by an intermediary of the employer, or by vouchers or assets easily converted into cash. PAYE applies to these payments. If the tax is not recovered from the employee or director within 30 days of the notional payment, then a benefit arises and the tax is shown in this section of form P11D. You do not need to know the detail of this box, just be aware of what should be entered here.

3.5 Section C: Vouchers or credit cards

The first 15p per day of luncheon vouchers are **tax free**. Any amounts over this figure, any other vouchers (including season tickets) provided by the employer that can be exchanged for money, goods or services, or any personal purchases made on company credit cards are entered in this section.

If the employer provides qualifying childcare vouchers, only the first £55 a week is exempt. Any excess over £55 a week needs to be entered here.

The cost is the cost to the employer. So, for example, if the employer gives each employee £100 of Debenham's vouchers but they only cost the employer £95, then the cost of the benefit is £95. Once again, any reimbursement by the employee or any amount taxed on form P11 is deducted in arriving at the benefit figure.

3.6 Section D: Living accommodation

The employer may provide the employee with living accommodation. Sometimes this is due to security problems (eg terrorist threats), because it is necessary for the employee to reside there in order to carry out his or her duties, or because it is usual to provide accommodation so that the job can be done better (eg warden in sheltered accommodation). In these cases, there is **no** taxable benefit and no entries are needed on form P11D.

In any other case, the rules for calculating the benefit are complex and you would need to use the Working Sheet 1 (P11DWS1). Remember the accommodation itself may not be a taxable benefit; but a benefit may exist if the employer pays any bills (eg gas, electricity) that would normally be the employee's **personal** liability.

Activity 6.1

Box Car Ltd, PAYE reference 890/B1234, provides the use of a company flat to one of its directors, Charlotte Bright. The flat is located at 1B Chelsea Arches, Embankment, London W12 7AA, and was available to Charlotte for the whole tax year. The flat cost Box Car Ltd £125,000 and Charlotte pays £5,000 a year rent. The flat is unfurnished and Charlotte meets all the running expenses. The annual value of the accommodation is the gross rating value. This is £4,000. Charlotte's National Insurance number is AB 12 34 56 C.

Compete WS1 to determine the benefit to be entered on form P11D. (*Note.* Work through WS1 methodically and carefully. You have all the information you need to calculate the benefit.) Please use an official rate of interest of 4.75% from 6 April 2009.

HM Revenue & Customs

P11D Working Sheet 1
Living accommodation 2008-09

Note to employer

You do not have to use this form, but, you may find it a useful way to calculate the cash equivalent if you provided living accommodation for a director or an employee during the year 2008-09 (that is 6 April 2008 to 5 April 2009).

Read the *P11D Guide* and Booklet 480 before you complete this form. Sections 1 and 2 apply to a director or an employee whatever their rate of pay. If you provided any benefits associated with accommodation you may find the checklist at Section 3 helpful.

If you use this form you must also fill in form P11D or P9D. You must also complete form P11D(b) *Return of Class 1A National Insurance contributions*, if you use this Working Sheet to fill in form P11D. CWG5(2009) *Class 1A National Insurance contributions on benefits in kind* gives more information.

You are advised to keep a copy of each completed working sheet as it could help you to deal with enquiries. You do not have to give a copy of the completed working sheet to the director or employee, or to your HM Revenue & Customs office.

The term employee is used to cover both directors and employees throughout the rest of this form.

The term accommodation refers to the living accommodation provided to the employee and the property consisting of that accommodation.

If the employee can choose between:

• taking living accommodation, **or**

• giving up the accommodation and taking a higher cash wage,

then the taxation value of the living accommodation may be greater than the cash equivalent calculated using this working sheet. That will be so if the extra wages the employee could have got (for the period the accommodation was provided) if he/she had given up the accommodation would have been more than the cash equivalent shown in box **E** or box **R**, in which case enter that amount of extra wages in section D box 14 of the P11D, or section C box 14 of the P9D.

Employer details

Employer name

Employer PAYE reference

Employee details

Employee name

Surname

Forename(s)

Works number or department   National Insurance number

The accommodation

Give the address of the accommodation provided

Was the accommodation provided for a full tax year?   Yes ☑   No ☑

If the answer is No, then when you are asked for amounts, enter the part of the rent or annual value which relates to the period for which the accommodation was provided. Booklet 480 tells you how to work out the annual value.

1   The basic benefit   *Complete this section in all cases.*

Amount of rent paid for the year (or part of the year) by you, or any other person at whose cost the accommodation is provided to the employee   **A** £

Enter the annual value (or part of the annual value) of the accommodation *see Booklet 480*   **B** £

Enter the greater of **A** and **B**   **C** £

Enter any amount made good to you by the employee for the living accommodation
If this amount is more than C, enter the amount at C here   **D** £

Subtract **D** from **C**   **E** £

The figure at **E** is the cash equivalent of the basic benefit.

Enter in section D box 14 on form P11D or section C box 14 on form P9D **unless** there is an additional yearly rent.

Please turn over to find out if you need to calculate the additional yearly rent.

P11D WS1 (2009)   HMRC 09/08

BPP
LEARNING MEDIA

2 **The additional yearly rent**

Complete this section if the cost of the accommodation was more than £75,000.

The cost of the accommodation is:
- the cost of acquiring the accommodation
  plus
- the cost of improvements made to the accommodation
  minus
- any payments made by the employee towards these costs or for the grant of a tenancy.

When considering the costs remember that they can be incurred by:
- you as the employer, or
- the person providing the accommodation, or
- any person connected with either of the above other than the employee.

There is a different rule if the employee first occupied the accommodation after 30 March 1983. If the person providing the accommodation held any interest in it throughout a period beginning **six years before the employee first occupied the accommodation**, then the figure to enter at box **F** is the market value of the accommodation at that date, plus the cost of subsequent improvements.

Cost of the accommodation (including the cost of improvements) **F** £

Payments made by the employee towards the cost or for the grant of tenancy **G** £

Subtract G from F **H** £

Excess of cost over £75,000 is H minus £75,000 **I** £

Multiply J by 6.25% *which is the official rate of interest on 6 April 2008* **K** £

If the accommodation was provided for part of the tax year only, enter the number of days it was provided here

Divide the number of days by 365 and multiply the result by **K** **L** £

Enter the rent paid by the employee for the accommodation **M** £

Enter any rent which you have included in box **D** **N** £

Subtract **N** from **M** **P** £

Subtract P from K (if the accommodation was provided throughout the tax year), or
Subtract P from L (if the accommodation was provided for only part of the tax year) and enter here **Q** £

Enter the amount shown in box E on the front of this form **E** £

Total of Q and E **R** £

The figure at **R** is the amount to be entered in section D box 14 on form P11D or section C box 14 on form P9D

3 **Other benefits**

This section is a checklist to help identify other benefits commonly associated with the provision of living accommodation.

Tick if appropriate

Expenses incurred by the provider of the accommodation on benefits or facilities connected with the accommodation ☐

Heating ☐

Lighting ☐

Repairs and decoration ☐

The benefit from furniture given or transferred to the employee ☐

The annual value of the use of furniture in the accommodation which is provided by reason of the employment ☐

Other *please describe in box below* ☐

Booklet 480 explains how to calculate these other benefits and give details of exemptions and limits to the charge.
Enter the benefits in the appropriate boxes on form P11D or P9D.

3.7 Section E: Mileage allowance and passenger payments

If an employee uses his own car on company business, the employer may give him a mileage allowance to reimburse him. HMRC issues a table of mileage rates called the Approved Mileage Allowance Payments. If the employer pays these rates or less, then no tax or NIC charge arises. Also you will not have to complete this section, or form P9D.

Approved Mileage Allowance Payments for 2009/10

	First 10,000 miles	Additional miles
Motor cars and vans*	40p	25p
Motor cycles	24p	24p
Bicycles	20p	20p

* For NIC purposes, use the first 10,000 miles rate for **all** business miles.

Passenger Payments for 2009/10

For each **employee** travelling as a passenger on a **business** journey 5p per mile

If the employer pays a mileage allowance **greater** than the approved rate, then the excess is taxable, and the excess amount needs to go on the P11D.

If the employer pays a mileage allowance **less** than the approved rate, the employee can claim the difference on their personal Tax Return. However, if the employer pays a rate lower than the approved passenger payment rate, the employee may **not** claim the difference on their Tax Return.

Note that the authorised mileage rates are only tax and NIC free when used to reimburse **business** mileage. Any reimbursement of travel from home to office is **fully taxable**, and will need to go on form P11D in this section.

There is a working sheet available (WS6), see the next two pages.

HM Revenue & Customs

P11D Working Sheet 6
Mileage allowance payments and passenger payments 2008-09

Note to employer

You do not have to use this form but you may find it a useful way to calculate the taxable amount to be reported on form P11D where you paid mileage allowances to a director, or an employee, using his or her own vehicle for business travel during the year 2008–09 (that is 6 April 2008 to 5 April 2009).

Read the *P11D (Guide)* and the section on taxation of mileage expense payments within booklet CWG2.

If you use this form to calculate a taxable amount in relation to mileage payments you must also fill in a form P11D. You are advised to keep a copy of each completed working sheet as it could help you to deal with enquiries. You do not have to give a copy of the completed working sheet to the director or employee, or to your HM Revenue & Customs office.

The term employee is used to cover both directors and employees throughout the rest of this form.

Employer details

Employer name

Employer PAYE reference

Employee details

Employee name

Surname

Forename(s)

Works number or department

National Insurance number

The calculation on this working sheet applies **only** to amounts actually paid to the employee in respect of the expenses of business travel. Amounts paid to the employee for more general purposes should normally have tax deducted at source. Items that are not payments to the employee should be reported in the relevant box of form P11D (or form P9D where appropriate).

1 Mileage allowance payments made to employee

Mileage allowance payments made to employee in 2008–09
Include total amounts paid to employee

A £ _____

Minus
Any amounts from which tax has been deducted

B £ _____

Net mileage allowance paid   (A minus B) = **C** £ _____

2 Vehicle used

	Car or van	Motorcycle	Cycle
Kind of vehicle *(tick one box only)*	☐	☐	☐

You need to use separate working sheets if the employee used more than one kind of vehicle above. If the employee used more than one vehicle of the same kind, the calculation is the same as if the employee had only used one vehicle and you only need to complete one working sheet.

Total business miles travelled by the employee in 2008–09
Include all miles travelled in the kind of vehicle above that counted as business miles for tax purposes, even if these were not miles that you reimburse under your mileage payments scheme

D _____

3 Table of mileage rates

Vehicle used	1 First 10,000 business miles in 2008–09	2 Each mile over 10,000 miles in 2008–09
Cars & Vans	40p	25p
Motorcycle	24p	24p
Cycles	20p	20p

Please turn over

P11D WS6 (2009)

HMRC 09/08

4 **Approved Mileage Allowance Payments (AMAPs)**

Mileage rates for the kind of vehicle used
*Use the appropriate rates as shown in the table
at section 3 on page 1. Enter the rate for the
first 10,000 business miles in box 1 and the rate
for each business mile over 10,000 miles in box 2*

1 ☐ p   **2** ☐ p

First 10,000 business miles
*If box D is more than 10,000 enter 10,000 in
box E, otherwise enter the figure from box D*

E ☐   X box **1** = **F** £ ☐

Balance of business miles
*If box D is more than 10,000 enter the excess
over 10,000 in box G, otherwise leave blank*

G ☐   X box **2** = **H** £ ☐

Total Approved Mileage Allowance Payments
*The maximum amount that can count as tax-free approved mileage
allowance payments for the kind of vehicle identified in section 2*

(F + H) = **J** £ ☐

Compare the amounts in box C and box J

- If the total at box J is the **same as** the amount at box C, the whole amount at box C is tax-free.
  Enter 0 (zero) in box N in section 6.

- If the total at box J is **more than** the amount at box C, the whole amount at box C is tax-free.
  Enter 0 (zero) in box N in section 6. Your employee may be able to get tax relief on the difference.

- If the total at box J is **less than** the amount at box C, **enter the excess (box C minus box J)
  in box N in section 6.**

5 **Passenger payments** *only complete this section once, however many working sheets are used*

Total of any passenger payments to the employee in 2008–09
*The payments must have been made **specifically** for the purpose of carrying
a fellow employee on a qualifying business journey in a car or van*

K £ ☐

Number of business miles for which
passenger payments made

L ☐   X 5p = **M** £ ☐

Compare the amounts in box **K** and box **M** and enter the following amounts in section 6 below.

- If the total at box **M** is the **same as** the amount in box **K**, the whole amount at box **K** is tax-free.
  Enter 0 (zero) in box P in section 6.

- If the total amount at box **M** is **more than** the amount at box **K**, the whole amount at box **K** is tax-free.
  Enter 0 (zero) in box P in section 6. No tax relief is available for the difference.

- If the total at box **M** is **less than** the amount at box **K**, **enter the excess (box K minus box M)
  in box P in section 6.**

6 **The taxable amount**

Taxable payments from section 4
plus
Taxable passenger payments from section 5

N £ ☐

P £ ☐

Total taxable payments   (N + P) = **Q** £ ☐

The amount at box **Q** (where more than zero) is the excess over the tax-free amounts for 2008–09. Enter this amount
in section E, box 12 on form P11D. If the amount at box **Q** is zero you do not need to report this on form P11D.

If you paid the employee mileage allowances for more than one kind of vehicle during 2008–09 and have completed more
than one working sheet, add together the amounts at box **Q** on each working sheet and enter the total in section **E**, box 12
on form P11D. If the total of the amounts at **Q** is zero you do not need to report this on form P11D.

3.8 Section F: Cars and car fuel

This is the most important section, as the company car is the commonest type of benefit provided by an employer.

HMRC provides a working sheet P11DWS2 to assist you in calculating car benefits. The form for 2008/09 is shown on pages 141 to 144.

3.8.1 Car benefits

In order to calculate the car benefit arising, work methodically though the WS2.

The basis of assessment is a percentage of list price (not cost). The percentage is determined according to carbon dioxide (CO_2) emissions.

The percentage varies from 15% of list price, for the cars with the lowest emissions, to a maximum of 35% of list price for cars with the highest emissions. However cars with emissions of 120 or less (figure **not** rounded down for this purpose) will qualify for a new 10% rate.

Diesel cars that do not meet the Euro 4 standard (and Euro 4 cars registered on or after 1 January 2006) will be subject to a 3% supplement, subject to the 35% maximum charge. The supplement does not apply to Euro 4 cars registered before 2006.

Cleaner, green technology attracts discounts, which can take the minimum charge below 15%, (see fuel codes, B, E and H on WS2). Cars manufactured to run on E85 fuel (a blend of petrol with 85% bioethanol) will qualify for a 2% reduction.

The emissions percentage is taken from the following table, with the charge building up by 1% for every 5g/km over the qualifying level.

2009/10 Emissions charge

CO_2 emissions in grams per kilometre	Percentage
120 or less	10
130	15
135	15
140	16
145	17
150	18
155	19
160	20
165	21
170	22
175	23
180	24
185	25
190	26
195	27
200	28
205	29
210	40
215	31

CO_2 emissions in grams per kilometre	Percentage
220	32
225	33
230	34
235	35

To use this table, round the emissions figure **down** to the nearest figure eg 204g/km are taxed on 200g/km (28%).

Indicative CO_2 emissions figures for all new cars can be viewed at www.vca.gov.uk.

A car first registered on 1 March 2001 or later will have the CO_2 emissions figure in the new vehicle registration document (V5). For cars first registered between 1 January 1998 and 28 February 2001, the CO_2 emissions figure can be obtained from the website of the Society of Motor Manufacturers and Traders Ltd (www.smmt.co.uk).

For cars first registered before 1 January 1998, the CO_2 percentage will be based on engine size:

Engine size (cc)	Pre-1998 Car	1998 or later car without an approved CO_2 emissions figure
0 – 1,400	15%	15%
1,401 – 2,000	22%	25%
2,001 and over (and cars without a cc value)	32%	35%

3.8.2 Car fuel benefit

This benefit arises where fuel is provided for the **private use** of the company car. The fuel benefit is charged **in full** unless the employee **fully reimburses** the employer for **all** private motoring.

The car fuel benefit is based on the CO_2 emission percentage. The benefit is calculated by taking the **same percentage as for the car benefit** and multiplying it by a set figure. The set figure is £16,900 for 2009/10.

Activity 6.2

During 2009/10, Roger Miller uses a company car (details below). Roger is not a director of the company, Comecon Ltd, but earns £30,000 pa.

Details of company car

Available: 6 April 2009 to 5 April 2010
Make: Rover 25 series
Engine capacity: 2.0 litres petrol
CO_2 emissions: 198g/km

First registration date: 6 January 2004
List price: £20,250
Cost: £18,225

Accessories: £500 (assume these were fitted at the time of purchase)

Contribution from employee: NIL

The company pays for all petrol and running expenses. Roger makes no contribution towards the costs.

Roger's NI number is CD 34 56 78 B and Comecon Ltd's PAYE reference is 889/C5675.

Task

Use the 2008/09 form P11D WS2 attached to calculate the car and car fuel benefit.

HM Revenue & Customs

P11D Working Sheet 2
Car and Car fuel benefit 2008-09

Note to employer

You do not have to use this form but you may find it a useful way to calculate the cash equivalent for each car made available to a director or an employee who earned at a rate of £8,500 a year or more during the year 2008-09 (that is 6 April 2008 to 5 April 2008).

A separate form is needed for each car provided to the director or employee during 2008-09.

Read the *P11D Guide* before you complete this form. It refers to paragraphs in Booklet 480(2009).

You are advised to keep a copy of each completed working sheet as it could help you to deal with enquiries. You do not have to give a copy of the completed working sheet to the director or employee, or to your HM Revenue & Customs office. But you must fill in forms *P11D* and *P11D(b) 'Return of Class 1A National Insurance contributions'* whether or not you use this form to calculate car and car fuel benefits.

The term employee is used to cover both directors and employees throughout the rest of this form.

Employer details

Employer name

Employer PAYE reference

Employee details

Employee name

Works number or department   National Insurance number

The car

Make and model of car available to employee

Date the car was first registered

/   /   Was this the only car made available to the employee   ✓ Yes ☐   No ☐

If 'No' please make sure that working sheets are completed for each car made available to the employee in 2008-09

If more than one working sheet 2 is completed for this employee, enter the number of sheets here

1   List price of the car

Complete box A as follows

- enter the list price of the car as published by its manufacturer, importer or distributor
- if the car had no list price when it was first registered you need to enter the notional price. That is, the price which might reasonably be expected to be its list price on that date if the car's manufacturer, importer or distributor had published a list price for an equivalent car for a single retail sale in the UK
- if the car is a classic car, enter the price that the car might reasonably be expected to fetch if you sold it on the open market on 5 April 2009. If the car was unavailable to the employee on 5 April 2009 then use the last day in the tax year 2008-09 that it was available to the employee. For this purpose, assume that all the qualifying accessories available on the car are included in the sale. A classic car is one which
  - is at least 15 years old on 5 April 2009
  - has a market value of at least £15,000, *and*
  - has a market value which is higher than the original list or notional price (including accessories).

Price of the car *including standard accessories*   **A** £

2   Accessories

Price of all accessories *see P11D Guide and paragraphs 12.7-12.14 of Booklet 480(2009)*   **B** £

A + B
C £

3   Capital contributions

Capital contributions made by the employee towards the cost of the car or the accessories *max £5,000*   **D** £

4   The price used to calculate the car benefit charge for 2008-09

C minus D
This box is subject to a maximum of £80,000   **E** £

5   **Calculating the appropriate percentage**

The appropriate percentage depends on when the car was first registered, the type of fuel used and whether it has an approved CO_2 emissions figure.

Approved CO_2 emissions figure, if the car has one *unrounded, for example 188*   **F** | g/km

Enter the key letter (B, C, D, E, G, H, L or P) for the car's fuel or power type from table 1 below.

TABLE 1	
Key letter	Fuel or power type description
P	Petrol
D	Diesel car not approved to Euro IV emissions standard
L	Diesel car approved to Euro IV emissions standard
E	Electric Only
H	Hybrid electric (combination of petrol engine and electric motor)
B	Gas only or bi-fuel car with approved CO_2 emissions figure for **Gas** when first registered
C	Conversion and all other bi-fuel cars with approved CO_2 emissions figure for **Petrol only** when first registered
G	Cars manufactured so as to be capable of running on E85, a blend of petrol and up to 85% bioethanol

Next step

- for cars registered on or after 1 January 1998 **with** an approved CO_2 emissions figure
  - if the figure in box F is more than 120, **Go to section 5a**
  - if the figure in box F is 120 or less, **Go to section 5b**
- for cars registered on or after 1 January 1998 **without** an approved CO_2 emissions figure, **Go to section 5c**
- for cars registered before 1 January 1998, **Go to section 5d**.

5a   **Cars registered on or after 1 January 1998 with an approved CO_2 emissions figure of more than 120**

Approved CO_2 emissions figure in box F, *rounded down to the next lowest 5g/km, for example 185*   **G** | g/km

Stage 1 - using table 2 below, use the figure in box G to work out the percentage to enter in box **H**
  - use column 1 for
    - all cars in fuel types B, C, G, H and P
    - cars in fuel type L which were first registered before 1 January 2006
  - use column 2 for
    - all cars in fuel type D
    - cars in fuel type L which were first registered on or after 1 January 2006.   **H** | %

TABLE 2								
CO_2 emissions (g/km)	Column 1 (%)	Column 2 (%)	CO_2 emissions (g/km)	Column 1 (%)	Column 2 (%)	CO_2 emissions (g/km)	Column 1 (%)	Column 2 (%)
135*	15	18	170	22	25	205	29	32
140	16	19	175	23	26	210	30	33
145	17	20	180	24	27	215	31	34
150	18	21	185	25	28	220	32	35
155	19	22	190	26	29	225	33	35
160	20	23	195	27	30	230	34	35
165	21	24	200	28	31	235*	35	35

These are the minimum and maximum CO_2 values for which different percentages apply.
*Use these values if the figure at box **G** is less than the minimum or greater than the maximum.*

Stage 2 - calculate reductions for alternative fuel/power types *fuel type letters H, B and G only*
  - fuel type H - insert 3% in box J
  - fuel types B and G - insert 2% in box J   **J** | %

Appropriate percentage
Go straight to section 6 – do not complete sections 5b, 5c or 5d   **N** | %   [H minus J]

2

5b Cars registered on or after 1 January 1998 with an unrounded approved CO_2 emissions figure of 120 or less

For these 'qualifying low emissions cars', or QUALECs
- enter 10% in box N for
  - all cars in fuel types B, C, G, H and P
  - cars in fuel type L which were first registered before 1 January 2006

- enter 13% in box N for
  - all cars in fuel type D
  - cars in fuel type L which were first registered on or after 1 January 2006

Appropriate percentage
Go straight to section 6 - do not complete sections 5c or 5d

`N          %`

5c Cars registered on or after 1 January 1998 without an approved CO_2 emissions figure

Stage 1 - using table 3 below, work out the percentage to enter in box **H**
- use column 1 for
  - all cars in fuel types C, G, H and P
  - cars in fuel type L which were first registered before 1 January 2006
- use column 2 for
  - all cars in fuel type D
  - cars in fuel L which were first registered on or after 1 January 2006
- for fuel type E, insert 15%
- for fuel type B, use section 5a (all such cars have CO_2 emissions figures)

`H          %`

TABLE 3		
Engine size of car (cc)	Column 1 %	Column 2 %
0 - 1400	15	18
1401 - 2000	25	28
over 2000	35	35
all rotary engines	35	35

Stage 2 - calculate reductions for alternative fuel/power types *fuel type letters G, H and E only*
- fuel type E - insert 6% in box J
- fuel type H - insert 3% in box J
- fuel type G - insert 2% in box J

`J          %`

Appropriate percentage
Go straight to section 6 - do not complete section 5d

`H minus J`
`N          %`

5d All cars registered before 1 January 1998

Enter the engine size, then work out the percentage to enter in box **N**

`          cc`

TABLE 4	
Engine size of car (cc)	Percentage
0 - 1400	15
1401 - 2000	22
over 2000	32
all rotary engines	32

Appropriate percentage

`N          %`

3

6 **Calculate the car benefit for a full year**

Ignore any decimals when completing box **P**

P £ | E x N

7 **Make any deductions for days the car was unavailable**

If the car was available to the employee for the whole of the tax year, put the figure in box **P** into box **S**. If not, state the period for which the car was available

from [/ /] to [/ /]

Total days for which the car was unavailable *see P11D Guide and Booklet 480(2009)*

Q [ ]

Deduction for unavailability *round up to next whole number*

R £ | (P x Q)/365

Car benefit for the period the car was **available**

S £ | P minus R

8 **Make any deductions for payments for private use**

Enter any required payments made for private use of the car in the year

T £

Car benefit charge for 2008-09 for this car *(ignore any decimals)*
Enter the figure at box **U** onto form *P11D*, at section F box 9
*If the employee had more than one car available in the year, add together all the figures at box **U** on each working sheet, then transfer the total to form P11D, at section F box 9*

U £ | S minus T

9 **Calculate the car fuel benefit charge** *if appropriate - see P11D Guide*

Car fuel benefit charge for the whole of this tax year

V £ | £16,900 x N

Calculate any required deductions
Days the **car** was unavailable *from section 7*

Q [ ]

If the provision of fuel was withdrawn and not reinstated later in the year, enter the date and complete box **W**, otherwise, go to box **X**

Date the provision of fuel was withdrawn *if applicable*

[/ /]

Additional days after fuel was withdrawn not already counted in box **Q**
do not include the same day in both box Q and box W

W [ ]

Total days for which no car fuel benefit charge applies

X [ ] | Q + W

Deduction *round up to next whole number*

Y £ | (V x X)/365

Car fuel benefit charge for 2008-09 for this car
Enter the figure at box **Z** onto form *P11D*, at section F box 10
If the employee had more than one car available in the year, add together all the figures at box Z on each working sheet, then transfer the total to form P11D, at section F box 10.

Z £ | V minus Y

4

BPP
LEARNING MEDIA

Activity 6.3

Using the facts in Activity 6.2, recalculate the car and car fuel benefits, assuming that the car is diesel and does not comply with the Euro 4 standards.

3.8.3 Accessories for the disabled

The costs of any accessories to enable a disabled employee to use the car **are ignored** for the purposes of calculating the cost of the car.

- Equipment designed solely for use by a chronically sick or disabled person (eg hand controls)
- If the employee is a **blue badge holder** when the car is first made available, other equipment fitted to enable the employee to use the car in spite of the disability for which the blue badge was awarded (eg power-assisted steering), where these are **not standard**.

From 6 April 2009, where an automatic car is required, the list price of the equivalent manual car can be used if this is lower.

3.9 Section G: Vans

Some organisations provide company vans instead of company cars. Where a van is made available to an employee and is available for private use, a benefit arises. However if the van is not available for private use, only for business travel, and any private use is insignificant, then there is no charge.

Guide 480 states that 'insignificant' is to mean ' too small or unimportant to be worth consideration.' Private use is to be considered insignificant in the following cases:

- Quantity in the tax year as a whole does not exceed a few days
- Quality eg a week's exclusive private use is **not** insignificant
- Intermittent and irregular
- Very much the exception

Examples of insignificant use

- Use the van to take an old mattress or other rubbish to the tip once or twice a year
- Regularly makes a **slight** detour to stop at a newsagent on the way to work
- Calls at the doctor on way home

Examples of not insignificant use

- Uses the van to do the supermarket shopping every week
- Takes the van away on a week's holiday
- Uses the van outside of work for social activities

For 2009/10 vans are given a taxable benefit of £3,000, with **no** reduction if the van is over 4 years old. In addition, a fuel charge of £500 is made for 2009/10, if any fuel is provided for private use.

The benefit may need to be calculated if the van was shared or not used for a whole year. The working sheet for 2008/09 (P11DWS3) on the next two pages helps you to calculate the relevant benefit if the van was only used for part of a year. However, regarding sharing, this is done on a 'just and reasonable' basis. HMRC gives the example of a father and son sharing a van. The son is exempt as his use is solely for business travel. However the father uses the van for the weekly shop. So the father will have a benefit of £3,000.

3.10 Section H: Interest-free and low interest loans

Figures only need to be entered in this section if the total of the loans exceed £5,000.

The idea of the section is to tax the benefit of receiving an interest-free or low interest rate loan from your employer. However, loans used wholly for a qualifying purpose (eg purchase of shares in an employee-controlled company) are excluded.

HMRC issues 'official' rates of interest and the total interest on the loan at the 'official' rate is calculated for the year. Any interest actually paid is then deducted to arrive at the 'benefit'.

There is a working sheet (P11DWS4) to help you calculate the benefit, as well as form P11D(INT) giving the official rates of interest. These are illustrated in activity 6.4 below, remember these are for tax year 2008/09!

Assessment focus point

The official rate of interest for 2009/10 is 4.75%.

HM Revenue & Customs

P11D Working Sheet 3
Vans available for private use 2008–09

Note to employer

You do not have to use this form but you may find it a useful way to calculate the cash equivalent if you provided a van which was available for private use by a director or employee who earned at a rate of £8,500 or more a year during the year 2008–09 (that is 6 April 2008 to 5 April 2009). Read the P11D(Guide) before you complete this form.

If you use this form you must also fill in forms P11D and P11D(b), 'Return of Class 1A National Insurance contributions'. You are advised to keep a copy of each completed working sheet as it could help you to deal with enquiries. You do not have to give a copy of the completed working sheet to the director or employee, or to your HM Revenue & Customs office.

The term employee is used to cover both directors and employees throughout the rest of this form and includes any member of their family or household.

Employer details

Employer name

Employer PAYE reference

Employee details

Employee name

Surname

Forename(s)

Works number or department

National Insurance number

The van

If the van is used mainly for business travel and the only other use is for ordinary commuting, there is no benefit charge and you need not complete this form.

Registration number

Was this the only van made available to the employee? Yes ☐ No ☐

If 'No' please make sure that working sheets are completed for each van made available to the employee in 2008–09.

If more than one working sheet 3 is completed for this employee, enter the number of sheets here ☐

VAN BENEFIT CHARGE

1 Standard charge for this van for the whole of 2008–09

A £ *3,000*

2 Make any reductions for days when the van was unavailable

If the van was not available to the employee for whole of the tax year, state the dates between which it was available, then calculate the number of days for which it was unavailable and enter this at box B

from __/__/__ to __/__/__ days unavailable **B**

If there were any other periods of at least 30 continuous days for which the van was not available to the employee, complete the boxes below (periods may span two tax years but only days in each tax year affect liability for that year). Complete box E in all cases

from __/__/__ to __/__/__ days unavailable **C**

from __/__/__ to __/__/__ days unavailable **D**

Total days for which the van was unavailable

B + C + D
E

Reduction for unavailability *round up to next whole number*

(A x E)/365
F £

Van benefit charge after reduction for unavailability

A minus F
G £

P11D WS3 (2009)

HMRC 09/08

Amount brought forward from page 1 — **G** £

3 **Make any reduction for sharing of this van**
If the van was shared by at least one other employee during the period when it was available to this employee, the benefit charge on this employee is reduced on a just and reasonable basis. Note that:

1. use by all sharing employees is taken into account, even if some were in excluded employment (they earn at a rate of less than £8,500 per annum) and so were not personally chargeable

2. except where any sharing employee in excluded employment is a member of this employee's family or household, in which case their use is disregarded when making the sharing reduction for this employee

3. in the majority of cases where vans are shared, the whole amount at box A will be chargeable but the charge will be allocated between two or more employees

Percentage reduction **H** % Reduction for sharing *round up to next whole number* — **J** £ *(G x H)*

Enter here an explanation of the basis for sharing reduction

Van benefit charge after reduction for sharing — **K** £ *(G minus J)*

4 **Make any reduction for payments for private use of this van**

Enter any payments the employee was required to, and did, make for private use of this van in the year — **L** £

Van benefit charge for this van in 2008–09 — **M** £ *(K minus L)*

Enter the figure at box M onto form P11D at **section G, box 9.**

If the employee had more than one van available in the year, add together all the figures at box **M** on each working sheet, then transfer the total to form P11D at **section G, box 9.**

VAN FUEL BENEFIT CHARGE – *if appropriate* – *see* P11D*(Guide)*

5 **Fuel benefit charge for the whole tax year** — **P** £ 500

6 **Reduction for days when the van was unavailable or fuel was not provided**

Days for which van was unavailable *from page 1* — **E**

If the provision of fuel was withdrawn and not reinstated later in the year, enter the date and complete box R, otherwise, go to box S.

Date the provision of fuel was withdrawn *if applicable*   /   /

Additional days after fuel was withdrawn not already counted in box E
do not include the same day in both box E and box R — **R**

Total days for which no fuel benefit charge applies — **S** *(E + R)*

Reduction *round up to next whole number* — **T** £ *(P X S)/365*

Van fuel benefit charge after reduction for unavailability — **V** £ *(P minus T)*

7 **Reduction for sharing of this van**

Percentage reduction **H** % Reduction for sharing *round up to next whole number* — **W** £ *(V x H)*

Van fuel benefit charge for this van in 2008–2009 — **X** £ *(V minus W)*

Enter the figure at box **X** onto form P11D at **section G, box 10.**

If the employee had more than one van available in the year, add together all the figures at box **X** on each working sheet, then transfer the total to form P11D at **section G, box 10.**

Activity 6.4

Roger Miller (from activity 6.2) has a non-qualifying loan from Comecon Ltd. The loan is for £10,000 outstanding for the whole tax year. Use the form P11D WS4 and P11D(INT) to calculate the benefit. For the purposes of this activity, use an interest rate of 4.75% for the whole year.

HM Revenue & Customs

P11D Working Sheet 4
Interest-free and low interest loans 2008–09

Note to employer

You do not have to use this form but you may find it a useful way to calculate the cash equivalent if you provided interest-free or low interest loans for a director, or an employee who earned at a rate of £8,500 or more during the year 2008–09 (that is 6 April 2008 to 5 April 2009).

Read the *P11D(Guide)* before you complete this form. Enter details of non-qualifying loans made to, or arranged for, a director or employee (or for any of his or her relatives) on which no interest was paid, or on which the amount of interest paid was less than interest at the official rate. Include 'notional loan' benefits of shares acquired by the director or employee at undervalue.

As a guide to whether a loan is a qualifying loan, and does not therefore need to be reported on the form P11D, see booklet 480.

If you use this form you must also fill in forms P11D and P11D(b) *Return of Class 1A National Insurance contributions*. Booklet CWG5(2009) *Class 1A National Insurance contributions on benefits in kind* gives more information. You are advised to keep a copy of each completed working sheet as it could help you to deal with enquiries. You do not have to give a copy of the completed working sheet to the director or employee, or to your HM Revenue & Customs office.

The term employee is used to cover both directors and employees throughout the rest of this form.

Employer details

Employer name

Employer PAYE reference

Employee details

Employee name

Surname

Forename(s)

Works number or department

National Insurance number

The loans

If the total amount outstanding on all the loans is not more than £5,000 at any time in the year, there is no need to complete this working sheet or Section H of form P11D.

You may find it helpful to complete the table below to identify:

- other small exempt loans
- for directors of close companies only, non-qualifying loans which may be treated as a single loan for the purpose of calculating the benefit.

	Loan 1	Loan 2	Loan 3	Loan 4	Loan 5
Maximum balance outstanding at any time in the year					
Currency if other than sterling					

If you know that the total amount outstanding on all non-qualifying loans does not exceed £5,000 at any time in the year, ignore such loans when completing the remainder of this working sheet and Section H of form P11D.

If you are a close company and the borrower is one of the company's directors, you can elect to treat all loans which are:

- in the same currency
- non-qualifying
- owing at the same time

as a single loan.

You can make the election by showing all such loans as a single loan in Section H on the form P11D. Please note that if you make the election and do not include all such loans within the single loan, you will be making an incorrect return.

Please turn over

P11D WS4 (2009)

HMRC 02/09

Official rates of interest

To calculate the cash equivalent of a loan you will need to know:

- the average official rate of interest for the year ended 5 April 2009 for loans made in sterling
- the official rate for Japanese Yen or Swiss Francs where the loan was made in one of those currencies and the conditions in paragraph 17.5 of Booklet 480 are met.

The average official rate of interest for 2008–09 for loans made in sterling is 6.10%. The official interest rates for loans in currencies other than sterling up to early November 2008 are printed in Booklet 480, but later changes are not known until the end of the tax year.

Form P11D(INT) is available from the Employer Orderline (Phone **08457 646 646**) and it gives details of the official rates of interest for 2008–09.

You can also get details of the official rates of interest from your HM Revenue & Customs office.

Calculating the cash equivalent

Use the formula below for each loan separately *except where an election has been made to treat a director's loans as a single loan.*

	Loan 1	Loan 2	Loan 3	Loan 4	Loan 5
A Maximum balance on either 5 April 2008 or the date the loan was taken out, whichever is later					
B Maximum balance on earlier of day loan was discharged or 5 April 2009					
C Total (A + B)					
D Divide C by 2					
E Number of complete tax months in tax year (6th of month to 5th of following month) throughout which loan was owing					
F Multiply D by E, then divide by 12					
G Official rate of interest	%	%	%	%	%
H Multiply F by G					
J Enter interest paid in 2008–09					
K Cash equivalent of loans H minus J					

The figures at K are the amounts to be entered in Section H boxes 15 on form *P11D*.

If the employee has more than two loans, you can write 'see attached' in Section H box 15 and attach a copy of this working sheet. But you must remember to add together the cash equivalents of all the loans for the purpose of calculating the total benefits liable to Class 1A NICs when completing form P11D(b) *'Return of Class 1A National Insurance contributions'*.

Employees may elect for a more complex but accurate method of calculating the benefit from interest-free or low interest loans. Employers are not responsible for providing such a calculation.

HM Revenue & Customs

Official rates of interest 2008-09

Interest-free and low interest loans

This form shows:
- the average official rates of interest, and
- the actual official rates of interest

for 2008-09 (that is 6 April 2008 to 5 April 2009).

This will help you calculate the cash equivalent of any interest-free or low interest loans you provided for a director or employee who earned at a rate of £8,500 or more.

Booklet 480(2009) *Expenses and benefits – A tax guide* contains details of the arrangements for taxing interest-free and low interest loans. You may also find that P11D *Working Sheet 4* is a useful way to calculate the cash equivalent.

Form P11D *Working Sheet 4* and booklet 480(2009) are both available from the Employer Orderline. See 'General information' below for details on how to contact the Orderline.

Official interest rates

For loans outstanding throughout, or for only part of, 2008-09.

The **average** official rate is 6.10%.

The **actual** official rate is as follows:

From	To	Rate	Number of days
06/04/2008	28/02/2009	6.25%	329
01/03/2009	05/04/2009	4.75%	36

Official interest rates for certain loans made in other currencies

Please read paragraph 17.5 of the booklet 480(2009). If the conditions set out in that paragraph are met, then the following rates apply.

For loans outstanding throughout, or for only part of 2008-09.

Japanese Yen

The **average** official rate is 3.9%.

The **actual** official rate is as follows:

From	To	Rate	Number of days
06/04/2008	05/04/2009	3.9%	365

Swiss Francs

The **average** official rate is 5.5%.

The **actual** official rate is as follows:

From	To	Rate	Number of days
06/04/2008	05/04/2009	5.5%	365

General information

If you require further copies of this form, please contact your local HM Revenue & Customs (HMRC) office, Enquiry Centre or from the Employer Orderline the contact details are as follows:

- internet **www.hmrc.gov.uk/employers**
- phone **08457 646 646**
- fax **08702 406 406**, or
- if you use a textphone, dial the Typetalk service on **0800 95 95 98**. Tell the operator the Orderline phone number. They will make contact and relay your order, at the end of the call they will give you your order number.

P11D(INT)(2009)   HMRC 02/09

3.11 Section I: Private medical treatment or insurance

Many employers now provide private medical insurance as a 'perk' to some or all of their employees.

The figure to be entered on the P11D is the **cost to the employer** for each employee. So if the employer gets a discount, it is the figure **after** discount that goes on the P11D.

The following types of medial treatment, are **not** taxable benefits.

- Medicals on behalf of the employer
- General medicals (eg Well Man, Well Woman clinics)
- Eye tests under the VDU Screen regulations
- Health checks under any other legislation, including the HSE
- Private medical insurance for employees whose duties are solely outside the UK

3.12 Section J: Qualifying relocation expenses payments and benefits

Qualifying relocation expenses occur when an employee has a new job and moves in order to be nearer his employment, so that he has a 'reasonable' journey; or when he is relocated to a job in another part of the country so he has to move. The employer may agree to pay his removal expenses and costs.

In order to qualify for relief, the removal expenses must normally be incurred before the end of the tax year following the one in which the employee starts the new job. So if the employee started the new job on 5 April 2009, the removal expenses must be incurred by 5 April 2010. If the employee started the new job on 6 April 2009, however, the removal expenses must be incurred by 5 April 2011.

The first £8,000 of qualifying relocation expenses are tax-free. Only the excess over £8,000 needs to be entered in this section. There is a working sheet P11DWS5 to calculate the excess over £8,000 if applicable (see the next two pages for the 2008/09 version).

If the move is not qualifying, however, the **total** costs reimbursed go into Sections M (professional fees eg solicitors, estate agents) and N (all other costs).

3.13 Section K: Services supplied

Any services supplied to the employee are included here. Note that the contract is between the service supplier and the employer for a benefit to arise.

Some employer provided services are exempt, if the private use of the service is insignificant compared to the use in the course of the employee's duties.

HM Revenue & Customs

P11D Working Sheet 5
Relocation expenses payments and benefits 2008–09

Note to employer

You do not have to use this form but you may find it a useful way to calculate the cash equivalent if you provided relocation expenses payments and benefits for a director or an employee who earned at a rate of £8,500 or more a year during the year 2008–09 (that is 6 April 2008 to 5 April 2009).

Read the *P11D(Guide)* before you complete this form.

If you use this form you must also fill in form P11D or P9D. You must also complete form P11D(b) *'Return of Class 1A National Insurance contributions'*, if you use this working sheet to fill in form P11D.

Booklet CWG5(2009) *Class 1A National Insurance contributions on benefits in kind* gives more information.

You are advised to keep a copy of each completed working sheet as it could help you to deal with enquiries. You do not have to give a copy of the working sheet to the director or employee, or to your HM Revenue & Customs office.

The term employee is used to cover both directors and employees throughout the rest of this form.

Employer details

Employer name

Employer PAYE reference

Employee details

Employee name

Surname

Forename(s)

Works number or department

National Insurance number

1 Qualifying expenses payments

Any items from last year (2007–08) that were incurred in connection with this relocation where you did not give details on the P11D (for 2007–08) because they were below the exemption limit should be included at item **4** below.

Enter the gross amount of all qualifying expenses payments **A** £

The cost to you as an employer of any qualifying benefits **1** £

less anything paid towards the cost by the employee (up to a maximum of the figure in box 1) **2** £

Enter the amount of qualifying benefits (1 minus 2) = **B** £

Enter the cost of qualifying living accommodation provided **C** £

Total of expenses and benefits (A + B + C) = **D** £

2 Calculating the exempt amount

For each relocation a fixed amount of qualifying relocation expenses and benefits can be exempt. Qualifying expenses and benefits which:

- were connected to this relocation
- were incurred in an earlier tax year

  and

- were below the exemption limit

have to be taken into account when working out the exempt amount for this employee for 2008–09.

Exempt amount for 2008–09 £8,000 **3** £ 8,000

minus amount of qualifying expenses and benefits incurred in 2007–08 **4** £

Exempt amount for this employee (3 minus 4) = **E** £
If 4 is more than 3, enter 'NIL' in box E

Total of expenses and benefits (D minus E) = **F** £
If E is more than D, enter 'NIL' in box F

Enter F in Section J, box 15 on form P11D *Please turn over*

P11D WS5 (2009) HMRC 09/08

Cheap or interest–free bridging loans 'made' by the employer

Reminder about relief which may be due

- There is a taxable benefit where the employer 'makes' a cheap or interest–free loan.
  See Section H of the P11D *(Guide)*, booklet 480 chapter 17, and P11D *Working Sheet 4*.

- The amount of the taxable benefit may be reduced if the loan in question is a bridging loan made in connection with a qualifying relocation. For conditions see booklet 480 Appendix 7, paragraph 7.1.

- This relief will not become due unless the total **for all years** of all other qualifying benefits is less than £8,000.

- It will only become clear whether or not this special relief arises when the relocation has been completed and you know the total of all of the other qualifying expenses and benefits.

- Guidance on the calculation of the relief is set out in booklet 480 Appendix 7, paragraph 7.3.

- In many cases you will not have enough information to know whether or not this relief is due for the year in which the bridging loan is first advanced. We would not, therefore, expect the employer to take this into account when calculating the cash equivalent.

- If it appears that the relief will be due, you may wish to advise your employees to contact their HM Revenue & Customs office to arrange for the relief to be calculated.

3.14 Section L: Assets placed at the employee's disposal

Assets owned by the employer but placed at the employee's disposal are included here. The benefit is calculated as the annual value of the use of the asset (20% of the market value of the asset when it was first used to provide a benefit).

However the first £500 of the value of a computer is exempt, provided that the loan of the computer is not restricted, or favourable, to directors. This exemption has been removed for computers provided on or after 6 April 2006, where the computer is supplied for **private use.**

Note that if the employer provides a mobile phone, no benefit arises even if the employee uses it for private calls. For mobile phones provided on or after 6 April 2006 , the exemption applies to **one** phone. There is no limit on the number of phones exempt if they were provided before 6 April 2006.

The exemption for insignificant private use (Section K above) also applies to this section.

If the employer provides equipment to enable disabled employees to take up or continue working (eg wheelchair, hearing aid), this is exempt from 9 July 2002.

3.15 Section M: Other items (including subscriptions and professional fees)

Notice that the first line of this section is '1A' but the second and third lines are not. Benefits that go on the '1A' line include subscriptions to leisure and sporting facilities, educational assistance to employees' children, and non-qualifying relocation benefits and expenses, and non-exempt incidental overnight expenses (see Section 3.16).

The non '1A' second line includes professional subscriptions, educational assistance to an employee, and nursery places provided for employees' and directors' children.

Employers often pay employees' subscriptions to a professional society. This will be entered in the second line of this section. If the subscription is to an 'approved' profession, then the employee can claim the expense on his or her personal Tax Return (eg AAT subscription).

Where loans to employees are waived (see your Level 2 studies) the waiver will go in this section. As will the cost of sports days and canteen facilities outside the concession (ie free or subsidised meals are **not** available to **all** staff.)

The final line of this section refers to income tax paid but not deducted from director's remuneration. Sometimes a director's personal tax liability may be paid on his behalf by the company. If this happens, it is a benefit and must be entered here.

3.16 Section N: Expenses payments made to, or on behalf of, the employee

This final section covers expenses reimbursed by the employer. Quite often an employer can get a 'dispensation' from HMRC covering some or all of these benefits. If your employer has a dispensation, then you do not need to enter any of the expenses covered by the dispensation on form P11D (see Chapter 5).

Sometimes the employer will reimburse business use of an employee's home telephone. Unless the phone is used solely for business purposes, a benefit arises. The employee can claim the cost of business calls as an expense on his or her personal tax return.

If the employee has a mobile phone contract, but the employer pays the whole bill (including private use), a benefit arises.

Other expenses that may need to be included, if not covered by a dispensation or statutory exemption, include the following.

- Entertaining
- Overnight subsistence
- Travel costs
- Taxis for late night working

HMRC has published **maximum** scale rates for employees required to buy meals while travelling.

- Breakfast £5 if the employee sets out before 6am
- Lunch £5 if out for over 5 hours
- £10 for both lunch and dinner if out for over 10 hours
- Additional £15 if working after 8pm

These amounts are exempt and do not need to be entered on from P11D. However, if these amounts are exceeded, the **whole amount** goes on form P11D.

Entertaining can include social events to which employees are invited. Employers can provide social events for employees costing up to £150 per head per annum, without incurring a benefit. However, entertaining fellow employees is always taxable, if the expense is reimbursed by the employer. Genuine business entertaining is allowable and the employee can claim a deduction in his or her Tax Return.

Overnight subsidence includes the room, meal and a reasonable drink with the meal (say half a bottle of wine per person or similar), business phone calls and incidental overnight expenses (IOE). These expenses will not usually be a taxable benefit if wholly and necessarily incurred for business purposes. However, IOE are limited to £5 per night in the UK and to £10 per night abroad averaged over the trip. If these limits are exceeded, the **whole** of the IOE are taxable. Any non-cash benefits go in Section M.

Travel costs for business purposes are not taxable, but the costs of travel between home and work are fully taxable.

When an employee has to work late, the employer may pay for a taxi to take the employee home. This is a taxable benefit; unless the employee finishes work after 9pm or there is public transport disruption, and this is not a regular occurrence where there is no taxable benefit.

An employer may contribute towards the additional household costs if an employee works wholly or partly at home. Up to £3 per week (£156 per year) can be claimed without supporting evidence and is exempt. Payments in excess of this amount require supporting evidence for the **whole** amount, otherwise the whole payment is taxable. Broadband charges may be reimbursed tax free if the service was installed **after** the employee begins to work from home, as this is an **additional cost** of working at home. If broadband was already installed, then no allowance is payable.

4 Class 1A NICs

For 2008/09, employers had to pay class 1A NICs on the following sections on form P11D.

- A: Assets transferred
- D: Living accommodation
- F: Cars and car fuel
- G: Vans
- H: Interest-free and low interest loans
- I: Private medical treatment or insurance
- J: Qualifying relocation expenses
- K: Services supplied
- L: Assets placed at the employee's disposal
- M: Other items (first line only)

All these sections are indicated by a '1A' box beside the cash equivalent (see pages 130 to 131). These will continue to attract Class 1A NICs in 2009/10.

Further details of Class 1A NIC are contained in booklet CWG5, which can be downloaded from the HMRC website if your employer does not have a copy.

Class 1A NICs are levied at the **employer's main rate** of NIC for the year ie 12.8% for 2009/10. They are paid only by the **employer.**

Example: Class 1A NICs

Ursula Johansson has a company car. Her car and car fuel benefits total £3,000 for tax year 2009/10. What Class 1A NICs are due?

Solution

The employer pays £3,000 × 12.8% = £384 Class 1A NIC.

Class 1A NICs have to be paid by 19 July. For example, the Class 1A NICs for 2009/10 will be due by 19 July 2010. They are paid separately from other deductions, using the separate payslip which will be sent to this employer by HMRC, along with a reminder to file the return. As Class 1A NICs are **employer's** NICs, they are not entered on form P11.

4.1 P11D(b)

HMRC will send your employer a form P11D(b). This acts as a calculator for the Class 1A NIC liability, as well as containing the declaration that all forms P11D have been completed, or that none are due.

Form P11D(b) has to be returned to HMRC by **6 July** following the end of the tax year (ie 6 July 2010 for tax year 2009/10). Forms P11D should either accompany form P11D(b) or have been submitted earlier.

Penalties are due if forms P11D(b) and P11D have not been received by 19 July, when payment of Class 1A NIC is due. The penalty is £100 per month (or part month) for every 50 directors and employees who get benefits (or part batch of 50).

A copy of form P11D(b) for 2007/08 follows. The format for 2009/10 is likely to be similar.

The first section acts as a summary of the total of all the benefits liable to Class 1A NICs on the forms P11D. The Class 1A NIC is then calculated by multiplying the benefits by the Class 1A NIC rate **(12.8% for 2009/10)** to arrive at the amount payable.

Example: Form P11D(b)

Comecon Ltd only has five employees. The total of the '1A' boxes on forms P11D is £7,650. Show the entries to be made in the first section of form P11D(b).

Solution

Box A   £7,650
Box B   12.8%
Box C   £979.20 (12.8% × £7,650)

The second section is the employer's declaration.

There are three types of declaration and you should only tick those that are relevant.

- If there are no P11Ds to be submitted, tick the first box only.

- If there are P11Ds and these are attached, tick the second box only to indicate that all the P11Ds due are enclosed.

- If P11Ds have already been submitted but for some reason the P11D(b) was not available, tick box three only and complete the date of submission.

The form has to be signed in the same way as form P35 is signed.

There is a penalty of £3,000 for **every** incorrect form P11D submitted.

By **6 July**, you must give each employee or director a copy of their form P11D to enable them to complete their personal Tax Returns.

The final section of form P11D(b) includes any adjustments needed to the Class 1A NIC figure. Full details of adjustments are given in paragraph 24 of CWG5.

HM Revenue & Customs

Return of Class 1A National Insurance contributions due
Return of expenses and benefits - Employer declaration

Employer PAYE reference

Accounts Office reference

Year ended 5 April 2008

Please return this form to the address shown below

Employer name and address

If this replaces a Return that was issued automatically it may not show all of your details. If this is so, please fill in the top of this Return before you send it to your HM Revenue & Customs office.

Please read the notes overleaf before completing this Return.
Do not declare any amounts already reported under the Taxed Award Scheme arrangements.

1 Class 1A National Insurance contributions (NICs) due

Enter the total benefits liable to Class 1A NICs from forms P11D. (This is the total of the brown Class 1A NICs boxes on forms P11D. There is a quick guide on page 5 of CWG5 if you are not sure.)

A £

If you need to adjust the figures entered in box A, do not complete box C below, tick this box and complete Section 4 overleaf.

Multiply by Class 1A NICs rate

B 12.8%

box A x rate in box B

Class 1A NICs payable

C £

2 Employer declaration

Tick the relevant box and fill in the appropriate details.

No expenses payments or benefits of the type to be returned on forms P11D have been or will be provided for the year ended 5 April 2008. For this reason no forms P11D are attached.

I confirm that all details of expenses payments and benefits that have to be returned on forms P11D for the year ended 5 April 2008 are enclosed with this declaration. I declare that the details on these forms are fully and truly stated to the best of my knowledge and belief.

Forms P11D for the year ended 5 April 2008 were sent to

HM Revenue & Customs office on   /   /

I confirm that details of expenses payments and benefits that have to be returned on forms P11D have been sent to HM Revenue & Customs.

I declare that all the details on this form are fully and truly stated to the best of my knowledge and belief.

Signature of employer

Date   /   /

The declaration should be signed by the employer or any person authorised to do so.

Capacity in which signed

P11D(b)(2008)Man

HMRC 11/07

---

3 Notes for employer

You should give each employee or director a copy of their P11D information and send the completed forms P11D and P11D(b) to your HM Revenue & Customs office by 6 July.

Pay Class 1A NICs shown on the Return to the Accounts Office using the attached payslip by:

- **19 July** if the payment is by post or cash, or
- **22 July** if the payment is by an approved electronic method.

Where **22 July** falls on a weekend or bank holiday, your payment should reach our bank account no later than the last bank working day before **22 July**. Interest is chargeable on payments paid late. If your Return is not received by 19 July, penalties will be charged automatically. You may also be penalised or prosecuted if you make false statements.

Please note if you have already indicated on your form P35 that forms P11D and P11D(b) are not due, there is no need to send this Return.

Class 1A National Insurance contributions (NICs) due

Employers pay Class 1A NICs on benefits which have to be returned on forms P11D except where Class 1 NICs or Class 1B NICs are due. To help you identify the benefits where Class 1A NICs are due the boxes on the form P11D are brown and are marked 1A. Before completing the forms P11D and this Return, read the P11D(Guide) and booklet CWG5 *class 1A National Insurance contributions on benefits in kind. A guide for employers.*

Forms P11D

As an employer you must complete a Return of expenses payments and benefits, form P11D, for each employee paid at a rate of £8,500 or more a year and for each director if:

- you have provided them with expenses or benefits which are not covered by a dispensation or PAYE Settlement Agreement
- you have arranged for expenses or benefits to be provided by a third party.

Send this declaration with the completed forms P11D to your HM Revenue & Customs office. If you choose to send the forms P11D in batches, send the declaration with the final batch.

References in this Return to forms P11D and HM Revenue & Customs office should be read as including the return of expenses payments and benefits by magnetic media to Shipley Data Centre.

4 Adjustments to Class 1A NICs

Complete this section if you need to adjust the total benefits shown as liable to Class 1A NICs.
Paragraph 18 of CWG5 explains circumstances in which you may need to make adjustments.

Enter the total benefits liable to Class 1A NICs from Section 1, box A overleaf	**A** £	**A**

Using the two boxes below enter any adjustment to the figures in box A

• Add any amounts not included in box A on which Class 1A NICs are due		Amount to be added
Brief description	**B** £	**A**

• Deduct any amounts included in box A on which Class 1A NICs are not due		Amount to be deducted
Brief description	**C** £	

Total of benefits on which Class 1A NICs are due	box A + box B minus box C	
	D £	**A**

Multiply by Class 1A NICs rate	**E** 12.8%	

Class 1A NICs payable	box D x rate in box E	
	F £	**A**

Activity 6.5

Using the information and forms for Activities 6.2 and 6.4, calculate the Class 1A NICs for 2009/10 in respect of Roger Miller's benefits.

5 Form P9D

Employees earning less than £8,500 (including the value of benefits), do not need a form P11D.

However certain benefits do need to be returned and these are entered on form P9D.

- Vouchers
- Assets transferred to an employee
- Assets provided for an employee to use personally
- Reimbursed expenses (except those wholly and necessarily for business purposes)
- Entertaining allowances not covered by a dispensation
- Income tax paid on the employee's behalf (and NICs)
- Living accommodation
- Private expenses met by the employer
- Relocation expenses (including the excess over £8,000 of qualifying relocation expenses).
- Round sum allowances.

Expenses totalling less than £25 do not need to be returned.

Form P9D for 2008/09 is shown on the next page.

Forms P9D also need to be submitted to HMRC by **6 July** and a copy should be given to the employee by the same date.

HM Revenue & Customs

P9D EXPENSES PAYMENTS AND INCOME FROM WHICH TAX CANNOT BE DEDUCTED 2008-09

Please ensure your entries are clear on both sides of the form.

Employer name

Employer PAYE reference

Employee name

Surname

Forename(s)

Works number/department

National Insurance number

Date of birth *in figures (if known)*

D D M M Y Y Y Y

Gender **M – Male F – Female**

Note to employer

Complete this return if you made expenses payments or provided benefits to an employee but you have not completed a form P11D, because he or she earned at a rate of less than £8,500 per year, during the year to 5 April 2009.

You do not need to include the information shown on this form in any return on form P11D(b). Send the completed form to your HM Revenue & Customs (HMRC) office by 6 July 2009.

Note to employee

Your employer has filled in this form, keep it in a safe place. You will need it to complete your 2008-09 Tax Return if you get one.

The box numbers on this P9D match the numbers on the the Employment Page of the Tax Return. Include the total figures in the corresponding box in the Tax Return.

A(1) Expenses payments

If the employee paid expenses solely and necessarily in the performance of his or her duties and/or business travelling expenses and you repaid the amount of those expenses, you do not need to include them here. Total all other expenses payments including:

* payments that included Value Added Tax (VAT), even if the VAT was later recovered from HMRC
* round sum allowances
* all relocation expenses payments and benefits (see note below).

Some relocation expenses qualify for relief *(see booklet 480)*. The maximum amount that can be paid for any one move is £8,000. You should total all the qualifying payments made for each move including:

* any payments made in 2007-08, and
* any benefits provided under the relocation package in 2008-09 or 2007-08.

The excess over £8,000 of any qualifying expenses payments and benefits for each move, should be included in the total expenses payments figure entered below.

If the above amounts total £25 or less they do not need to be included.

If more than £25 enter the total amount. **16** £

A(2) Any other payments or benefits

Include here:

* payments made to the employee and not included on the Employer's Annual Return for 2008-09
* payments made on the employees behalf
* gifts in kind – enter the second-hand value of any goods provided, that is, the price at which the employee could sell the items as soon as he or she got them
* any other payments or benefits which could be turned into money not included elsewhere.

Employees own National Insurance contributions paid by you	**15** £	
Employees personal phone bills paid by you	**15** £	
Gifts in kind	**15** £	
Anything bought for, or paid to, the employee other than at market value	**15** £	
Any payment or benefit not included elsewhere enter the value here and give details in the box overleaf	**15** £	

P9D(2009)   HMRC 09/08

B Vouchers and credit cards

Enter the expense of providing the vouchers, and the goods and services for which they can be exchanged.
(For qualifying childcare vouchers the excess over £55 per week.)

Exclude the value of any vouchers, such as cash vouchers, which have been taxed already under PAYE.

Travel and transport vouchers, including season tickets	12 £

Gift vouchers, including National Savings Certificates and Premium Bonds	12 £

Meal vouchers – *as requested in booklet CWG2 'Employer's further Guide to PAYE and NICs'*	12 £

Any other vouchers exchangeable for goods and services	12 £

Credit cards provided for the employee and his or her family – *enter the total amount of expenses met by credit cards provided by you for the employee to use unless you have already entered these expenses under one of the above headings.*

	12 £

C Accommodation

Give the cash equivalent of accommodation provided for the employee and/or his or her family. Deduct any amounts paid by the employee towards the cost of providing the accommodation – for example, rent.

If the employee is provided with living accommodation give details of the rateable value. This is the gross value that applied before Community Charge was introduced. If the property does not have a gross value, enter 'No rateable value established' and give your estimate of what the gross value would have been if rates had continued. If the cost of the property, including improvements, is greater than £75,000 you will have to calculate the additional yearly rent, see booklet 480 to arrive at the cash equivalent at box 14 below.

If, as well as providing the accommodation, you paid some of the employees bills (such as heat and light), show these in the appropriate box or boxes overleaf, whether or not the value of the accommodation itself is exempt from tax.

Enter property address

Postcode

Enter rateable value of property	£

Enter rent and insurance paid by you	£

Enter the cash equivalent of the accommodation provided to the employee. This will be:
- the greater of the two figures entered above, **or**
- if there is additional yearly rent, you **must** enter the cash equivalent you have calculated **instead.** 14 £

Where necessary use this box to describe the benefits mentioned above and overleaf

6 PSAs and Class 1B NICS

Your employer may agree with HMRC to pay the tax cost of certain benefits provided. This is called a PAYE Settlement Agreement (PSA). PSAs are only available for minor or irregular expenditure, or where it is impractical to work out the PAYE liability for each employee.

Under a PSA, the employer agrees to pay the PAYE due on certain non cash benefits. Examples include the following.

- Food provided for staff working late
- Incentive awards
- Shared use of taxi or pooled cars
- Overseas conferences
- Meals to celebrate success or to welcome new staff
- Refreshments at group meetings

These items are excluded from form P11D and are also excluded from the employee's own tax return.

The PSA has to be agreed by 6 July following the tax year (so 6 July 2010 for 2009/10).

The **employer** has to pay Class 1B NICs on benefits covered by a PSA and the tax paid under the PSA. The rate is 12.8% for 2008/09 and it is due by 19 October at the latest (19 October 2010 for 2009/10).

Taxed award schemes are similar but cover third party benefits paid to employees.

Example: PSA

Comecon Ltd provides its employees with refreshments at group meetings. The total expenditure (and tax thereon) for 2009/10 is £500. How much class 1B NIC does Comecon Ltd pay?

Solution

Class 1B NIC on £500 @ 12.8% = £64.00

Key learning points

- ☑ Taxable benefits are detailed on forms **P9D** and **P11D**, which must be submitted with a form **P11D(b)**.

- ☑ Administration can be cut by the use of **statutory exemptions** and **dispensations.**

- ☑ **Class 1A NICs** are due on taxable benefits by **19 July** following the end of the tax year.

- ☑ Employers can meet the employee's tax liability on certain non cash benefits covered by a **PAYE Settlement Agreement**. However a liability to **Class 1B NICs** arises.

Quick quiz

1   Which employees need a P9D?

2   All employees with a company car need a form P11D. True or false?

3   All benefits can be the subject of a dispensation. True or false?

4   What is a PSA used for?

Answers to quick quiz

1   Where employees earn less than £8,500 pa, certain benefits must be reported on form P9D.

2   False. Only if the salary plus benefits exceed £8,500 pa is a form P11D needed.

3   False. Benefits subject to Class 1A NICs cannot be the subject of a dispensation.

4   A PSA is used to enable employers to pay the tax liability for employees on non cash benefits.

Activity checklist

This checklist shows which performance criteria, range statement or knowledge and understanding point is covered by each activity in this chapter. Tick off each activity as you complete it.

Activity

6.1   This activity cover performance criteria 75.3.A.

6.2   This activity cover performance criteria 75.3.A.

6.3   This activity cover performance criteria 75.3.A.

6.4   This activity cover performance criteria 75.3.A.

6.5   This activity cover performance criteria 75.3.C and 75.3.E.

P A R T   C

Maintaining working relations
with external bodies

chapter 7

Payments to and
from external bodies

Contents

Performance criteria

76.1.A Reconcile payroll records with the organisation's financial reports

76.1.B Make **payments** to **statutory bodies** in accordance with statutory deadline dates and ensure they are accompanied by the applicable statutory documentation

76.1.C Make payments to non-statutory bodies in accordance with business agreements and ensure they are accompanied by the applicable documentation

76.1.D Ensure all payments are made in accordance with organisational regulations and procedures

Range statement

1   **Payments:** cheque; electronic lodgement

2   **Statutory bodies:** Collector of Taxes; Local Authorities; Child Support Agency; Courts

Knowledge and understanding

1   Data Protection legislation (Elements 76.1 & 76.2)

2   PAYE regulations in respect of deadlines for Tax and NI payments (Element 76.1)

3   Reporting requirements in respect of attachments of earnings (Elements 76.1 & 76.2)

5   Signatories and authorisations (Elements 76.1 & 76.2)

6   Timescales and schedules for updating, presenting and despatching data (Elements 76.1 & 76.2)

Knowledge and understanding (continued)

8   Procedures for the security and confidentiality of information (Elements 76.1 & 76.2)

9   Systems for the transmission of disbursements to external agencies (Elements 76.1 & 76.2)

10   External agency requirements for information (Elements 76.1 & 76.2)

11   Sources of information for the resolution of discrepancies (Elements 76.1 & 76.2)

1 The problem

We have looked at paying wages to employees at Level 2. However, what about all the amounts deducted from wages? In this chapter, we will look at paying these amounts to the appropriate organisations.

2 The solution

The most important deductions, in terms of amounts, are going to be tax and NICs. Section 3 looks at paying these amounts to HMRC.

Where the employer has a pension scheme, deductions must be paid to the Trustees. We look at this in Section 4.

There are various other statutory and non-statutory deductions (eg Court orders and Trade Union subscriptions respectively). Section 5 deals with payments to those bodies.

3 HM Revenue and Customs

Before you make any payments to external bodies, you will want to make sure that your records of deductions are correct.

If you think about it carefully, you will realise that the following formula is true.

> Total payroll = Gross pay + SSP + SMP + SPP + SAP + Employer's NIC + Employer's pension contributions – SSP, SMP, SPP and SAP recovered

Another way of stating this follows.

> Total payroll = Net pay + PAYE + Employee's NICs + Employer's NICs + Employee's pension contributions + Employer's pension Contributions – SSP, SMP, SPP and SAP recovered + other deductions.

Therefore you need to produce a monthly report showing that these two equations are equal. A suggested format follows.

PAYROLL SUMMARY – MONTH 1	£
Staff costs – Gross pay (excl. SSP and SMP)	31,200
– SSP	200
– SMP	500
– Employer's NICs	2,000
– Employer's pension contributions	1,500
– SSP recovered	(10)
– SMP recovered	(460)
	34,930
Net pay	25,700
HMRC – PAYE	3,900
– Student Loan Deductions	100
– Employees' NICs	1,000
– Employer's NICs	2,000
– SSP recovered	(10)
– SMP recovered	(460)
Pension fund – Employee's contribution	1,200
– Employer's contributions	1,500
	34,930

The above report also provides the information needed by the accounts department to post the wages, so you may be able to save time by agreeing the detail with the accounts department first.

The report can also be adjusted to account for other deductions, such as trade union subscriptions. These deductions from wages are added to the bottom part of the report.

3.1 Payments to HMRC

We looked at completing HMRC payslip in Chapter 4 (Section 4). Revise this section now if you cannot remember how to complete payslip P30B and the payment summary form P32.

Payment is due to reach HMRC by the 19th of each month, unless you pay electronically (22nd of month) or quarterly.

Payment be made by any of these methods, unless the employer has more than 250 employees, in which case electronic payments are **compulsory**:

- Cheque
- Bank giro at the employer's bank
- By internet or telephone banking
- By direct debit
- By debit or credit card over the internet using the Bill Pay service provided by Alliance & Leicester Commercial Bank (1.25% charge for credit cards)
- At a post office
- By direct credit (BACS, CHAPS)

These methods were all dealt with in detail in your Level 2 studies on paying wages.

Activity 7.1

Using details from the report above, calculate the total amount payable to HMRC.

4 Pension schemes

The pension fund will usually be invested by a insurance company.

Therefore payment of the employee's and employer's contributions will need to be made each month to the insurance company, as soon after the end of the period as possible. The insurance company will set the date.

The insurance company may provide you with a payslip to be sent with each payment. If not, you will need to provide a covering letter (called a remittance advice) detailing the payment and giving your employer's pension scheme reference number.

It is likely that the insurance company will also need a report detailing contributions by employee but this is dealt with in Chapter 8.

5 Other external bodies

You may need to make other statutory deductions from employees' wages.

- Court orders (including Child Support Agency)
- Local authority orders (for payment of council tax).

In each case, you will need to send a cheque, together with details of the order. It will save time if you photocopy the order and send the photocopy with the cheque. Payment can also be made through the CHAPS system.

The payment should be sent in accordance with the instructions on the order, to arrive by the date stipulated in the order. Council tax regulations require payment by 19th of following month.

There are many voluntary deductions that can be made from employee's wages.

- Pensions (see Section 4 above)
- Trade Union subscriptions
- Charity donations under payroll giving
- Savings under SAYE

In each case payment must be made promptly after the month end and details of the deductions provided.

- Name of employee
- Trade Union membership number
- Other reference numbers
- Amount deducted for the month

The details can be provided by reports on paper, tape or disc.

In additional there may be payments for medical insurance due from the employer only. Sometimes employees may contribute to get a higher level of cover or to include their families.

If your organisation provides medical insurance free of charge to employees or with an employee contribution, you will need to send the payment to the insurance company in accordance with the agreement. This may be monthly, quarterly or annually.

Do not forget to keep a record of the split of the premium paid by the employer between the different employees, as this will need to be entered on form P11D.

Key learning points

- ☑ Deductions must be paid over to the relevant authority **promptly**.
- ☑ You must reconcile the wages to ensure that you are paying the correct deductions to each external body.
- ☑ PAYE and NIC must be paid by the 19th of each month (or 22nd of month if sent electronically).
- ☑ Other deductions must be paid promptly.
- ☑ Remittance advices or reports must be sent with the payment, where a payslip is not provided.

Quick quiz

1   When must payments be made to HMRC, if your employer is allowed to pay quarterly?

2   Is it sufficient to send a report listing all employee deductions to the pension fund?

3   Deductions under Court Order can be sent with a copy of the order. True or false?

4   Voluntary deductions do not need to be authorised. True or false?

Answers to quick quiz

1 | Quarter end | Payment due |
    |-------------|-------------|
    | 5 July | 19 July |
    | 5 October | 19 October |
    | 5 January | 19 January |
    | 5 April | 19 April |

2   No. The pension fund will need details of employer's contributions too.

3   True. The copy order should give all the details needed. You may want to add a covering letter, giving details of the period covered (eg for the month of July).

4   False. All voluntary deductions must be authorised in writing by the employee.

Activity checklist

This checklist shows which performance criteria, range statement or knowledge and understanding point is covered by each activity in this chapter. Tick off each activity as you complete it.

Activity

7.1   This activity covers performance criteria 76.1.B.

chapter 8

Providing information to authorised agencies

Contents

Performance criteria

76.2.A Deal with enquiries from statutory agencies and non-statutory bodies in accordance with the organisation's customer care requirements

76.2.B Comply with all aspects of the provision of information covered by current Data Protection legislation

76.2.C Respond to enquiries in the required **medium**

76.2.D Obtain employee authorisation where required prior to the release of information

76.2.E Supply information within the specified timescale

76.2.F File copies of responses in a logical and accessible manner and in accordance with the requirements of the organisation

76.2.G Follow up requests for information from other departments or individuals in an appropriate manner

76.2.H Verify the source of all enquiries prior to the release of information

Range statement

1   **Medium of communication:** proformas; letters; telephone calls; face to face; e-mail; internet

Knowledge and understanding

1	Data Protection legislation (Elements 76.1 & 76.2)
3	Reporting requirements in respect of attachments of earnings (Elements 76.1 & 76.2)
4	Policies, practices and procedures for filing (Element 76.2)
5	Signatories and authorisations (Elements 76.1 & 76.2)
6	Timescales and schedules for updating, presenting and despatching data (Elements 76.1 & 76.2)
7	Information flows within the organisation (Element 76.2)
8	Procedures for the security and confidentiality of information (Elements 76.1 & 76.2)
9	Systems for the transmission of disbursements to external agencies (Elements 76.1 & 76.2)
10	External agency requirements for information (Elements 76.1 & 76.2)
11	Sources of information for the resolution of discrepancies (Elements 76.1 & 76.2)

1 The problem

This chapter provides useful revision of communications, as most of the rules are the same as for internal communications (see Chapter 2).

2 The solution

In Section 3, we will revise the general rules for responding to enquiries.

Pension funds need detailed reports and we will consider this in Section 4.

Finally, we will review communications with statutory bodies in Section 5 and non-statutory bodies in Section 6.

3 Responding to enquiries

In Chapter 2, we looked at internal communications. The rules for external communications are very similar.

All enquiries should be treated as if they were from a customer of the business. After all, HMRC is to a certain extent a customer of the payroll department. However, unlike other customers, if payments are late or enquiries are not answered, HMRC can fine your employer.

All communications to external bodies should be dealt with in the following ways.

- In a professional manner (eg be polite at all times even if the enquirer is rude)
- Answers supplied are correct and accurate
- Security and confidentiality are maintained
- The reply is in the required format
- The reply is sent before the deadline

Remember that, unless the enquiry is from a statutory body, you must have the employee's written authorisation to reply to third party enquiries.

Copies of all enquiries, authorisations and replies should be kept and filed in the employee records. If the enquiry is important, it might be a good idea to file a copy on the employee's permanent file. Otherwise the correspondence can be filed with the current tax year's documents for the employee.

Replies should be made in an appropriate format.

- Proformas (eg monthly report in a set format)
- Letters
- Telephone calls (not recommended with third parties, where you are unlikely to know the caller)
- Person to person
- E-mail

Go back to Chapter 2 to revise the use of these formats and the problems that may occur. In particular, remember to check the identity of the enquirer, if appropriate. Only release information when you are certain that the enquiry is authorised.

Remember the provisions of the Data Protection Acts. You cannot use computer records to reply to external bodies without the employee's permission. However, this does not apply to enquiries from statutory bodies.

If some of the information requested has to come from another department (eg personnel), make sure that you keep a diary note to follow this up if the data is not received within a reasonable time. Never feel that you have passed on the request and so it is now the other department's responsibility. The request came to you in the first place and you must deal with it.

IMPORTANT!

AAT guidance states that personal information should never be given to third parties over the telephone.

---

4 Pension funds

A lot of time is likely to be spent dealing with pension fund queries.

Not only will you have to send payments and information monthly to the trustees and their agents, you are going to have to process details of employees joining or leaving the scheme.

4.1 Joining a company scheme

It is **illegal** to **require** an employee to join a company scheme as a condition of his or her employment.

An employee also has the **right to leave** a company scheme if he or she so wishes, and take up some other pension arrangement.

In terms of **administration**, what should be done when someone joins the company scheme?

(a) Like most deductions from pay, the **deduction for payments** to the company pension fund must be **authorised** by the employee. In practice, this will mean that the payroll department will receive instructions from the **personnel department** to begin deducting pension contributions.

(b) You will be told the amount of **pensionable earnings** on which to base the deductions.

(c) In some schemes an employee may only be permitted to join the pension scheme after he or she has completed a **specified period of service** (eg six months).

(d) The **contracted-out rate of NICs** only applies if the employer has received a contracting-out certificate from the Contracted-Out Employments Group.

(e) Every pay day, or as soon as possible afterwards, the **pension fund** should be credited with the employees' and employer's contributions for the period. You should ensure that the right amounts of contributions are credited to the right accounts. These can involve:

    (i) A **manual system**, sending a detailed contribution schedule with the funds

    (ii) Ensuring, in a **computer-based system**, that the program automatically analyses the total contribution by employee (basic and AVCs)

4.2 Leaving a company scheme

An employee ceases contributions to a company scheme:

- On death
- On retirement
- On leaving the employment
- On changing over to a personal pension plan

4.2.1 Employees leaving within two years

An employee who leaves **within two years** is entitled to a **refund** of his or her own contributions, **but not the employer's contributions**.

- The employer does not have to pay **interest** on the refund.
- Tax must be deducted from the contributions at the rate of 20% on the first £10,800 and 40% on the excess.

Example: Early leavers

Fred Lighty has contributed to the pension scheme run on behalf of Buggins and Terne Ltd for 18 months. His pensionable earnings were £10,000 for the first year and £10,800 thereafter. Fred contributes 5% of his pensionable earnings. Buggins and Terne contribute a further 10% of Fred's pensionable earnings.

Fred leaves Buggins and Terne Ltd. What will be the amount of his refund from the pension fund?

Solution

	£
(5% × 10,000) + (5% × £10,800 × 6/12)	770
Less tax of 20% × £770	(154)
Net refund	616

The scheme might offer alternatives to a refund. The employee might be offered a **deferred pension** for the contributions, or might be able to **transfer** the amount to another scheme.

4.2.2 Employees leaving after two years

Leavers with more than two years' pensionable service have two options.

- The contributions can be **transferred** to another scheme, such as another company scheme or a personal pension scheme, at a determined **transfer value**.
- They may **freeze** the pension.

Freezing the pension involves keeping the contributions made so far in the fund. A pension will be given to an employee on the basis of those frozen contributions when that employee reaches State retirement age.

Example: Later leavers

Phil Aupered contributes four years' worth of contributions to a pension scheme whose benefits are based on 1/60 of final salary for each year's service (up to 40 years). His salary on leaving was £2,100 per annum. Had he stayed, his final salary in 36 years time would have been, say, £30,000.

- If the contributions are frozen, Phil will receive from that employment:

  £2,100 × 4/60 = £140 per annum. Since 1988, such a 'deferred' pension must be increased by either 5% a year or the rate of inflation (if lower) between the date of leaving and the date of retirement.

- He has lost the chance to base his final salary on his last years of employment, in which case the pension based on those four years' contributions would have been:

  £30,000 4/60 = £2,000 per annum (out of a total annual pension of £30,000 × 0/60 = £20,000 per annum).

This detail is given so that you understand why, in some cases, you will need to maintain contribution records for **former employees** who no longer contribute to the scheme.

- They will eventually be paid a **small pension** from the fund.
- This will be based on the **salary** and **contribution records** that you have maintained.

Activity 8.1

How would you answer the following queries about your company pension scheme?

(a) The scheme rules require employees to pay contributions of 6% of annual salary. The employer pays 8%. Charlotte Bax tells you that she would like to pay more as a way of regular saving. How much more can she pay? She earns £24,000 per year.

(b) Richard Pierce has left the company. He joined the scheme 12 months ago and paid contributions of £1,200 in that time. The company paid £1,600. He asks for a refund of contributions. How much will the cheque be?

(c) Marlene Drayton has left the company after 20 years service. She joined the pension scheme 18 years ago. She is going to work for another company which has no occupational pension scheme. She asks what her options are in respect of her contributions to your scheme.

4.3 Reporting

If the pension scheme is run by an **outside agency**, you will probably have to provide a **return** every time you run the payroll, to accompany the document transferring the funds from the employer's to the pension fund's accounts.

The return should indicate:

- Joiners and leavers
- Employees' contributions
- Employer's contributions

which should be **reconciled** with the payroll record.

In addition, you are likely to have to provide the scheme trustees with an annual return at the tax year end. This will include the following information.

- Employee's name
- Date of joining/leaving the scheme
- Employee's contributions analysed between basic, supplementary and AVCs.
- Employer's contribution in respect of that employee

Other reports would be needed for a member on retirement.

- Average past three year's salary (for salary related schemes)
- Contribution record
- How long he or she has been a member of the scheme
- Any purchase of extra years

5 Statutory bodies

The statutory agencies that you are likely to deal with include the following.

- HM Revenue and Customs
- DWP
- Child Support Agency (CSA)
- Courts
- Local authorities
- Other government departments

Enquiries from these bodies **must** be answered by law even if the employee does not want you to provide information (eg to the CSA).

However, you must satisfy yourself that the enquiry is from a statutory authority. Never give information over the phone, if at all possible. Instead, get details of the address, check this (eg to the telephone directory) and only when you are satisfied that the caller is genuine, should you reply preferably by letter. Keep a note of the enquiry and a copy of your reply.

If information is given over the telephone (eg to clarify a letter sent to HMRC), you should keep a note on the file as follows.

- Agency that made the enquiry
- The person you spoke to and their extension
- The enquiry
- Your reply

This detail is essential, if further queries arise later. Never give detailed, confidential information over the telephone.

6 Non-statutory bodies

In addition to pension fund trustees, you are likely to deal with non-statutory bodies for voluntary deductions.

- Trade unions and associations
- Financial institutions (eg SAYE)
- Charities
- Solicitors

In all cases, remember that you can only reply to enquiries from these bodies with the **prior written agreement of the employee**. If the employee does not authorise the release of information, then you must tell the enquirer so.

Remember to verify the source of the enquiry, especially telephone enquiries. **Never** give information over the phone. Tell the caller that you will need the employee's authorisation and you will write with the information once this is received.

Financial institutions or solicitors may write for details of pay for mortgage purposes. These enquiries may be accompanied by an authorisation signed by the employee. If possible check the employee's signature to ensure that it is genuine and check with the employee to ensure that the authorisation is still in force. This may be relevant where a further advance has been applied for and the enquirer is using an authorisation signed some years ago when the first mortgage was taken out.

6.1 GAYE reports

You are likely to have to make a monthly report to the CAF when forwarding employees' deductions. The usual format is shown on the next page.

INSTRUCTIONS FOR SUBMITTING DONATIONS

1. Quote your CONTRACT NUMBER and PAYROLL NAME on all documentation.

2. Check that the Employee identification number on each Charity Choice Form is correct.

3. Check that the Employee identification number which you quote on your monthly deduction list is also the same on the Charity Choice form.

4. Send us the completed TOP SECTION of the Charity Choice form AND keep a copy or the yellow carbonated copy on your file for future reference.

5. Please arrange for your monthly lists to be in this format or PHOTOCOPY FREELY and write or type the information required.

6. Please arrange for your monthly lists to show the MONTH OF DEDUCTION where possible.

7. Please submit donations by cheque. Other means of payment should be agreed with Give As You Earn prior to any change.

8. Please arrange for all Give As You Earn documentation to come to us in one monthly packet.

9. Use this as an example of the format needed for computer printouts.

10. It will help us if we could have both these numbers. If this poses a problem, please submit one or the other (see * overleaf).

GIVE AS YOU EARN EMPLOYEE DONATIONS   PAYLISTING/DEDUCTION STATEMENT

CONTRACT NUMBER: _ _ _ _ _ _ _ _ _ _ _   EMPLOYER NAME: _ _ _ _ _ _ _ _ _ _ _ _ _ _ _ _ _ _
MONTH OF DEDUCTION: _ _ _ _ _ _ _ _ _   EMPLOYER ADDRESS: _ _ _ _ _ _ _ _ _ _ _ _ _ _ _ _ _
PAYROLL NAME/ID/CODE: _ _ _ _ _ _ _ _ _ _ _ _ _ _   _ _ _ _ _ _ _ _ _ _ _ _ _ _ _ _ _
                                                          _ _ _ _ _ _ _ _ _ _ _ _ _ _ _ _ _

*NI NUMBER AND *PAYROLL NUMBER	DONATION	NAME	STARTER/ LEAVER
			—
			—
			—
			—
PAGE TOTAL			
OPTIONAL 5% ADMIN			
REMITTANCE ENCLOSED		MUST AGREE WITH ENCLOSED CHEQUE	

6.2 SAYE

You will have to make monthly returns of the following.

- Scheme code number
- Building society account number
- Monthly contribution
- Number of shares allocated (if a sharesave scheme)

6.3 Other reports

In all cases where voluntary deductions are made, you are likely to have to provide a monthly report to go with the payment (a remittance advice). This will normally include at least the following information.

- Employer's name
- Employee's membership number
- Employee's contribution

Activity 8.2

You are the payroll assistant for Comecon Ltd. Roger Miller's solicitor has rung you to ask for details of his income for mortgage purposes. You do not hold an authorisation from Roger to divulge this information, but the solicitor is being very pushy and wants the information now. What do you do?

Key learning points

☑ Check the identity of the enquirer.

☑ Respond in an appropriate, professional manner.

☑ If the enquiry is from a non-statutory body, obtain the employee's prior written approval before replying.

Quick quiz

1 If a telephone call is made, is it acceptable to slam down the phone?

2 Can a non-statutory body demand information?

3 You do not need to keep details of telephone queries. True or false?

4 Pension funds can demand information. True or false?

5 You must reply to enquiries from the Child Support Agency. True or false?

Answers to quick quiz

1   No. Always act in a professional manner. Be polite but firm and do not allow yourself to get angry during the call.

2   No. You can only reply to queries after the employee has authorised it.

3   False. You must make a note and file it. In case further queries arise, it is useful to keep a note of exactly what was said and who you spoke to.

4   Pension funds do need information about employees, particularly when a pension is due to be paid. However, employee's permission will be needed, so false.

5   True. The CSA has legal powers to force employers to reveal confidential information about their employees (see your Level 2 studies).

Activity checklist

This checklist shows which performance criteria, range statement or knowledge and understanding point is covered by each activity in this chapter. Tick off each activity as you complete it.

Activity

8.1   ☐   This activity covers performance criteria 76.2.A.

8.2   ☐   This activity covers performance criteria 76.2.A and 76.2.D.

BPP LEARNING MEDIA

Answers to Activities

Answers to activities

Chapter 1

Answer 1.1

(a) **Pensionable earnings** are based on salary at 1 January each year. Therefore pensionable earnings for October 20X3 are:

	£
£36,000/12	3,000

(b) **Taxable earnings**

	£	£
Gross pay (£37,500/12)		3,125
Bonus		500
		3,625
Less: pension contributions – basic (10% × £3,000)	300	
– AVCs	25	
GAYE	75	
		400
Taxable earnings		3,225

Tutorial note. Remember from Section 3.4.1 that both basic contributions and AVCs are deducted from pay before tax. Sharesave contributions of £20 pa are deducted from net pay.

(c) **NICable earnings**

	£
Gross pay	3,125
Bonus	500
NICable earnings	3,625

Answer 1.2

(a) A general schedule of hourly rates by grade is probably not confidential. However, check with your supervisor before giving a copy to Jacob, if you are not sure that he is entitled to see it.

(b) Jacob can only receive details of Judith's pay if she has given her written permission. Explain to Jacob that Judith's pay details are confidential, but that you are willing to give that information to her if she requests it. Alternatively you can give such information to Jacob if Judith signs an authority to do so.

Answer 1.3

At first sight, there is a discrepancy somewhere. You need to check whether Judith is really Grade D.

(a)   Look at her employee record
(b)   Check her contract of employment
(c)   If necessary, contact personnel/human resources to confirm her current grading.

If Judith is Grade D, then she is entitled to more pay. If this was a recent promotion, it may well be that payroll records were late being updated, and you may need to do this now. If Judith wants her backpay now, you may need to make a special payment to her.

If the promotion was some time ago and the payroll records are up to date, you may need to check the payroll parameters.

(a)   Has the employee's master file been updated to show her as Grade D?
(b)   Is the schedule of pay rates by grade up to date?

If the schedule of pay rates by grade is out of date, other employees may also be affected.

Answer 1.4

The payment of £3,260 comprises $£(3,260 - 2,650) = £610$ for June and £2,650 for July.

Employees' NIC

June: $(610 - 476) \times 11\% = £14.74$
July: $(2,650 - 476) \times 11\% = £239.14$

Employer's NIC

June: $(610 - 476) \times 12.8\% = £17.15$
July: $(2,650 - 476) \times 12.8\% = £278.27$

Answer 1.5

(a) As tax is calculated as if paid on the usual pay day, use month 11 table A for allowances. Also use the month 11 limits and subtraction tables.

		Tax code		Amended							
		461L		WK/mnth							
					K codes				K codes		K codes
W e e k	M o n t h	Pay in the week	Total pay to date	Total free pay to date	Total additional pay to date	Total taxable pay to date	Total tax due to date	Tax due at end of current period	Regulatory limit	Tax deducted in the week	Tax not deducted owing to the regulatory limit
		2	3	4a	4b	5	6	6a	6b	7	8
43	10	2,000.00	20,000.00	3,849.20		16,150.80	3,230.00			323.00	
44											
45		500.00	20,500.00	4,234.12		16,265.88	3,253.00			23.00	
46											
47	11	2,000.00	22,500.00	4,234.12		18,265.88	3,653.00			400.00	

(b) Although the £500 is paid in week 45, we use the normal pay day rates for 'additional pay' ie month 11. Use the limits and subtraction tables for month 11 also.

		Tax code		Amended							
		K461		WK/mnth							
					K codes				K codes		K codes
W e e k	M o n t h	Pay in the week	Total pay to date	Total free pay to date	Total additional pay to date	Total taxable pay to date	Total tax due to date	Tax due at end of current period	Regulatory limit	Tax deducted in the week	Tax not deducted owing to the regulatory limit
		2	3	4a	4b	5	6	6a	6b	7	8
43	10	2,000.00	20,000.00		3,849.20	23,849.20	4,769.80	476.98	1,000.00	476.98	
44											
45		500.00	20,500.00		4,234.12	24,734.12	4,946.80	177.00	250.00	177.00	
46											
47	11	2,000.00	22,500.00		4,234.12	26,734.12	5,346.80	400.00	1,000.00	400.00	

Answer 1.6

£

April

Total earnings to date	10,000
Employees' NICs (£10,000 – £5,715) × 11%	471.35
Employer's NICs (£10,000 – £5,715) × 12.8%	548.48
Total NICs due this pay day	1,109.83

May

Total earnings to date: 2 × £10,000	20,000

Employees' NICs

Total due to date (£20,000 – £5,715) × 11%	1,571.35
Less: NICs paid in April	(471.35)
Total due this pay day	1,100.00

Employer's NICs

(£20,000 – £5,715) × 12.8%	1,828.48
Less: NICs paid in April	(548.48)
Due this pay day	1,280.00
Total NICs due this pay day	2,380.00

June

Total earnings to date: 3 × £10,000	30,000
Bonus	4,000
	34,000

Employees' NICs

Total due to date: (£34,000 – £5,715) × 11%	3,111.35
Less: NICs paid in April and May	(1,571.35)
Due this pay day	1,540.00

£

Employer's NICs: (£34,000 – £5,715) × 12.8%	3,620.48
Less: NICs paid in April and May	(1,828.48)
Due this pay day	1,792.00
Total NICs due this pay day	3,332.00

Answer 1.7

- **Arun Misra** was not a director in the tax year 2009/10 so he had no earnings period!

- **John Birch** and **Sally Hill** have a full year's earnings period for 2009/10 as they were both directors at the start of the tax year.

- **Sean Heaney** also has an annual earnings period even though he resigned before the end of the year. The effect of this is that any earnings he received between 6 April 2009 and 10 December 2009 would be charged to NIC on a cumulative basis using the ET, UAP and UEL, not pro rata but for the whole tax year.

- **Bill Rogerson** and **Lucille James** both have a pro rata annual earnings period.
    - Bill Rogerson: 10 May 2009 falls in Week 5
    - Lucille James: 12 November 2009 falls in Week 32

    Including the week of appointment:

    - Bill Rogerson is a director for 48 weeks of this tax year.
    - Lucille James is a director for 21 weeks of this tax year.

    Remember not to include Week 53.

Answer 1.8

You need Table A for both directors.

Peggy Ainsworth

Annual earnings period

Monthly earnings = £45,000 ÷ 12 = £3,750

By the end of August, Peggy's earnings to date are 5 × £3,750 = £18,750

	£
Employee's NIC: (18,750 − 5,715) × 11%	1,433.85
Employer's NIC: (18,750 − 5,715) × 12.8%	1,668.48
Total due to date at the end of August	3,102.33

Vijay Parmar

Monthly earnings = £32,000 ÷ 12 = £2,666.67

Pro rata earnings period: appointed in tax week 17, so 36 weeks in year.

		£
LEL	£95 × 36	3,420
ET	£5,715/52 × 36	3,957
UAP	£770 × 36	27,720
UEL	£43,875/52 × 36	30,375

As Vijay's earnings have not exceeded the pro-rated LEL, there is no NI due at the end of August.

Answer 1.9

(a) **Week 1**

	£
Net pay	150
Protected earnings	(100)
Leaves	50

So the full deduction of £50 is made. Mr Tweed receives:

	£
Net pay	150
DEO deduction (paid to CSA)	(50)
Administrative fee (kept by Harris Ltd)	(1)
Take home pay	99

(b) **Week 2**

	£
Net pay	175
Protected earnings	(100)
Leaves	75

Full deduction is made. Mr Tweed receives:

	£
Net pay	175
DEO deduction	(50)
Administrative fee	(1)
Take home pay	124

(c) **Week 3**

	£
Net pay	100

As this is the protected earnings rate, no deduction is made. Harris Ltd cannot take the administrative fee. Mr Tweed receives:

	£
Net pay = take home pay	100

The £50 not deducted is carried forward.

(d) **Week 4**

	£
Net pay	250
Protected earnings	(100)
Leaves	150

Therefore £100 is deducted this week (£50 week 3 b/f + £50 week 4). Mr Tweed receives:

	£
Net pay	250
DEO deduction (weeks 3 & 4)	(100)
Administrative fee	(1)
Take home pay	149

Answer 1.10

Yes this is an *ex-gratia* payment and so is partly exempt from tax. The redundancy pay and ex-gratia payment are added together. The first £30,000 of the total is exempt, the excess is taxable. However it is not NICable.

BPP
LEARNING MEDIA

Answer 1.11

Unfortunately the letter states that the payment is to reward loyalty. Therefore, it is due to her employment and not *ex-gratia*. Therefore, it is fully taxable and NICable.

Tutorial note. If an employer is considering making an *ex-gratia* payment, it is very important that any documentation does not link the payment to the employment. If it does, then the payment is not *ex-gratia*.

Answer 1.12

Parsifal Ltd
Reconciliation of actual payroll costs to budget for June 20X5

	£	£
Budget		120,000
Unbudgeted costs:		
Bonuses	12,733	
Employer's NIC @ 12.8%	1,630	
Employer's pension costs @ 5%	637	
		15,000
Actual wages		135,000

Chapter 2

Answer 2.1

This request is suspicious. Why should the personnel manager want the information sent to his home address? Of course, he could be working at home this week. However, you need to do some checking. You are probably familiar with Arthur Brown's signature. However, you should double check the signature to the authorised signatory list and check Arthur Brown's home address to your employee records (he is an employee of the organisation so you should have his address on file). If the address is wrong, you need to tell your supervisor that you are suspicious of the request. You should say that the signature does not agree with the authorised signatory list and that the address given is not Arthur Brown's home address. Under no circumstance should you comply with the request unless authorised to do so by your supervisor (it could be that Arthur Brown is ill, causing a shaky signature, and is working from a relative's home this week!).

This scenario may seem far-fetched, but it has happened in practice. A jealous worker felt that his colleague was being paid more than him and so sent a request for salary details, with the forged signature of the personnel manager. An alert payroll clerk spotted the forgery.

Answer 2.2

The request seems genuine. However you should check Alice Cooper to the authorised signatory list. If she is on the list and her signature looks genuine, then you should let her have the information. However, if you are not sure, then you should get your supervisor's authority first.

Answer 2.3

You could wait for the repairman and hope he can repair the printer in time to print out your report. However, it would be sensible to phone Ms Cooper, tell her your problem and ask if you can send her a disc of the report instead. She can then print out the report herself. This also has the advantages of enabling her to have the figures well before the deadline, in case of any queries, and to be able to use the figures in any reports she needs to produce.

Answer 2.4

The first option of getting Ms Cooper's secretary to print off the report and then faxing it to Ms Cooper at a customer's office is not recommended. You do not know if Ms Cooper's secretary is authorised to see payroll information and there are the security problems of faxing the report to a customer's office. It is far easier and more secure to send the report as an attachment to an e-mail to Ms Cooper's laptop. That way no third party will be able to read the information.

Answer 2.5

Anna Christianson is perfectly entitled to information about her pay. The fact that the information is going to be produced at a Tribunal is beside the point. You should send her a letter setting out the information she requires. You should also inform your supervisor of the query and let personnel have a copy of your reply to Ms Christianson, since this is going to be evidence at the Tribunal.

Answer 2.6

You should explain to George Jones that, legally, you can not alter or reissue a form P45. If he has genuine concerns (for example, his NI number is wrongly recorded on the form P45), then you should write a letter to your tax office informing them of the error, with a copy for George Jones. HMRC will then sort out George's problem.

Answer 2.7

Legally, you are only required to keep payroll information for three years. Although as it is advisable to keep this information for longer (at least six years since PAYE audits can go back that far), the data may be in storage. If your organisation has guidelines for dealing with these kinds of enquiries, you should follow them. If not, it is advisable to speak to your supervisor **before** getting records back from storage. It may be that the research needed to reply to this query is going to take a lot of time and effort. If you can provide Rosemary Clark with the information fairly easily, then you should do so. If it is going to take a disproportionate amount of time and effort, then Ms Clark may be asked to make a payment towards the costs (maximum £10). If the records no longer exist, then Ms Clark should be told that.

Answer 2.8

Even though Jack Smith is the union representative, he does not have Sid's authorisation to disclose his pay. You must explain politely to Jack that he will need Sid's written authorisation before you can give him this information. Alternatively, you can send a report to Sid and then it is up to Sid if he passes the details onto Jack.

Answer 2.9

Explain to Sid that you can not give details of his pay to anyone without his authorisation. As Sid is now in your office, you can offer to let him have a letter giving his pay details which he can pass to Jack Smith. Alternatively, if Sid wants to give you written authorisation, you can give the information direct to Jack Smith yourself.

Answer 2.10

You will need to do some identity checks. You could ask Reeza for some or all of the following details.

- Staff number
- Home address
- Bank account details
- Next of kin (if this is shown in employee records)

Only when you are satisfied that you are actually talking to Reeza herself, should you answer her enquiry. If in doubt, politely refuse to answer the query over the phone. You could ask Reeza to put the request in writing or tell her that you will not give that information over the phone but you will send her a letter at her home address.

Note. Remember this is an internal phone call. For external phone calls even greater caution is needed. The above checks may not be enough if a third party has got hold of a stolen cheque book for example. As a general rule, do not give information over the phone, unless you know the person you are talking to, use an alternative method.

Answer 2.11

You must tell the employee that the CSA has statutory powers to force employers to provide information, in cases where the alleged parent will not comply with the CSA's enquiries. Therefore if you get a demand from the CSA for details of his earnings, you will have to provide this information. It is up to the employee (and his solicitors) to convince the CSA that they have the wrong person.

Answer 2.12

(a) You should explain to Mona Lott that you cannot give her details of other employees' pay without their permission. If she gets annoyed, remind her how she would feel if you gave her salary details to one of her colleagues! It sounds as if her complaint would be most usefully discussed with her manager or supervisor, who could ask the Personnel Department to consider this matter further if they think Mona has a point.

(b) This is a very difficult problem for you personally, but professionally your answer is obvious: you would be giving Jim confidential information without authorisation and as such would be risking dismissal for misconduct. Jim should understand this and respect your professionalism.

(c) Sharon's behaviour is suspicious and should be reported to your supervisor. She should certainly not be allowed into your office while there is cash about. The reasons should be obvious to her, but if she is simply naïve, rather than dishonest, perhaps it would help if you pointed out that in the event of cash disappearing from the payroll office, she would be under suspicion if she had been allowed in.

(d) Harry is entitled under the Data Protection Act 1984 to access to his file unless your company uses personal data on employees solely for payroll processing. Your company may have procedures laid down to deal with requests like Harry's: if so, follow them. Otherwise it might be best to refer him to your supervisor. The Act only requires information to be provided 'at reasonable intervals and without undue delay and expense.' Ex-employees' records may not be readily available any more so Harry may have to wait.

Chapter 3

Answer 3.1

(a) Martha has worked for 10 years, all of them since she was 41 and so is entitled to 10 years' pay at 1½ weeks per year. Her weekly pay exceeds the maximum.

Therefore she is due: $10 \times 1½ \times £350 = £5,250$.

(b) Simon has worked 5 years since age 22 and so is entitled to 5 weeks pay at £130 per week.

He is due: $5 \times 1 \times £130 = £650$.

(c) Ranjit has worked 2 years below age 22 and 18 years between the ages of 22 and 40.

He is due: $(½ \times 2 \times £200) + (18 \times 1 \times £200) = £3,800$.

Answer 3.2

(a) Alnoor was 20 when he joined the firm on 1 January 1981. On 1 January 2010 he will have worked for exactly 29 years and will be 49 years old. He was 22 on 26 June 1982 and 41 on 26 June 2001. His first **full** year at work after the age of 22 commenced on 1 January 1983 and his first **full** year of work after the age of 41 commenced on 1 January 2002. Therefore he has 2 whole years at ½ week's pay, 19 years at 1 week's pay and 8 years at the 1½ week's pay (total 29 years). As only 20 years count, we take the last 20 years as this gives a higher figure of statutory redundancy pay. His pay exceeds the statutory maximum and so £380 is used.

SRP = $(8 \times 1½ \times £380) + (12 \times 1 \times £380) = £9,120$

(b) Janet was 16 when she joined the firm on 1 July 2006 and will have worked for 3 years 6 months. She is 19 on 1 January 2010. Therefore she is entitled to SRP of $3 \times ½ \times £140 = £210$.

(c) Mark Canter was 19 when he joined the firm on 1 July 1968. On 1 January 2010, he will have worked for the firm for 41 years 6 months and will be 61 years old. The number of years counting for SRP is the last 20 years.

Mark was 41 on 27 September 1989 and so his first full year after the age of 41 started on 1 January 1990. He has 20 full years at 1½ weeks' pay at 1 January 2010. Part years do not count for SRP. Once again the statutory maximum of £380 per week applies.

Therefore his entitlement is: $(20 \times 1½ \times £380) = £11,400$

Answer 3.3

The redundancy pay is over £30,000 and so £15,000 will be taxed.

(a) On 1 January 2010, Jack Jones is paid £25,000

	£
Payment	25,000
Exempt	(25,000)
Taxable	NIL

(b) On 1 January 2011, Jack Jones is paid £20,000

	£
Payment	20,000
Exempt (£30,000 – £25,000)	(5,000)
Taxable	15,000

A deduction card will need to be set up for Jack Jones for the tax year 2010/11 (as he left on 1 January 2010, in the 2009/10 tax year, you will not have a deduction card in use). You do **not** bring forward his tax code from 2009/10. Instead you will use BR code and tax the £15,000 accordingly. No NIC will be due on the payment.

Payment due

	£
Redundancy payment	20,000
Tax @ 20% on £15,000	(3,000)
Paid to Jack Jones	17,000

Chapter 4

Answer 4.1

The average payment is found by adding all the monthly totals together (which gives £18,000) and dividing this by 12.

£18,000 ÷ 12 = £1,500.00 monthly

So Bob cannot pay quarterly, as he is not a small employer by HMRC's criteria. Note that if one month's payment was just £1 lower, the average would be £1,499.92 monthly and Bob would qualify for quarterly payments.

Answer 4.2

	£	£
Net Income Tax		
Income Tax		40,000
Less: refund		(500)
Add Student Loan Deductions		1,500
		41,000
Net NICs		
Employees' NICs		7,500
Employer's NICs		14,900
		22,400
SMP recovery (W2)	414	
SPP recovery (W3)	460	
SAP recovery (W4)	828	
		(1,702)
		20,698
Amount due		61,698

Workings

1 *SSP recovery*

13% of total NICs = 13% × £22,400

= £2,912

As SSP paid out of £200 is less than 13% of NICs, no recovery is due.

2 *SMP recovery*

92% × £450 = £414

3 *SPP recovery*

92% × £500 = £460

4 *SAP recovery*

92% × £900 = £828

Answer 4.3

The totals of the pension report are as follows.

Basic	Supplementary	AVCs	Employer's	Total
37,900	5,000	8,300	102,400	153,600

Therefore total employee contributions are £37,900 + £5,000 + £8,300 = £51,200, which agrees to the report.

Total employer's contributions are £102,400, which also agrees to the report.

Answer 4.4

You should by now have a good collection of sample forms, documentation and so on. It would be particularly worthwhile to study any which are computer-generated versions of HMRC stationery to see how they show the essential items of information even when the layout has been changed.

Alternatively visit the HMRC website to see the latest versions of the forms mentioned in this text. These can be printed out for future reference.

Answer 4.5

P14 End of Year Summary 2009-10 007

For help to fill in this form, see Employer Helpbook E10

Please use black ink and write firmly to ensure your entries are clear on all three sheets. If spaces should be filled from the right hand side.

Your name and address as employer

BIX LTD
HIGHTOWN, BUCKS

HM Revenue & Customs office name
HIGHTOWN

for employer's use 007

Employer PAYE reference
1 2 3 / 4 5 6 7 8

Tax Year to 5 April 2010

Expenses payments and benefits paid to directors and employees:
Complete form P11D or P9D if appropriate and provide a copy of the information to your employee by 6 July. See booklet CWG2 Employer Further Guide to PAYE and NICs for more details

Employee's details Copy from P11

Postcode A B 1   2 C D

National Insurance number: A B 1 2 3 4 5 6 C

Surname: B R A G G

First two forenames: P R I S C I L L A   M A R Y

Works/payroll number: A29

Date of birth in figures
DD MM YYYY
0 1 ; 0 3 ; 1 9 5 0

Gender F ☐ male M ☑ female

Employer's name and address (if known)
7 HUNTINGDON ROAD
HIGHTOWN
BUCKS

Postcode A B 1   5 X T

National Insurance contributions in this employment

(Note: LEL = Lower Earnings Limit, ET = Earnings Threshold, UAP = Upper Accrual Point, UEL = Upper Earnings Limit)

NIC table letter 1a	Earnings at the LEL (where earnings are equal to or exceed the LEL) (whole £s) from col.1a on P11 1a	Earnings above the LEL, up to and including the ET (whole £s) from col.1b on P11 1b	Earnings above the ET, up to and including the UEL (whole £s) from col.1c on P11 1c	Earnings above the UAP, up to and including the UEL (whole £s) from col.1d on P11 1d	Total of employee's and employer's contributions from col.1e on P11 1e	If amount in col.1e is a minus amount, enter 'R' here	Employee's contributions due on all earnings above the ET from col.1f on P11 1f
A	4 ,5 3 2	7 ,0 4	5 ;9 4 0	0	1 4 1 3 ; 7 2		6 5 3 ; 4 0
C	,4 1 2	6 ,4	5 4 0	0	6 ;9 ; 1 2		0 ; 0 0

Statutory payments included in the pay in this employment figure below

Statutory Sick Pay (SSP) 1g	Statutory Maternity Pay (SMP) 1h	Statutory Paternity Pay (SPP) 1i	Statutory Adoption Pay (SAP) 1j

Pay and Income Tax details

	Pay	Tax deducted
In previous employment(s)		
In this employment	1 2 2 0 0 ; 0 0	1 3 5 2 ; 2 0
Total for year	1 2 2 0 0 ; 0 0	1 3 5 2 ; 2 0

Employee's Widows & Orphans/Life Assurance contributions in this employment

Final tax code 5 4 3 L

Student Loan deductions

In this employment (whole £) from col.1k on P11

Enter 'R' in this box if not refund

Scheme Contracted-out Number (for Contracted-out Money Purchase schemes (Contracted-out Money Purchase Stakeholder Pension schemes only))

£
£
£
£

Date of starting if during tax year to 5 April 2010 DD MM YYYY

Date of leaving if during tax year to 5 April 2010

Payment in Week 53: If included in Pay and Tax, enter '53' '54' or '56' here (see Employer Helpbook E10)

Please detach sheets and make separate bundles of National Insurance and Tax copies before sending in

For official use

Answer 4.6

HM Revenue & Customs

P35 – Employer Annual Return for

⌐   ⌐
└   └

*
*

Please return to

For information only

Employer PAYE reference   /   Your reference

HMRC office phone number   Accounts Office reference

PAYE Income Tax, National Insurance contributions (NICs) and related payments

If in the tax year you were required to prepare any P11 *Deductions Working Sheets*, **you are required by law to:**

- complete and sign this Return or send it online. **If you send your Return online you must not send this form**

- send the 'National Insurance copy' and 'Tax copy' of form P14 *End of Year Summary* (or online equivalent), for each employee for whom you were required to complete a form P11 *Deductions Working Sheet* (or equivalent record) during the year

- send, where applicable, P35(CS) *Continuation Sheets* and form P38A *Employer Supplementary Return*. (Forms P38(S) *Student employees* should not be sent with this Return, but must be kept for at least three years)

- send the Return, including any of the above, in time to **reach the above HM Revenue & Customs office by 19 May** following the end of the tax year.

You may be charged a penalty if your Return is received late.

Help

For step-by-step guidance on completing this Return:

- see the Employer Helpbook E10 *Finishing the tax year* included on the *Employer CD-ROM*

- go to **www.hmrc.gov.uk/employers**

- phone our Employer Helpline on **08457 143 143**

- contact your HM Revenue & Customs office at the address shown above.

You can get paper copies of all the forms and booklets mentioned on this Return from our Employer Orderline.

- Order online at **www.hmrc.gov.uk/employers/emp-form.htm**
- Phone **08457 646 646**
- Fax **08702 406 406**

Other important dates following the end of the tax year

By 19 April — if you do not pay electronically and you post your payment, please pay all outstanding tax and NICs so your payment reaches us no later than 19 April to avoid being charged interest

By 22 April — if you pay by an approved electronic payment method, please pay all outstanding tax and NICs so that cleared funds for your payment reach us no later than 22 April to avoid being charged interest (and a surcharge in the case of employers who have to pay electronically)

By 31 May — give a P60 *End of Year Certificate* to each relevant employee

By 6 July — submit online or on paper, forms:
- P9D *Expenses payments and income from which tax cannot be deducted*
- P11D *Expenses and Benefits*, and
- P11D(b) *Return of Class 1A National Insurance contributions due, Return of expenses and benefits – Employer declaration*
- give a copy of forms P11D or P9D (or equivalent information) to each relevant employee

By 19 July — if you post your payment, please pay any Class 1A NICs so your payment reaches us no later than 19 July

By 22 July — if you pay by an approved electronic payment method, please pay any Class 1A NICs so that cleared funds for your payment reach us no later than 22 July.

Do not include payment with this form. If a payment is due, please use one of our recommended methods to pay direct to our Accounts Office. There is 'How to pay' guidance in your P30BC *Payslip Booklet* notes or in the letter we issue in place of your booklet or go to **www.hmrc.gov.uk/howtopay/paye.htm**   *Now fill in pages 2 and 3* ▶

P35(2008)   Page 1   HMRC 11/07

Answer 4.5

P14 End of Year Summary 2009-10   007

Employer PAYE reference: 1 2 3 / 4 5 6 7 8

Tax Year to 5 April 2 0 1 0

For help to fill in this form, see Employer Helpbook E10

Please use black ink and write firmly to ensure your entries are clear on all three sheets. If spaces should be filled from the right hand side.

HM Revenue & Customs office name: HIGHTOWN

For employer's use: 007

Your name and address as employer:

BIX LTD
HIGHTOWN, BUCKS

Postcode: A B 1   2 C D

Expenses payments and benefits paid to directors and employees:
Complete form P11D or P9D if appropriate and provide a copy of the information to your employee by 6 July. See booklet CWG2 Employer Further Guide to PAYE and NICs for more details

Employee's details Copy from P11

National Insurance number: A B 1 2 3 4 5 6 C

Date of birth in figures DD MM YYYY: 0 1 0 3 1 9 5 0

Gender: F M/female

Surname: B R A G G

First two forenames: P R I S C I L L A   M A R Y

Weekly/payroll number: A29

Employee's private address (if known): 7 HUNTINGDON ROAD
HIGHTOWN
BUCKS

Postcode: A B 1   5 X Y

National Insurance contributions in this employment

(Note: LEL = Lower Earnings Limit, ET = Earnings Threshold, UAP = Upper Accrual Point, UEL = Upper Earnings Limit)

NIC table letter	Earnings at the LEL (where earnings are equal to or exceed the LEL) (whole £s) 1a	Earnings above the LEL, up to and including the ET (whole £s) 1b	Earnings above the ET, up to and including the UAP (whole £s) 1c	Earnings above the UAP, up to and including the UEL (whole £s) 1d	Total of employee's and employer's contributions 1e	Employee's contributions due on all earnings above the ET 1f
A	4 5 3 2	1 7 0 4	5 5 9 4 0	0	1 4 1 3 · 7 2	6 5 3 · 4 0
C	4 1 2	6 4	5 4 0 0		6 9 · 1 2	0 · 0 0

If amount in col.1e is a minus amount, enter 'R' here

Statutory payments included in the pay 'In this employment' figure below

Statutory Sick Pay (SSP) 1g	Statutory Maternity Pay (SMP) 1h	Statutory Paternity Pay (SPP) 1i	Statutory Adoption Pay (SAP) 1j

Pay and Income Tax details

	Pay	Tax deducted
In previous employment(s)	1 2 2 0 0 · 0 0	1 3 5 2 · 2 0
In this employment	1 2 2 0 0 · 0 0	1 3 5 2 · 2 0
Total for year		Final tax code 5 4 3 L

Employee's Widow's & Orphans'/Life Assurance contributions in this employment

Student Loan deductions

In this employment (whole £)

Enter 'R' in this box if not refund

Date of starting if during tax year to 5 April 2010: DD MM YYYY

Date of leaving if during tax year to 5 April 2010:

Scheme Contracted-out Number (For Contracted-out Money Purchase schemes OR Contracted-out Money Purchase Stakeholder Pension schemes only):
S
S
S
S

Payment in Week 53: If included Pay and Tax under Week 53, '54' or '56' here. See your employer Helpbook E10

Please detach sheets and make separate bundles of National Insurance and Tax copies before sending in

Answer 4.6

HM Revenue & Customs

P35 – Employer Annual Return for

⌐ ⌐

∗
∗

Please return to

For information only

Employer PAYE reference　　/　　　　　Your reference

HMRC office phone number　　　　　　Accounts Office reference

PAYE Income Tax, National Insurance contributions (NICs) and related payments

If in the tax year you were required to prepare any P11 *Deductions Working Sheets*, you are required by law to:

- complete and sign this Return or send it online. If you send your Return online you must not send this form
- send the 'National Insurance copy' and 'Tax copy' of form P14 *End of Year Summary* (or online equivalent), for each employee for whom you were required to complete a form P11 *Deductions Working Sheet* (or equivalent record) during the year
- send, where applicable, P35(CS) *Continuation Sheets* and form P38A *Employer Supplementary Return*. (Forms P38(S) *Student employees* should not be sent with this Return, but must be kept for at least three years)
- send the Return, including any of the above, in time to **reach the above HM Revenue & Customs office by 19 May** following the end of the tax year.

You may be charged a penalty if your Return is received late.

Help

For step-by-step guidance on completing this Return:
- see the Employer Helpbook E10 *Finishing the tax year* included on the *Employer CD-ROM*
- go to **www.hmrc.gov.uk/employers**
- phone our Employer Helpline on **08457 143 143**
- contact your HM Revenue & Customs office at the address shown above.

You can get paper copies of all the forms and booklets mentioned on this Return from our Employer Orderline.
- Order online at **www.hmrc.gov.uk/employers/emp-form.htm**
- Phone **08457 646 646**
- Fax **08702 406 406**

Other important dates following the end of the tax year

By 19 April – if you do not pay electronically and you post your payment, please pay all outstanding tax and NICs so your payment reaches us no later than 19 April to avoid being charged interest

By 22 April – if you pay by an approved electronic payment method, please pay all outstanding tax and NICs so that cleared funds for your payment reach us no later than 22 April to avoid being charged interest (and a surcharge in the case of employers who have to pay electronically)

By 31 May – give a P60 *End of Year Certificate* to each relevant employee

By 6 July – submit online or on paper, forms:
- P9D *Expenses payments and income from which tax cannot be deducted*
- P11D *Expenses and Benefits*, and
- P11D(b) *Return of Class 1A National Insurance contributions due, Return of expenses and benefits – Employer declaration*
- give a copy of forms P11D or P9D (or equivalent information) to each relevant employee

By 19 July – if you post your payment, please pay any Class 1A NICs so your payment reaches us no later than 19 July

By 22 July – if you pay by an approved electronic payment method, please pay any Class 1A NICs so that cleared funds for your payment reach us no later than 22 July.

Do not include payment with this form. If a payment is due, please use one of our recommended methods to pay direct to our Accounts Office. There is 'How to pay' guidance in your P30BC *Payslip Booklet* notes or in the letter we issue in place of your booklet or go to **www.hmrc.gov.uk/howtopay/paye.htm**　　*Now fill in pages 2 and 3* ▶

P35(2008)　　　　　　　　　　　　　Page 1　　　　　　　　　　　　　HMRC 11/07

BPP LEARNING MEDIA

Part 1 Summary of employees and directors

- If you are sending your form P35 and **all** of your forms P14 on paper you must:
  a. list **each employee or director** for whom you have completed a form P11 *Deductions Working Sheet* (or equivalent record).
     If you have more than ten entries, please prepare P35(CS) *Continuation Sheets*
  b. ensure that all forms P14 are enclosed with this Return.
- If some or all of your forms P14 are not enclosed with this Return because they are being sent by Internet, Electronic Data Interchange (EDI) or magnetic media, there is no need to complete the 'Part 1 Summary of employees and directors' section of this Return. Instead you must begin by completing boxes 3 and 6 of the 'Part 2 Summary of payments for the year' section below.

Guidance notes
Some useful hints are given below.
For step-by-step guidance refer to the 'Help' section on page 1.

If any of the boxes do not apply to you, please leave them blank.

If you make a mistake and record the wrong entry:
- draw a line through the entry so that it can still be read, and
- record the correct figure alongside.

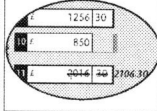

Employee name Put an asterisk (*) by the name if the person is a director	National Insurance contributions (NICs) Enter the total NICs from **column 1d** on form P11. Write 'R' beside any minus amounts.	Income Tax deducted or refunded **in this employment.** Write 'R' beside an amount to show a net refund.
FINCH C A*	£ 2,797.80	£ 2,773.50
GULL S E	£ 2,186.88	£ 1,957.50
HERON G T	£ 3,088.68	£ 3,082.50
IBIS M A	£ 2,090.20	£ 2,174.00
	£	£
	£	£
	£	£
	£	£
	£	£
	£	£

Total NICs shown above *after deducting amounts marked 'R'* **1** £ 10,163 56

Total tax shown above *after deducting amounts marked 'R'* **4** £ 9,987 50

Totals from P35(CS) *Continuation Sheets* **2** £ –

Totals from P35(CS) *Continuation Sheets* **5** £ –

Part 2 Summary of payments for the year

Total NICs 1 + 2 **3** £ 10,163 56 *see Note 2*

Total tax 4 + 5 **6** £ 9,987 50 *see Note 2*

Advance received from HM Revenue & Customs to refund tax **7** £ –

Total tax 6 + 7 **8** £ 9,987 50

Combined amounts

Total NICs and tax 3 + 8 **9** £ 20,151 06

Total Student Loan deductions *see Note 3* **10** £ –

9 + 10 **11** £ 20,151 06

Statutory payments recovered *see Note 4*

Statutory Sick Pay (SSP) recovered **12** £

Statutory Maternity Pay (SMP) recovered **13** £

NIC compensation on SMP **14** £

Statutory Paternity Pay (SPP) recovered **15** £

NIC compensation on SPP **16** £

Statutory Adoption Pay (SAP) recovered **17** £

NIC compensation on SAP **18** £

Total of boxes 12 to 18 **19** £

Funding received from HM Revenue & Customs to pay SSP/SMP/SPP/SAP **20** £

19 minus 20 **21** £ –

11 minus 21 **22** £ 20,151 06 *see Note 5*

For information only

Deductions made from subcontractors *see Note 6* **23** £ –

Amount payable for the year 22 + 23 **24** £ 20,151 06

NICs and tax paid already **25** £ 18,307 52

Tax-free incentive payment received during the year *see Note 7* **26** £ –

NOW PAYABLE 24 minus 25 and 26 **27** £ 1,843 54

► Do not include a payment with this Return. If a payment is due, please make it immediately. See page 1 for notes on how to pay.

Fill in boxes 28 and 29 only if you are a **limited company** that has had CIS deductions made from payments received for work in the construction industry.

CIS deductions suffered *Total of column E on form CIS132* **28** £ –

Revised amount now payable 27 minus 28 **29** £ –

Note 1
Boxes **1** to **6** Enter 'R' beside any minus amounts.

Note 2
Boxes **3** and **6** If you are not required to complete the 'Part 1 Summary of employees and directors' section you should begin by entering the respective NICs and Income Tax totals for all employees for whom you have completed a form P11 (or equivalent record).

Note 3
Box **10** Whole pounds only. Do not enter pence in shaded area.

Note 4
Boxes **12** to **18** Do not enter the totals paid.
Only enter the amounts you are entitled to recover. You will find this in your P30BC *Payslip Booklet* or your own equivalent payment record.

Note 5
Box **22** If box **22** is a minus figure then add box **21** to box **11**

Note 6
Box **23** Enter the total CIS deductions on account of tax from box 4.6 on your CIS300 monthly Returns.

Note 7
Box **26** If a tax-free payment was credited to your PAYE payment record for this year, for having sent any previous year's Return online, enter the amount. If the tax-free payment was repaid directly to you or your adviser by cheque, leave this box blank.

Please now fill in page 4 ►

Page 2

Page 3

Part 3 Checklist

You must answer each question

1 Have you sent a form P14 *End of Year Summary* or completed and retained a form P38(S) *Student employees* for every person in your paid employment, either on a casual basis or otherwise, during the tax year shown on the front of this form?

No ☐   Yes ☒

If 'No', please send a form P38A *Employer Supplementary Return*.

2 Did you make any 'free of tax' payments to an employee? In other words, did you bear any of the tax yourself rather than deduct it from the employee?

No ☒   Yes ☐

3 As far as you know, did anyone else pay expenses, or in any way provide vouchers or benefits to any of your employees while they were employed by you during the year?

No ☒   Yes ☐

4 Did anyone **employed** by a person or company **outside the UK** work for you in the UK for 30 or more days in a row?

No ☒   Yes ☐

If 'Yes', have you sent a form P14 for them?

No ☐   Yes ☐

5 Have you **paid** any of an employee's pay to **someone other than the employee**, for example, to a school?

No ☒   Yes ☐

If 'Yes', have you included this pay on their form P14?

No ☐   Yes ☐

6 Are you a Service Company?

No ☒   Yes ☐

If 'Yes', have you operated the Intermediaries legislation (sometimes known as **IR35**) or the Managed Service Companies legislation?

No ☐   Yes ☐

For more detailed information, see CWG2 *Employer Further Guide to PAYE and NICs.*

For information only

Part 4 Contracted-out pension schemes *if applicable*

If you have a Contracted-out pension scheme, enter your Employer Contracted-out number (ECON) from your contracting-out certificate

E 3 ☐☐☐☐☐☐☐

Part 5 Employer certificate and declaration

Tick one box to complete each statement below. *This certificate and declaration covers any documents authorised by us as substitutes for the forms mentioned below. We may penalise or prosecute you if you make false statements.*

I declare and certify that

- forms P14 *End of Year Summary* for each employee or director for whom I was required to complete a form P11 *Deductions Working Sheet* (or equivalent record) during the year,

are all enclosed   ☒

or

have been sent separately in one or more parts† ☐

† If forms P14 have been sent in more than one part, please enter the number of parts sent, **not the total number of forms P14,** and note that only one P35 is required reflecting all P14 parts. For more detailed information, see the *Guide to filing PAYE forms online and paying electronically.* ☐

- completed form P38A *Employer Supplementary Return*

is enclosed ☐   is not due ☒

- completed forms P11D and P11D(b) *Returns of expenses payments, benefits and Class 1A contributions*

are due ☒   are not due ☐

All the details on this Return and any forms enclosed or sent separately are fully and truly stated to the best of my knowledge and belief.

Employer signature

V Sparrow

Please print your name

V SPARROW

Capacity in which signed

PAYROLL OFFICER

Date

15 / 04 / 10

Please give a daytime phone number. It will help speed things up if we need to talk to you about your Return.

By law this Return must reach us by 19 May.

Page 4

Answer 4.7

The reconciliation in part 2 of form P35 identifies any tax and NIC outstanding. Therefore it is sensible to complete this before 19 April to ensure that the correct amount is paid to the collector by 19 April. This avoids interest charges.

Answer 4.8

Unless instructed otherwise, give the auditors details of the total salary and benefits for each of the two tax years. An extract from the payroll might be as follows.

	Director A £	Director B £
Gross pay (including bonus) – 2008/09	112,000	200,000
– 2009/10	150,000	222,000
Bonus year end 30/9/08, paid 1/12/08	25,000	50,000
Bonus year end 30/9/09, paid 1/12/09	30,000	60,000
P11D benefits – 2007/08	5,600	7,800
– 2009/10	8,000	9,000

This will enable the auditors to apportion the details between the company years. As always, when preparing reports, make sure you know exactly what is required **before** doing the report.

Chapter 5

Answer 5.1

		£
(a)	Salary	5,000
	Benefits	2,500
		7,500

Total is less than £8,500 and so no form P11D is needed. Also the car benefit is not entered on form P9D, so this is not needed either. Therefore, no annual returns are needed.

		£
(b)	Salary	8,000
	Benefits	2,500
		10,500

The total exceeds £8,500 and so form P11D is needed.

(c) If Melanie has the use of a company credit card, then she will need a form P9D return in case (a). In case (b), the form P11D is still needed, so there is no change to the requirements.

Answer 5.2

Each employee is taxable on £1.35 per day (£1.50 – £0.15).

Chapter 6

Answer 6.1

HM Revenue & Customs

P11D Working Sheet 1
Living accommodation 2008-09

Note to employer

You do not have to use this form, but, you may find it a useful way to calculate the cash equivalent if you provided living accommodation for a director or an employee during the year 2008-09 (that is 6 April 2008 to 5 April 2009).

Read the *P11D Guide* and Booklet 480 before you complete this form. Sections 1 and 2 apply to a director or an employee whatever their rate of pay. If you provided any benefits associated with accommodation you may find the checklist at Section 3 helpful.

If you use this form you must also fill in form P11D or P9D. You must also complete form P11D(b) *Return of Class 1A National Insurance contributions*, if you use this Working Sheet to fill in form P11D. CWG5(2009) *Class 1A National Insurance contributions on benefits in kind* gives more information.

You are advised to keep a copy of each completed working sheet as it could help you to deal with enquiries. You do not have to give a copy of the completed working sheet to the director or employee, or to your HM Revenue & Customs office.

The term employee is used to cover both directors and employees throughout the rest of this form.

The term accommodation refers to the living accommodation provided to the employee and the property consisting of that accommodation.

If the employee can choose between:
• taking living accommodation, **or**
• giving up the accommodation and taking a higher cash wage,

then the taxation value of the living accommodation may be greater than the cash equivalent calculated using this working sheet. That will be so if the extra wages the employee could have got (for the period the accommodation was provided) if he/she had given up the accommodation would have been more than the cash equivalent shown in box E or box **R**, in which case enter that amount of extra wages in section D box 14 of the P11D, or section C box 14 of the P9D.

Employer details

Employer name

BOX CAR LTD

Employer PAYE reference

890/B1234

Employee details

Employee name

Surname   BRIGHT

Forename(s)   CHARLOTTE

Works number or department   National Insurance number

A B 1 2 3 4 5 6 C

The accommodation

Give the address of the accommodation provided

1B CHELSEA ARCHES
EMBANKMENT
LONDON W12 7AA

Was the accommodation provided for a full tax year?   Yes [X]   No [ ]

If the answer is No, then when you are asked for amounts, enter the part of the rent or annual value which relates to the period for which the accommodation was provided. Booklet 480 tells you how to work out the annual value.

1   **The basic benefit**   *Complete this section in all cases.*

Amount of rent paid for the year (or part of the year) by you, or any other person at whose cost the accommodation is provided to the employee   **A** £ –

Enter the annual value (or part of the annual value) of the accommodation *see Booklet 480*   **B** £ 4,000

Enter the greater of **A** and **B**   **C** £ 4,000

Enter any amount made good to you by the employee for the living accommodation *if this amount is more than C, enter the amount at C here*   **D** £ 4,000

Subtract **D** from **C**   **E** £ nil

The figure at **E** is the cash equivalent of the basic benefit.

Enter in section D box 14 on form P11D or section C box 14 on form P9D **unless** there is an additional yearly rent.

Please turn over to find out if you need to calculate the additional yearly rent.

P11D WS1 (2009)   HMRC 09/08

2 **The additional yearly rent**

Complete this section if the cost of the accommodation was more than £75,000.

The cost of the accommodation is:

- the cost of acquiring the accommodation

  plus
- the cost of improvements made to the accommodation

  minus
- any payments made by the employee towards these costs or for the grant of a tenancy.

When considering the costs remember that they can be incurred by:
- you as the employer, or
- the person providing the accommodation, or
- any person connected with either of the above other than the employee.

There is a different rule if the employee first occupied the accommodation after 30 March 1983. If the person providing the accommodation held any interest in it throughout a period beginning **six years before the employee first occupied the accommodation**, then the figure to enter at box **F** is the market value of the accommodation at that date, plus the cost of subsequent improvements.

Cost of the accommodation (including the cost of improvements)	**F**	£125,000
Payments made by the employee towards the cost or for the grant of tenancy	**G**	£ -
Subtract **G** from **F**	**H**	£125,000
Excess of cost over £75,000 is **H** minus £75,000	**J**	£ 50,000
Multiply J by 6.25% *which is the official rate of interest on 6 April 2008*	**K**	£ 2,375
If the accommodation was provided for part of the tax year only, enter the number of days it was provided here		
Divide the number of days by 365 and multiply the result by **K**	**L**	£
Enter the rent paid by the employee for the accommodation	**M**	£ 5,000
Enter any rent which you have included in box **D**	**N**	£ 4,000
Subtract **N** from **M**	**P**	£ 1,000
Subtract **P** from **K** (if the accommodation was provided throughout the tax year), or Subtract **P** from **L** (if the accommodation was provided for only part of the tax year) and enter here	**Q**	£ 1,375
Enter the amount shown in box **E** on the front of this form	**E**	£ -
Total of **Q** and **E**	**R**	£ 1,375

Total of Q and E

The figure at **R** is the amount to be entered in section D box 14 on form P11D or section C box 14 on form P9D

3 **Other benefits**

This section is a checklist to help identify other benefits commonly associated with the provision of living accommodation.

Tick if appropriate

Expenses incurred by the provider of the accommodation on benefits or facilities connected with the accommodation	☐
Heating	☐
Lighting	☐
Repairs and decoration	☐
The benefit from furniture given or transferred to the employee	☐
The annual value of the use of furniture in the accommodation which is provided by reason of the employment	☐
Other *please describe in box below*	☐

Booklet 480 explains how to calculate these other benefits and give details of exemptions and limits to the charge. **Enter the benefits in the appropriate boxes on form P11D or P9D.**

NB: Did you remember to use the official interest rate of 4.75% for 2009/10?

Answer 6.2

HM Revenue & Customs

P11D Working Sheet 2
Car and Car fuel benefit 2008-09

Note to employer

You do not have to use this form but you may find it a useful way to calculate the cash equivalent for each car made available to a director or an employee who earned at a rate of £8,500 a year or more during the year 2008-09 (that is 6 April 2008 to 5 April 2008).

A separate form is needed for each car provided to the director or employee during 2008-09.

Read the *P11D Guide* before you complete this form. It refers to paragraphs in Booklet *480(2009)*.

You are advised to keep a copy of each completed working sheet as it could help you to deal with enquiries. You do not have to give a copy of the completed working sheet to the director or employee, or to your HM Revenue & Customs office. But you must fill in forms P11D and P11D(b) *'Return of Class 1A National Insurance contributions'* whether or not you use this form to calculate car and car fuel benefits.

The term employee is used to cover both directors and employees throughout the rest of this form.

Employer details

Employer name

COMECON LTD

Employer PAYE reference

889/C5675

Employee details

Employee name

ROGER MILLER

Works number or department

National Insurance number

C D 3 4 5 6 7 8 B

The car

Make and model of car available to employee

ROVER 25 SERIES

Date the car was first registered

6 / 1 / 04

Was this the only car made available to the employee ✓ Yes ☑ No ☐

If 'No' please make sure that working sheets are completed for each car made available to the employee in 2008-09

If more than one working sheet 2 is completed for this employee, enter the number of sheets here [ ]

1 List price of the car

Complete box **A** as follows

- enter the list price of the car as published by its manufacturer, importer or distributor
- if the car had no list price when it was first registered you need to enter the notional price. That is, the price which might reasonably be expected to be its list price on that date if the car's manufacturer, importer or distributor had published a list price for an equivalent car for a single retail sale in the UK
- if the car is a classic car, enter the price that the car might reasonably be expected to fetch if you sold it on the open market on 5 April 2009. If the car was unavailable to the employee on 5 April 2009 then use the last day in the tax year 2008-09 that it was available to the employee. For this purpose, assume that all the qualifying accessories available on the car are included in the sale. A classic car is one which
  - is at least 15 years old on 5 April 2009
  - has a market value of at least £15,000, *and*
  - has a market value which is higher than the original list or notional price (including accessories).

Price of the car *including standard accessories* **A** £ 20,250

2 Accessories

Price of all accessories *see P11D Guide and paragraphs 12.7-12.14 of Booklet 480(2009)* **B** £ 500

C A + B £ 20,750

3 Capital contributions

Capital contributions made by the employee towards the cost of the car or the accessories *max £5,000* **D** £ –

4 The price used to calculate the car benefit charge for 2008-09

This box is subject to a maximum of £80,000 **E** C minus D £ 20,750

P11D WS2 (2009) v9.5　　　　1　　　　IMS OX/OX

5 **Calculating the appropriate percentage**

The appropriate percentage depends on when the car was first registered, the type of fuel used and whether it has an approved CO_2 emissions figure.

Approved CO_2 emissions figure, if the car has one *unrounded, for example 188*

| **F** | 198 g/km |

Enter the key letter (B, C, D, E, G, H, L or P) for the car's fuel or power type from table 1 below.

| P |

TABLE 1	
Key letter	Fuel or power type description
P	Petrol
D	Diesel car not approved to Euro IV emissions standard
L	Diesel car approved to Euro IV emissions standard
E	Electric Only
H	Hybrid electric (combination of petrol engine and electric motor)
B	Gas only or bi-fuel car with approved CO_2 emissions figure for **Gas** when first registered
C	Conversion and all other bi-fuel cars with approved CO_2 emissions figure for **Petrol only** when first registered
G	Cars manufactured so as to be capable of running on E85, a blend of petrol and up to 85% bioethanol

Next step

- for cars registered on or after 1 January 1998 **with** an approved CO_2 emissions figure
  - if the figure in box F is more than 120, **Go to section 5a**
  - if the figure in box F is 120 or less, **Go to section 5b**
- for cars registered on or after 1 January 1998 **without** an approved CO_2 emissions figure, **Go to section 5c**
- for cars registered before 1 January 1998, **Go to section 5d.**

5a **Cars registered on or after 1 January 1998 with an approved CO_2 emissions figure of more than 120**

Approved CO_2 emissions figure in box **F**, *rounded down to the next lowest 5g/km, for example 185*

| **G** | 195 g/km |

Stage 1 - using table 2 below, use the figure in box **G** to work out the percentage to enter in box **H**
- use column 1 for
  - all cars in fuel types B, C, G, H and P
  - cars in fuel type L which were first registered before 1 January 2006
- use column 2 for
  - all cars in fuel type D
  - cars in fuel type L which were first registered on or after 1 January 2006.

| **H** | 27 % |

TABLE 2								
CO_2 emissions (g/km)	Column 1 (%)	Column 2 (%)	CO_2 emissions (g/km)	Column 1 (%)	Column 2 (%)	CO_2 emissions (g/km)	Column 1 (%)	Column 2 (%)
135*	15	18	170	22	25	205	29	32
140	16	19	175	23	26	210	30	33
145	17	20	180	24	27	215	31	34
150	18	21	185	25	28	220	32	35
155	19	22	190	26	29	225	33	35
160	20	23	195	27	30	230	34	35
165	21	24	200	28	31	235*	35	35

*These are the minimum and maximum CO_2 values for which different percentages apply.
Use these values if the figure at box G is less than the minimum or greater than the maximum.*

Stage 2 - calculate reductions for alternative fuel/power types *fuel type letters H, B and G only*
- fuel type H - insert 3% in box J
- fuel types B and G - insert 2% in box J

| **J** | - % |

Appropriate percentage
Go straight to section 6 - do not complete sections 5b, 5c or 5d

| **H minus J** | |
| **N** | 27 % |

5b Cars registered on or after 1 January 1998 with an unrounded approved CO_2 emissions figure of 120 or less

For these 'qualifying low emissions cars', or QUALECs
- enter 10% in box N for
  - all cars in fuel types B, C, G, H and P
  - cars in fuel type L which were first registered before 1 January 2006

- enter 13% in box N for
  - all cars in fuel type D
  - cars in fuel type L which were first registered on or after 1 January 2006

Appropriate percentage
Go straight to section 6 - do not complete sections 5c or 5d

N _____ %

5c Cars registered on or after 1 January 1998 without an approved CO_2 emissions figure

Stage 1 - using table 3 below, work out the percentage to enter in box H
- use column 1 for
  - all cars in fuel types C, G, H and P
  - cars in fuel type L which were first registered before 1 January 2006
  use column 2 for
  - all cars in fuel type D
  - cars in fuel type L which were first registered on or after 1 January 2006
- for fuel type E, insert 15%
  for fuel type B, use section 5a (all such cars have CO_2 emissions figures)

H _____ %

TABLE 3		
Engine size of car (cc)	Column 1 %	Column 2 %
0 - 1400	15	18
1401 - 2000	25	28
over 2000	35	35
all rotary engines	35	35

Stage 2 - calculate reductions for alternative fuel/power types *fuel type letters G, H and E only*
- fuel type E - insert 6% in box J
- fuel type H - insert 3% in box J
- fuel type G - insert 2% in box J

J _____ %

Appropriate percentage
Go straight to section 6 - do not complete section 5d

N H minus J _____ %

5d All cars registered before 1 January 1998

Enter the engine size, then work out the percentage to enter in box **N**

_____ cc

TABLE 4	
Engine size of car (cc)	Percentage
0 - 1400	15
1401 - 2000	22
over 2000	32
all rotary engines	32

Appropriate percentage

N _____ %

6 Calculate the car benefit for a full year

Ignore any decimals when completing box **P**

	f x N
P	£ 5,602

7 Make any deductions for days the car was unavailable

If the car was available to the employee for the whole of the tax year, put the figure in box **P** into box **S**. If not, state the period for which the car was available

from [/ /]   to [/ /]

Total days for which the car was unavailable *see P11D Guide and Booklet 480(2009)*

Q	–

Deduction for unavailability *round up to next whole number*

	(P x Q)/365
R £	–

Car benefit for the period the car was **available**

	P minus R
S £	5,602

8 Make any deductions for payments for private use

Enter any required payments made for private use of the car in the year

T £	–

Car benefit charge for 2008-09 for this car *(ignore any decimals)*
Enter the figure at box **U** onto form *P11D*, at section F box 9
If the employee had more than one car available in the year, add together all the figures at box U on each working sheet, then transfer the total to form P11D, at section F box 9

	S minus T
U £	5,602

9 Calculate the car fuel benefit charge *if appropriate - see P11D Guide*

Car fuel benefit charge for the whole of this tax year

	£16,900 x N
V £	4,563

Calculate any required deductions
Days the **car** was unavailable *from section 7*

Q	

If the provision of fuel was withdrawn and not reinstated later in the year, enter the date and complete box **W**, otherwise, go to box **X**

Date the provision of fuel was withdrawn *if applicable*

[/ /]

Additional days after fuel was withdrawn not already counted in box **Q**
do not include the same day in both box Q and box W

W	

Total days for which no car fuel benefit charge applies

	Q + W
X	

Deduction *round up to next whole number*

	(V x X)/365
Y £	–

Car fuel benefit charge for 2008-09 for this car
Enter the figure at box **Z** onto form *P11D*, at section F box 10
If the employee had more than one car available in the year, add together all the figures at box Z on each working sheet, then transfer the total to form P11D, at section F box 10.

	V minus Y
Z £	4,563

4

Tutorial note

Box A – did you remember to use **list price** not cost?
Box G – did you remember to round **down** to 195 g/km?

Answer 6.3

The CO_2 emissions percentage is still 27%, but this time you have to add the 3% diesel supplement, giving a total of 30% for the car and car fuel benefit.

	£
Car benefit: 30% × £20,750	6,225
Car fuel benefit: 30% × £16,900	5,070
	11,295

Answer 6.4

HM Revenue & Customs

P11D Working Sheet 4
Interest-free and low interest loans 2008–09

Note to employer

You do not have to use this form but you may find it a useful way to calculate the cash equivalent if you provided interest-free or low interest loans for a director, or an employee who earned at a rate of £8,500 or more during the year 2008–09 (that is 6 April 2008 to 5 April 2009).

Read the *P11D(Guide)* before you complete this form. Enter details of non-qualifying loans made to, or arranged for, a director or employee (or for any of his or her relatives) on which no interest was paid, or on which the amount of interest paid was less than interest at the official rate. Include 'notional loan' benefits of shares acquired by the director or employee at undervalue.

As a guide to whether a loan is a qualifying loan, and does not therefore need to be reported on the form P11D, see booklet 480.

If you use this form you must also fill in forms P11D and P11D(b) *Return of Class 1A National Insurance contributions.* Booklet CWG5(2009) *Class 1A National Insurance contributions on benefits in kind* gives more information. You are advised to keep a copy of each completed working sheet as it could help you to deal with enquiries. You do not have to give a copy of the completed working sheet to the director or employee, or to your HM Revenue & Customs office.

The term employee is used to cover both directors and employees throughout the rest of this form.

Employer details

Employer name

COMECON LTD

Employer PAYE reference

889/C5675

Employee details

Employee name

Surname MILLER

Forename(s) ROGER

Works number or department

National Insurance number

C D 3 4 3 5 7 8 B

The loans

If the total amount outstanding on all the loans is not more than £5,000 at any time in the year, there is no need to complete this working sheet or Section H of form P11D.

You may find it helpful to complete the table below to identify:

- other small exempt loans
- for directors of close companies only, non-qualifying loans which may be treated as a single loan for the purpose of calculating the benefit.

	Loan 1	Loan 2	Loan 3	Loan 4	Loan 5
Maximum balance outstanding at any time in the year	10,000				
Currency if other than sterling					

If you know that the total amount outstanding on all non-qualifying loans does not exceed £5,000 at any time in the year, ignore such loans when completing the remainder of this working sheet and Section H of form P11D.

If you are a close company and the borrower is one of the company's directors, you can elect to treat all loans which are:

- in the same currency
- non-qualifying
- owing at the same time

as a single loan.

You can make the election by showing all such loans as a single loan in Section H on the form P11D. Please note that if you make the election and do not include all such loans within the single loan, you will be making an incorrect return.

Please turn over

P11D WS4 (2009)

HMRC 02/09

BPP LEARNING MEDIA

Official rates of interest

To calculate the cash equivalent of a loan you will need to know:

- the average official rate of interest for the year ended 5 April 2009 for loans made in sterling
- the official rate for Japanese Yen or Swiss Francs where the loan was made in one of those currencies and the conditions in paragraph 17.5 of Booklet 480 are met.

The average official rate of interest for 2008–09 for loans made in sterling is 6.10%. The official interest rates for loans in currencies other than sterling up to early November 2008 are printed in Booklet 480, but later changes are not known until the end of the tax year.

Form P11D(INT) is available from the Employer Orderline (Phone **08457 646 646**) and it gives details of the official rates of interest for 2008–09.

You can also get details of the official rates of interest from your HM Revenue & Customs office.

Calculating the cash equivalent

Use the formula below for each loan separately *except where an election has been made to treat a director's loans as a single loan.*

	Loan 1	Loan 2	Loan 3	Loan 4	Loan 5
A Maximum balance on either 5 April 2008 or the date the loan was taken out, whichever is later	10,000				
B Maximum balance on earlier of day loan was discharged or 5 April 2009	10,000				
C Total (A + B)	20,000				
D Divide C by 2	10,000				
E Number of complete tax months in tax year (6th of month to 5th of following month) throughout which loan was owing	12				
F Multiply D by E, then divide by 12	10,000				
G Official rate of interest	4.75%	%	%	%	%
H Multiply F by G	475				
J Enter interest paid in 2008–09	–				
K Cash equivalent of loans H minus J	475				

The figures at K are the amounts to be entered in Section H boxes 15 on form P11D.

If the employee has more than two loans, you can write 'see attached' in Section H box 15 and attach a copy of this working sheet. But you must remember to add together the cash equivalents of all the loans for the purpose of calculating the total benefits liable to Class 1A NICs when completing form P11D(b) *'Return of Class 1A National Insurance contributions'*.

Employees may elect for a more complex but accurate method of calculating the benefit from interest-free or low interest loans. Employers are not responsible for providing such a calculation.

Answer 6.5

	£
Car benefit	
Total of boxes F9 (£5,602) and F10 (£4,563) is	10,165
Loan benefit	
Amount to be entered in box 15 of Section H	475
Total benefits liable to Class 1A NICs	10,640
Class 1A NICs due at 12.8%	1,361.92

Chapter 7

Answer 7.1

Net Income Tax

	£
PAYE	3,900.00
Student Loan Deductions	100.00
	4,000.00

Net NIC

	£
Employees' NICs	1,000.00
Employers' NICs	2,000.00
SSP recovered	(10.00)
SMP recovered	(460.00)
	2,530.00
Total amount due	6,530.00

Chapter 8

Answer 8.1

(a) Charlotte can obtain tax relief on contributions up to 100% of her salary.

(b) The employer's contributions will not be refunded. The employee's contributions will be refunded net of 20% tax.

	£
Contributions	1,200
Less tax at 20%	(240)
Amount of cheque	960

(c) Marlene has two options:

   (i) Transfer her pension contributions to a personal pension scheme at an agreed **transfer value**.
   (ii) **Freeze** the pension until retirement age.

She should seek advice on which option to choose from a financial adviser.

Answer 8.2

Without Roger's express permission, you can do nothing. Politely explain to the solicitor that Roger has not authorised release of this information. Therefore, you can not reply to his query now. However you can suggest that you will send a letter detailing this information to Roger and he can then pass it on to the solicitor if he wishes.

Appendix
(tax and NI tables)

HM Revenue & Customs

Taxable Pay Tables
Manual Method

Tables B to D (April 2009)

Keep using Tables A 1993 issue – Pay Adjustment Tables

Use from 6 April 2009

Monthly paid

Column A	Column B
Month	Use Table B on pages 7 and 8
1	3117
2	6234
3	9350
4	12467
5	15584
6	18700
7	21817
8	24934
9	28050
10	31167
11	34284
12	37400

If you do your payroll on a monthly basis use this table. If it's weekly use the table on page 6.
- Work out which month the pay is for – there is a chart on page 26 of the Helpbook E13 *Day-to-day payroll.*
- Pick the month you need from the month column in the table. Look at the figure in Column B.
- Is your employee's total taxable pay to date **less than or equal to** the figure in Column B? If so, use Table B on pages 7 and 8.
- If your employee's total taxable pay to date is **more than** the amount in Column B, use Tables C and D on pages 9 and 11.

Example 3
You are working out the tax due for Month 5. Your employee's total taxable pay to date is £1,200 which is **less than** £15,584 in Column B. So, use Tables B on pages 7 and 8.

Example 4
You are working out the tax due for Month 5. Your employee's total taxable pay to date is £17,500 which is **more than** £15,584 in Column B. So, use Tables C and D on pages 9 and 11.

Weekly paid

Column A	Column B
Week	Use Table B on pages 7 and 8
1	720
2	1439
3	2158
4	2877
5	3597
6	4316
7	5035
8	5754
9	6474
10	7193
11	7912
12	8631
13	9350
14	10070
15	10789
16	11508
17	12227
18	12947
19	13666
20	14385
21	15104
22	15824
23	16543
24	17262
25	17981
26	18700
27	19420
28	20139
29	20858
30	21577
31	22297
32	23016
33	23735
34	24454
35	25174
36	25893
37	26612
38	27331
39	28050
40	28770
41	29489
42	30208
43	30927
44	31647
45	32366
46	33085
47	33804
48	34524
49	35243
50	35962
51	36681
52	37400

If you do your payroll on a weekly basis use this table. If it's monthly use the table on page 4.

- Work out which week the pay is for – there is a chart on page 26 of the Helpbook E13, *Day-to-day payroll*
- Pick the week you need from the week column in the table. Look at the figure in Column B.
- Is your employee's total taxable pay to date **less than or equal to** the figure in Column B? If so, use Table B on pages 7 and 8.
- If your employee's total taxable pay to date is **more than** the amount in Column B, use Tables C and D on pages 10 and 11.

Example 7
You are working out the tax due for Week 22. Your employee's total taxable pay to date is £1,200 which is **less than** £15,824 in Column B. So, use Table B on pages 7 and 8.

Example 8
You are working out the tax due for Week 22. Your employee's total taxable pay to date is £17,500 which is **more than** £15,824 in Column B. So, use Tables C and D on pages 10 and 11.

Table B

To work out tax at 20%. Pages 3 and 5 tell you when to use this table.

Table B
Tax due on taxable pay from £1 to £15,000

Total taxable pay to date	Total tax due to date	Total taxable pay to date	Total tax due to date	Total taxable pay to date	Total tax due to date	Total taxable pay to date	Total tax due to date	Total taxable pay to date	Total tax due to date
1	0.20	51	10.20	100	20.00	5100	1020.00	10100	2020.00
2	0.40	52	10.40	200	40.00	5200	1040.00	10200	2040.00
3	0.60	53	10.60	300	60.00	5300	1060.00	10300	2060.00
4	0.80	54	10.80	400	80.00	5400	1080.00	10400	2080.00
5	1.00	55	11.00	500	100.00	5500	1100.00	10500	2100.00
6	1.20	56	11.20	600	120.00	5600	1120.00	10600	2120.00
7	1.40	57	11.40	700	140.00	5700	1140.00	10700	2140.00
8	1.60	58	11.60	800	160.00	5800	1160.00	10800	2160.00
9	1.80	59	11.80	900	180.00	5900	1180.00	10900	2180.00
10	2.00	60	12.00	1000	200.00	6000	1200.00	11000	2200.00
11	2.20	61	12.20	1100	220.00	6100	1220.00	11100	2220.00
12	2.40	62	12.40	1200	240.00	6200	1240.00	11200	2240.00
13	2.60	63	12.60	1300	260.00	6300	1260.00	11300	2260.00
14	2.80	64	12.80	1400	280.00	6400	1280.00	11400	2280.00
15	3.00	65	13.00	1500	300.00	6500	1300.00	11500	2300.00
16	3.20	66	13.20	1600	320.00	6600	1320.00	11600	2320.00
17	3.40	67	13.40	1700	340.00	6700	1340.00	11700	2340.00
18	3.60	68	13.60	1800	360.00	6800	1360.00	11800	2360.00
19	3.80	69	13.80	1900	380.00	6900	1380.00	11900	2380.00
20	4.00	70	14.00	2000	400.00	7000	1400.00	12000	2400.00
21	4.20	71	14.20	2100	420.00	7100	1420.00	12100	2420.00
22	4.40	72	14.40	2200	440.00	7200	1440.00	12200	2440.00
23	4.60	73	14.60	2300	460.00	7300	1460.00	12300	2460.00
24	4.80	74	14.80	2400	480.00	7400	1480.00	12400	2480.00
25	5.00	75	15.00	2500	500.00	7500	1500.00	12500	2500.00
26	5.20	76	15.20	2600	520.00	7600	1520.00	12600	2520.00
27	5.40	77	15.40	2700	540.00	7700	1540.00	12700	2540.00
28	5.60	78	15.60	2800	560.00	7800	1560.00	12800	2560.00
29	5.80	79	15.80	2900	580.00	7900	1580.00	12900	2580.00
30	6.00	80	16.00	3000	600.00	8000	1600.00	13000	2600.00
31	6.20	81	16.20	3100	620.00	8100	1620.00	13100	2620.00
32	6.40	82	16.40	3200	640.00	8200	1640.00	13200	2640.00
33	6.60	83	16.60	3300	660.00	8300	1660.00	13300	2660.00
34	6.80	84	16.80	3400	680.00	8400	1680.00	13400	2680.00
35	7.00	85	17.00	3500	700.00	8500	1700.00	13500	2700.00
36	7.20	86	17.20	3600	720.00	8600	1720.00	13600	2720.00
37	7.40	87	17.40	3700	740.00	8700	1740.00	13700	2740.00
38	7.60	88	17.60	3800	760.00	8800	1760.00	13800	2760.00
39	7.80	89	17.80	3900	780.00	8900	1780.00	13900	2780.00
40	8.00	90	18.00	4000	800.00	9000	1800.00	14000	2800.00
41	8.20	91	18.20	4100	820.00	9100	1820.00	14100	2820.00
42	8.40	92	18.40	4200	840.00	9200	1840.00	14200	2840.00
43	8.60	93	18.60	4300	860.00	9300	1860.00	14300	2860.00
44	8.80	94	18.80	4400	880.00	9400	1880.00	14400	2880.00
45	9.00	95	19.00	4500	900.00	9500	1900.00	14500	2900.00
46	9.20	96	19.20	4600	920.00	9600	1920.00	14600	2920.00
47	9.40	97	19.40	4700	940.00	9700	1940.00	14700	2940.00
48	9.60	98	19.60	4800	960.00	9800	1960.00	14800	2960.00
49	9.80	99	19.80	4900	980.00	9900	1980.00	14900	2980.00
50	10.00			5000	1000.00	10000	2000.00	15000	3000.00

Table B ~ continued

To work out tax at 20%. Pages 3 and 5 tell you when to use this table.

Table B
Tax due on taxable pay from £15,100 to £37,400

Total taxable pay to date	Total tax due to date	Total taxable pay to date	Total tax due to date	Total taxable pay to date	Total tax due to date	Total taxable pay to date	Total tax due to date	Total taxable pay to date	Total tax due to date
15100	3020.00	20100	4020.00	25100	5020.00	30100	6020.00	35100	7020.00
15200	3040.00	20200	4040.00	25200	5040.00	30200	6040.00	35200	7040.00
15300	3060.00	20300	4060.00	25300	5060.00	30300	6060.00	35300	7060.00
15400	3080.00	20400	4080.00	25400	5080.00	30400	6080.00	35400	7080.00
15500	3100.00	20500	4100.00	25500	5100.00	30500	6100.00	35500	7100.00
15600	3120.00	20600	4120.00	25600	5120.00	30600	6120.00	35600	7120.00
15700	3140.00	20700	4140.00	25700	5140.00	30700	6140.00	35700	7140.00
15800	3160.00	20800	4160.00	25800	5160.00	30800	6160.00	35800	7160.00
15900	3180.00	20900	4180.00	25900	5180.00	30900	6180.00	35900	7180.00
16000	3200.00	21000	4200.00	26000	5200.00	31000	6200.00	36000	7200.00
16100	3220.00	21100	4220.00	26100	5220.00	31100	6220.00	36100	7220.00
16200	3240.00	21200	4240.00	26200	5240.00	31200	6240.00	36200	7240.00
16300	3260.00	21300	4260.00	26300	5260.00	31300	6260.00	36300	7260.00
16400	3280.00	21400	4280.00	26400	5280.00	31400	6280.00	36400	7280.00
16500	3300.00	21500	4300.00	26500	5300.00	31500	6300.00	36500	7300.00
16600	3320.00	21600	4320.00	26600	5320.00	31600	6320.00	36600	7320.00
16700	3340.00	21700	4340.00	26700	5340.00	31700	6340.00	36700	7340.00
16800	3360.00	21800	4360.00	26800	5360.00	31800	6360.00	36800	7360.00
16900	3380.00	21900	4380.00	26900	5380.00	31900	6380.00	36900	7380.00
17000	3400.00	22000	4400.00	27000	5400.00	32000	6400.00	37000	7400.00
17100	3420.00	22100	4420.00	27100	5420.00	32100	6420.00	37100	7420.00
17200	3440.00	22200	4440.00	27200	5440.00	32200	6440.00	37200	7440.00
17300	3460.00	22300	4460.00	27300	5460.00	32300	6460.00	37300	7460.00
17400	3480.00	22400	4480.00	27400	5480.00	32400	6480.00	37400	7480.00
17500	3500.00	22500	4500.00	27500	5500.00	32500	6500.00		
17600	3520.00	22600	4520.00	27600	5520.00	32600	6520.00		
17700	3540.00	22700	4540.00	27700	5540.00	32700	6540.00		
17800	3560.00	22800	4560.00	27800	5560.00	32800	6560.00		
17900	3580.00	22900	4580.00	27900	5580.00	32900	6580.00		
18000	3600.00	23000	4600.00	28000	5600.00	33000	6600.00		
18100	3620.00	23100	4620.00	28100	5620.00	33100	6620.00		
18200	3640.00	23200	4640.00	28200	5640.00	33200	6640.00		
18300	3660.00	23300	4660.00	28300	5660.00	33300	6660.00		
18400	3680.00	23400	4680.00	28400	5680.00	33400	6680.00		
18500	3700.00	23500	4700.00	28500	5700.00	33500	6700.00		
18600	3720.00	23600	4720.00	28600	5720.00	33600	6720.00		
18700	3740.00	23700	4740.00	28700	5740.00	33700	6740.00		
18800	3760.00	23800	4760.00	28800	5760.00	33800	6760.00		
18900	3780.00	23900	4780.00	28900	5780.00	33900	6780.00		
19000	3800.00	24000	4800.00	29000	5800.00	34000	6800.00		
19100	3820.00	24100	4820.00	29100	5820.00	34100	6820.00		
19200	3840.00	24200	4840.00	29200	5840.00	34200	6840.00		
19300	3860.00	24300	4860.00	29300	5860.00	34300	6860.00		
19400	3880.00	24400	4880.00	29400	5880.00	34400	6880.00		
19500	3900.00	24500	4900.00	29500	5900.00	34500	6900.00		
19600	3920.00	24600	4920.00	29600	5920.00	34600	6920.00		
19700	3940.00	24700	4940.00	29700	5940.00	34700	6940.00		
19800	3960.00	24800	4960.00	29800	5960.00	34800	6960.00		
19900	3980.00	24900	4980.00	29900	5980.00	34900	6980.00		
20000	4000.00	25000	5000.00	30000	6000.00	35000	7000.00		

Where the exact amount of taxable pay is not shown add together the figures for two (or more) entries that make up the amount of taxable pay to the nearest £1.

Table C - monthly paid

Page 4 tells you when to use this table.

Month	Column 1 If total taxable pay to date exceeds £	Column 2 Total tax due to date on pay in column 1 £
1	3117	623.46
2	6234	1246.93
3	9350	1870.00
4	12467	2493.46
5	15584	3116.93
6	18700	3740.00
7	21817	4363.46
8	24934	4986.93
9	28050	5610.00
10	31167	6233.46
11	34284	6856.93
12	37400	7480.00

Table C — Employee paid at monthly rates

Add tax at 40% as shown in Table D on the amount by which the total taxable pay to date exceeds the figure in column 1.

Table C calculation

Employee's code is **431L**

The pay is in **month 4**

	£
Pay in the month	5,800.80
Plus previous pay to date	9,332.64
Total pay to date	15,133.44
Minus pay adjustment Table A figure at **month 4** code **431L**	1,439.68
Total taxable pay to date	13,693.76
Round down to the nearest pound	13,693
Minus amount in column 1 for **month 4**	12,467
Excess to be taxed at 40%	1,226

Tax due

Tax due on £12,467 from column 2	2,493.46
Tax due on £1,226 from tables D	490.40
Total tax due	**2,983.86**

Table C – weekly paid

Page 6 tells you when to use this table.

Table C Employee paid at weekly rates		
Week	**Column 1** If total taxable pay to date exceeds £	**Column 2** Total tax due to date on pay in column 1 £
1	720	144.15
2	1439	287.90
3	2158	431.66
4	2877	575.41
5	3597	719.56
6	4316	863.32
7	5035	1007.07
8	5754	1150.83
9	6474	1294.98
10	7193	1438.73
11	7912	1582.49
12	8631	1726.24
13	9350	1870.00
14	10070	2014.15
15	10789	2157.90
16	11508	2301.66
17	12227	2445.41
18	12947	2589.56
19	13666	2733.32
20	14385	2877.07
21	15104	3020.83
22	15824	3164.98
23	16543	3308.73
24	17262	3452.49
25	17981	3596.24
26	18700	3740.00
27	19420	3884.15
28	20139	4027.90
29	20858	4171.66
30	21577	4315.41
31	22297	4459.56
32	23016	4603.32
33	23735	4747.07
34	24454	4890.83
35	25174	5034.98
36	25893	5178.73
37	26612	5322.49
38	27331	5466.24
39	28050	5610.00
40	28770	5754.15
41	29489	5897.90
42	30208	6041.66
43	30927	6185.41
44	31647	6329.56
45	32366	6473.32
46	33085	6617.07
47	33804	6760.83
48	34524	6904.98
49	35243	7048.73
50	35962	7192.49
51	36681	7336.24
52	37400	7480.00

Add tax at 40% as shown in Table D on the amount by which the total taxable pay to date exceeds the figure in column 1.

Table C calculation

Employee's code is **431L**

The pay is in **week 12**

	£
Pay in the week	812.21
Plus previous pay to date	9,961.55
Total pay to date	10,773.76
Minus pay adjustment Table A figure at **week 12 code 431L**	996.72
Total taxable pay to date	9,777.04
Round down to the nearest pound	9,777
Minus amount in column 1 for **week 12**	8,631
Excess to be taxed at 40%	1,146

Tax due

Tax due on £8,631 per column 2	1,726.24
Tax due on £1,146 per tables D	458.40
Total tax due	**2,184.64**

Table D - Tax at 40%

Also to be used for Code D0. Pages 3, 4 and 6 tell you when to use this table.

Table D

Taxable Pay £	Tax £	Taxable Pay £	Tax £	Taxable Pay £	Tax £	Taxable Pay £	Tax £
1	0.40	50	20.00	100	40.00	6100	2440.00
2	0.80	51	20.40	200	80.00	6200	2480.00
3	1.20	52	20.80	300	120.00	6300	2520.00
4	1.60	53	21.20	400	160.00	6400	2560.00
5	2.00	54	21.60	500	200.00	6500	2600.00
6	2.40	55	22.00	600	240.00	6600	2640.00
7	2.80	56	22.40	700	280.00	6700	2680.00
8	3.20	57	22.80	800	320.00	6800	2720.00
9	3.60	58	23.20	900	360.00	6900	2760.00
10	4.00	59	23.60	1000	400.00	7000	2800.00
11	4.40	60	24.00	1100	440.00	7100	2840.00
12	4.80	61	24.40	1200	480.00	7200	2880.00
13	5.20	62	24.80	1300	520.00	7300	2920.00
14	5.60	63	25.20	1400	560.00	7400	2960.00
15	6.00	64	25.60	1500	600.00	7500	3000.00
16	6.40	65	26.00	1600	640.00	7600	3040.00
17	6.80	66	26.40	1700	680.00	7700	3080.00
18	7.20	67	26.80	1800	720.00	7800	3120.00
19	7.60	68	27.20	1900	760.00	7900	3160.00
20	8.00	69	27.60	2000	800.00	8000	3200.00
21	8.40	70	28.00	2100	840.00	8100	3240.00
22	8.80	71	28.40	2200	880.00	8200	3280.00
23	9.20	72	28.80	2300	920.00	8300	3320.00
24	9.60	73	29.20	2400	960.00	8400	3360.00
25	10.00	74	29.60	2500	1000.00	8500	3400.00
26	10.40	75	30.00	2600	1040.00	8600	3440.00
27	10.80	76	30.40	2700	1080.00	8700	3480.00
28	11.20	77	30.80	2800	1120.00	8800	3520.00
29	11.60	78	31.20	2900	1160.00	8900	3560.00
30	12.00	79	31.60	3000	1200.00	9000	3600.00
31	12.40	80	32.00	3100	1240.00	9100	3640.00
32	12.80	81	32.40	3200	1280.00	9200	3680.00
33	13.20	82	32.80	3300	1320.00	9300	3720.00
34	13.60	83	33.20	3400	1360.00	9400	3760.00
35	14.00	84	33.60	3500	1400.00	9500	3800.00
36	14.40	85	34.00	3600	1440.00	9600	3840.00
37	14.80	86	34.40	3700	1480.00	9700	3880.00
38	15.20	87	34.80	3800	1520.00	9800	3920.00
39	15.60	88	35.20	3900	1560.00	9900	3960.00
40	16.00	89	35.60	4000	1600.00	10000	4000.00
41	16.40	90	36.00	4100	1640.00	20000	8000.00
42	16.80	91	36.40	4200	1680.00	30000	12000.00
43	17.20	92	36.80	4300	1720.00	40000	16000.00
44	17.60	93	37.20	4400	1760.00	50000	20000.00
45	18.00	94	37.60	4500	1800.00	60000	24000.00
46	18.40	95	38.00	4600	1840.00	70000	28000.00
47	18.80	96	38.40	4700	1880.00	80000	32000.00
48	19.20	97	38.80	4800	1920.00	90000	36000.00
49	19.60	98	39.20	4900	1960.00	100000	40000.00
		99	39.60	5000	2000.00	200000	80000.00
				5100	2040.00	300000	120000.00
				5200	2080.00	400000	160000.00
				5300	2120.00	500000	200000.00
				5400	2160.00	600000	240000.00
				5500	2200.00	700000	280000.00
				5600	2240.00	800000	320000.00
				5700	2280.00	900000	360000.00
				5800	2320.00	1000000	400000.00
				5900	2360.00		
				6000	2400.00		

Where the exact amount of taxable pay is not shown, add together the figures for two (or more) entries to make up the amount of taxable pay to the nearest £1 below.

BPP LEARNING MEDIA

HM Revenue & Customs

National Insurance contributions Tables A and J

Use from 6 April 2009 to 5 April 2010 inclusive

Not Contracted-out Tables

CA38

Earnings limits and NICs rates

Earnings limits	Employee's contribution		Employer's contribution
	Contribution Table letter A	Contribution Table letter J	Contribution Table letters A and J
Below £95 weekly, or below £412 monthly, or below £4,940 yearly	Nil	Nil	Nil
£95 to £110 weekly, or £412 to £476 monthly, or £4,940 to £5,715 yearly	0%	0%	0%
£110.01 to £770 weekly, or £476.01 to £3,337 monthly, or £5,715.01 to £40,040 yearly	11% on earnings above the ET	1% on earnings above the ET	12.8% on earnings above the ET
£770.01 to £844 weekly, or £3,337.01 to £3,656 monthly, or £40,040.01 to £43,875 yearly	11% on earnings above the ET	1% on earnings above the ET	12.8% on earnings above the ET
Over £844 weekly, or over £3,656 monthly, or over £43,875 yearly	11% on earnings above the ET, up to and including the UEL, then 1% on all earnings above the UEL	1% on all earnings above the ET	12.8% on all earnings above the ET

Table
letter **A**

Monthly table for not contracted-out standard rate contributions
for use from 6 April 2009 to 5 April 2010

Use this table for

- employees who are age 16 or over and under State Pension age (65 for men, 60 for women)
- employees who have an Appropriate Personal Pension or Appropriate Personal Pension Stakeholder Pension.

Do not use this table for

- any year other than 2009-10
- married women or widows who have the right to pay reduced rate employee's contributions, see Table B, in booklet CA41
- employees who are State Pension age or over, see Table C, in booklet CA41
- employees for whom you hold form CA2700, see Table J.

Completing form P11 Deductions Working Sheet or substitute

- enter 'A' in the space provided in the 'End of Year Summary' box of form P11
- copy the figures in columns 1a - 1f of the table to columns 1a - 1f of form P11 on the line next to the tax week in which the employee is paid.

If the employee's total earnings fall between the LEL and the UEL and the exact gross pay is not shown in the table, use the next smaller figure shown. If the employee's total earnings exceed the UEL, see page 70.

The figures in the left-hand column of each table show steps between the LEL and the UEL. The NICs liability for each step, with the exception of the LEL, ET, UAP and UEL, is calculated at the mid-point of the steps so you and your employee may pay slightly more or less than if you used the exact percentage method.

▼ Employee's earnings up to and including the UEL	Earnings at the LEL (where earnings are equal to or exceed the LEL)	Earnings above the LEL, up to and including the ET	Earnings above the ET, up to and including the UAP	Earnings above the UAP, up to and including the UEL	Total of employee's and employer's contributions	Employee's contributions due on all earnings above the ET	▼ Employer's contributions
	1a	1b	1c	1d	1e	1f	
£	£	£ p	£ p	£ p	£ p	£ p	£ p
Up to and including 411.99		No NICs liability, make no entries on forms P11 and P14					
412	412	0.00	0.00	0.00	0.00	0.00	0.00
416	412	4.00	0.00	0.00	0.00	0.00	0.00
420	412	8.00	0.00	0.00	0.00	0.00	0.00
424	412	12.00	0.00	0.00	0.00	0.00	0.00
428	412	16.00	0.00	0.00	0.00	0.00	0.00
432	412	20.00	0.00	0.00	0.00	0.00	0.00
436	412	24.00	0.00	0.00	0.00	0.00	0.00
440	412	28.00	0.00	0.00	0.00	0.00	0.00
444	412	32.00	0.00	0.00	0.00	0.00	0.00
448	412	36.00	0.00	0.00	0.00	0.00	0.00
452	412	40.00	0.00	0.00	0.00	0.00	0.00
456	412	44.00	0.00	0.00	0.00	0.00	0.00
460	412	48.00	0.00	0.00	0.00	0.00	0.00
464	412	52.00	0.00	0.00	0.00	0.00	0.00
468	412	56.00	0.00	0.00	0.00	0.00	0.00
472	412	60.00	0.00	0.00	0.00	0.00	0.00
476	412	64.00	0.00	0.00	0.00	0.00	0.00
480	412	64.00	4.00	0.00	1.43	0.66	0.77
484	412	64.00	8.00	0.00	2.38	1.10	1.28
488	412	64.00	12.00	0.00	3.33	1.54	1.79
492	412	64.00	16.00	0.00	4.28	1.98	2.30
496	412	64.00	20.00	0.00	5.24	2.42	2.82
500	412	64.00	24.00	0.00	6.19	2.86	3.33
504	412	64.00	28.00	0.00	7.14	3.30	3.84
508	412	64.00	32.00	0.00	8.09	3.74	4.35
512	412	64.00	36.00	0.00	9.04	4.18	4.86
516	412	64.00	40.00	0.00	10.00	4.62	5.38
520	412	64.00	44.00	0.00	10.95	5.06	5.89
524	412	64.00	48.00	0.00	11.90	5.50	6.40
528	412	64.00	52.00	0.00	12.85	5.94	6.91

▼ for information only - do not enter on form P11 *Deductions Working Sheet*

Table letter **A**

Monthly table

Employee's earnings up to and including the UEL	Earnings at the LEL (where earnings are equal to or exceed the LEL)	Earnings above the LEL, up to and including the ET	Earnings above the ET, up to and including the UAP	Earnings above the UAP, up to and including the UEL	Total of employees and employer's contributions	Employee's contributions due on all earnings above the ET	Employer's contributions
		1a	1b	1c	1d	1e	1f
£	£	£ p	£ p	£ p	£ p	£ p	£ p
1852	412	64.00	1376.00	0.00	327.96	151.58	176.38
1856	412	64.00	1380.00	0.00	328.92	152.02	176.90
1860	412	64.00	1384.00	0.00	329.87	152.46	177.41
1864	412	64.00	1388.00	0.00	330.82	152.90	177.92
1868	412	64.00	1392.00	0.00	331.77	153.34	178.43
1872	412	64.00	1396.00	0.00	332.72	153.78	178.94
1876	412	64.00	1400.00	0.00	333.68	154.22	179.46
1880	412	64.00	1404.00	0.00	334.63	154.66	179.97
1884	412	64.00	1408.00	0.00	335.58	155.10	180.48
1888	412	64.00	1412.00	0.00	336.53	155.54	180.99
1892	412	64.00	1416.00	0.00	337.48	155.98	181.50
1896	412	64.00	1420.00	0.00	338.44	156.42	182.02
1900	412	64.00	1424.00	0.00	339.39	156.86	182.53
1904	412	64.00	1428.00	0.00	340.34	157.30	183.04
1908	412	64.00	1432.00	0.00	341.29	157.74	183.55
1912	412	64.00	1436.00	0.00	342.24	158.18	184.06
1916	412	64.00	1440.00	0.00	343.20	158.62	184.58
1920	412	64.00	1444.00	0.00	344.15	159.06	185.09
1924	412	64.00	1448.00	0.00	345.10	159.50	185.60
1928	412	64.00	1452.00	0.00	346.05	159.94	186.11
1932	412	64.00	1456.00	0.00	347.00	160.38	186.62
1936	412	64.00	1460.00	0.00	347.96	160.82	187.14
1940	412	64.00	1464.00	0.00	348.91	161.26	187.65
1944	412	64.00	1468.00	0.00	349.86	161.70	188.16
1948	412	64.00	1472.00	0.00	350.81	162.14	188.67
1952	412	64.00	1476.00	0.00	351.76	162.58	189.18
1956	412	64.00	1480.00	0.00	352.72	163.02	189.70
1960	412	64.00	1484.00	0.00	353.67	163.46	190.21
1964	412	64.00	1488.00	0.00	354.62	163.90	190.72
1968	412	64.00	1492.00	0.00	355.57	164.34	191.23
1972	412	64.00	1496.00	0.00	356.52	164.78	191.74
1976	412	64.00	1500.00	0.00	357.48	165.22	192.26
1980	412	64.00	1504.00	0.00	358.43	165.66	192.77
1984	412	64.00	1508.00	0.00	359.38	166.10	193.28
1988	412	64.00	1512.00	0.00	360.33	166.54	193.79
1992	412	64.00	1516.00	0.00	361.28	166.98	194.30
1996	412	64.00	1520.00	0.00	362.24	167.42	194.82
2000	412	64.00	1524.00	0.00	363.19	167.86	195.33
2004	412	64.00	1528.00	0.00	364.14	168.30	195.84
2008	412	64.00	1532.00	0.00	365.09	168.74	196.35
2012	412	64.00	1536.00	0.00	366.04	169.18	196.86
2016	412	64.00	1540.00	0.00	367.00	169.62	197.38
2020	412	64.00	1544.00	0.00	367.95	170.06	197.89
2024	412	64.00	1548.00	0.00	368.90	170.50	198.40
2028	412	64.00	1552.00	0.00	369.85	170.94	198.91
2032	412	64.00	1556.00	0.00	370.80	171.38	199.42
2036	412	64.00	1560.00	0.00	371.76	171.82	199.94
2040	412	64.00	1564.00	0.00	372.71	172.26	200.45
2044	412	64.00	1568.00	0.00	373.66	172.70	200.96
2048	412	64.00	1572.00	0.00	374.61	173.14	201.47
2052	412	64.00	1576.00	0.00	375.56	173.58	201.98
2056	412	64.00	1580.00	0.00	376.52	174.02	202.50
2060	412	64.00	1584.00	0.00	377.47	174.46	203.01
2064	412	64.00	1588.00	0.00	378.42	174.90	203.52
2068	412	64.00	1592.00	0.00	379.37	175.34	204.03

▼ for information only - do not enter on form P11 *Deductions Working Sheet*

BPP LEARNING MEDIA

Table letter **A**

Monthly table

Employee's earnings up to and including the UEL	Earnings at the LEL (where earnings are equal to or exceed the LEL)	Earnings above the LEL, up to and including the ET	Earnings above the ET, up to and including the UAP	Earnings above the UAP, up to and including the UEL	Total of employee's and employer's contributions	Employee's contributions due on all earnings above the ET	Employer's contributions
1a		1b	1c	1d	1e	1f	
£	£	£ p	£ p	£ p	£ p	£ p	£ p
2292	412	64.00	1816.00	0.00	432.68	199.98	232.70
2296	412	64.00	1820.00	0.00	433.64	200.42	233.22
2300	412	64.00	1824.00	0.00	434.59	200.86	233.73
2304	412	64.00	1828.00	0.00	435.54	201.30	234.24
2308	412	64.00	1832.00	0.00	436.49	201.74	234.75
2312	412	64.00	1836.00	0.00	437.44	202.18	235.26
2316	412	64.00	1840.00	0.00	438.40	202.62	235.78
2320	412	64.00	1844.00	0.00	439.35	203.06	236.29
2324	412	64.00	1848.00	0.00	440.30	203.50	236.80
2328	412	64.00	1852.00	0.00	441.25	203.94	237.31
2332	412	64.00	1856.00	0.00	442.20	204.38	237.82
2336	412	64.00	1860.00	0.00	443.16	204.82	238.34
2340	412	64.00	1864.00	0.00	444.11	205.26	238.85
2344	412	64.00	1868.00	0.00	445.06	205.70	239.36
2348	412	64.00	1872.00	0.00	446.01	206.14	239.87
2352	412	64.00	1876.00	0.00	446.96	206.58	240.38
2356	412	64.00	1880.00	0.00	447.92	207.02	240.90
2360	412	64.00	1884.00	0.00	448.87	207.46	241.41
2364	412	64.00	1888.00	0.00	449.82	207.90	241.92
2368	412	64.00	1892.00	0.00	450.77	208.34	242.43
2372	412	64.00	1896.00	0.00	451.72	208.78	242.94
2376	412	64.00	1900.00	0.00	452.68	209.22	243.46
2380	412	64.00	1904.00	0.00	453.63	209.66	243.97
2384	412	64.00	1908.00	0.00	454.58	210.10	244.48
2388	412	64.00	1912.00	0.00	455.53	210.54	244.99
2392	412	64.00	1916.00	0.00	456.48	210.98	245.50
2396	412	64.00	1920.00	0.00	457.44	211.42	246.02
2400	412	64.00	1924.00	0.00	458.39	211.86	246.53
2404	412	64.00	1928.00	0.00	459.34	212.30	247.04
2408	412	64.00	1932.00	0.00	460.29	212.74	247.55
2412	412	64.00	1936.00	0.00	461.24	213.18	248.06
2416	412	64.00	1940.00	0.00	462.20	213.62	248.58
2420	412	64.00	1944.00	0.00	463.15	214.06	249.09
2424	412	64.00	1948.00	0.00	464.10	214.50	249.60
2428	412	64.00	1952.00	0.00	465.05	214.94	250.11
2432	412	64.00	1956.00	0.00	466.00	215.38	250.62
2436	412	64.00	1960.00	0.00	466.96	215.82	251.14
2440	412	64.00	1964.00	0.00	467.91	216.26	251.65
2444	412	64.00	1968.00	0.00	468.86	216.70	252.16
2448	412	64.00	1972.00	0.00	469.81	217.14	252.67
2452	412	64.00	1976.00	0.00	470.76	217.58	253.18
2456	412	64.00	1980.00	0.00	471.72	218.02	253.70
2460	412	64.00	1984.00	0.00	472.67	218.46	254.21
2464	412	64.00	1988.00	0.00	473.62	218.90	254.72
2468	412	64.00	1992.00	0.00	474.57	219.34	255.23
2472	412	64.00	1996.00	0.00	475.52	219.78	255.74
2476	412	64.00	2000.00	0.00	476.48	220.22	256.26
2480	412	64.00	2004.00	0.00	477.43	220.66	256.77
2484	412	64.00	2008.00	0.00	478.38	221.10	257.28
2488	412	64.00	2012.00	0.00	479.33	221.54	257.79
2492	412	64.00	2016.00	0.00	480.28	221.98	258.30
2496	412	64.00	2020.00	0.00	481.24	222.42	258.82
2500	412	64.00	2024.00	0.00	482.19	222.86	259.33
2504	412	64.00	2028.00	0.00	483.14	223.30	259.84
2508	412	64.00	2032.00	0.00	484.09	223.74	260.35

▼ for information only - do not enter on form P11 *Deductions Working Sheet*

Index

Review Form & Free Prize Draw – AAT Certificate in Payroll Administration Level 3 Text (8/09)

All original review forms from the entire BPP range, completed with genuine comments, will be entered into one of two draws on 31 January 2010 and 31 July 2010. The names on the first four forms picked out on each occasion will be sent a cheque for £50.

Name: _____   Address: _____

_____

_____

How have you used this Course Companion?
(Tick one box only)

☐ Home study (book only)

☐ On a course: college _____

☐ With 'correspondence' package

☐ Other _____

Why did you decide to purchase this Course Companion? *(Tick one box only)*

☐ Have used BPP Texts in the past

☐ Recommendation by friend/colleague

☐ Recommendation by a lecturer at college

☐ Saw advertising

☐ Other _____

During the past six months do you recall seeing/receiving any of the following?
(Tick as many boxes as are relevant)

☐ Our advertisement in *Accounting Technician* magazine

☐ Our advertisement in *Pass*

☐ Our brochure with a letter through the post

Which (if any) aspects of our advertising do you find useful?
(Tick as many boxes as are relevant)

☐ Prices and publication dates of new editions

☐ Information on Course Companion content

☐ Facility to order books off-the-page

☐ None of the above

Have you used the companion Revision Companion for this subject?   ☐ Yes   ☐ No

Your ratings, comments and suggestions would be appreciated on the following areas

	Very useful	Useful	Not useful
Introduction	☐	☐	☐
Chapter contents lists	☐	☐	☐
Examples	☐	☐	☐
Activities and answers	☐	☐	☐
Key learning points	☐	☐	☐
Quick quizzes and answers	☐	☐	☐
Activity checklist	☐	☐	☐

	Excellent	Good	Adequate	Poor
Overall opinion of this Text	☐	☐	☐	☐

Do you intend to continue using BPP Course Companions/Revision Companions?   ☐ Yes   ☐ No

Please note any further comments and suggestions/errors on the reverse of this page.

The BPP author of this edition can be e-mailed at: janiceross@bpp.com

Please return this form to: Janice Ross, BPP Learning Media, FREEPOST, London, W12 8BR

Review Form & Free Prize Draw (continued)

Please note any further comments and suggestions/errors below

Free Prize Draw Rules

1   Closing date for 31 January 2010 draw is 31 December 2009. Closing date for 31 July 2010 draw is 30 June 2010.

2   Restricted to entries with UK and Eire addresses only. BPP employees, their families and business associates are excluded.

3   No purchase necessary. Entry forms are available upon request from BPP Learning Media. No more than one entry per title, per person. Draw restricted to persons aged 16 and over.

4   Winners will be notified by post and receive their cheques not later than 6 weeks after the relevant draw date.

5   The decision of the promoter in all matters is final and binding. No correspondence will be entered into.